SEVENTH EDITION

MASS COMMUNICATION LAW
^{IN} GEORGIA

Gregory C. Lisby

NEW FORUMS
Stillwater, Oklahoma
U.S.A.

Table of Contents

List of Figures

About the Author

GREGORY C. LISBY, professor of Communication at Georgia State University, holds a Ph.D. from the University of Tennessee – where he was awarded the Chancellor's Citation for Extraordinary Academic Achievement and Professional Promise – and a J.D. degree from the G.S.U. College of Law. Prior to that, he earned a B.A. degree in journalism from Auburn University and a M.A. degree in journalism from the University of Mississippi. Professor Lisby currently teaches communication law, regulation, and policy, as well as communication ethics, and also practices law (Georgia Bar No. 452022) in Gwinnett County. He serves on the editorial boards of *Communication Law & Policy*, *Newspaper Research Journal*, the *Online Journal of Communication & Media Technologies*, and *Studies in Media & Information Literacy Education*, and is a past editorial board member of *American Journalism* and past head of the Law & Policy Division of the Association for Education in Journalism & Mass Communication. He is the author of two books and his research has been published in *Journalism Monographs*, *Communication Law & Policy*, *Journalism Quarterly*, *Journal of Communication Inquiry*, *Communication & the Law*, *Free Speech Yearbook*, *Newspaper Research Journal*, *Critical Studies*, and *Georgia Historical Quarterly*, from which he received the E. Merton Coulter Award for the best article of the year for his legal history of the Georgia Literature Commission. His documentary on film censorship in Atlanta was broadcast on Georgia public television and his biography of Pulitzer Prize-winning Georgia journalist Julian Harris won the book of the year award from the American Journalism Historians Association in 2003. He currently serves as associate chair of the Department of Communication at Georgia State University. He is currently working on a comparative appraisal of testimonial privilege among professionals – attorneys and clients, doctors and patients, ministers and penitents, and journalists and sources – to examine its effects on the ultimate purpose of American trials, which is the discovery of truth and the accomplishment of justice.

Preface

As every student of mass communication law is aware, most of the law with which journalists deal on a day-to-day basis originates not in our nation's capital but in the statehouse. This is true even though the U.S. Supreme Court has "federalized" much of communication law, setting standards for the states to follow. Because these standards allow for differences of opinion and approach, laws affecting freedom of expression still vary significantly from state to state, and even more today than when Dewey Benefield published *Georgia Laws and Cases Affecting Newspapers* in 1955.

This book has been developed as a comprehensive survey of key mass communication law issues and problems in the state of Georgia. For more than twenty years now, it has served as a primer or introduction to communication law in Georgia and as a supplement to other texts which discuss mass communication law from a national perspective. Because of continual changes in the law on all levels of government and in our understanding of those changes, updated material will be made available online at: gsu.academia.edu/GregLisby/.

Although by no means a substitute for legal counsel, this material has been prepared for reference use by journalists and students of mass communication. Because of this, though the book's style generally follows the *Uniform System of Citation* used in legal writing, some stylistic modifications have been made to simplify references cited herein.

For example, abbreviations have been restricted to those most commonly used: U.S. stands for *United States Reports* (the official case reporter of the U.S. Supreme Court); F. for

West Publishing's *Federal Reporter* (the official case reporter of the federal appellate courts, with first, second, and third editions); and F. Supp. for West's *Federal Supplement* (the official case reporter of the federal district courts, with first and second editions). On the state level, Ga. stands for *Georgia Reports* (the official case reporter of the Georgia Supreme Court); Ga. App. for *Georgia Appeals Reports* (the official case reporter of the Georgia Court of Appeals); S.E. for West's *Southeastern Reporter* (a compilation of regional appellate decisions, with first and second editions); and O.C.G.A. for the *Official Code of Georgia Annotated*. The names of other books and periodicals have been spelled out. In addition, two reference locations are included for all Georgia cases discussed, where possible. However, page references for quoted material are always from the official source. The location of law cases and articles in legal periodicals may be easily determined: 24 *Georgia Law Review* 635 simply means volume 24 of the *Georgia Law Review* beginning at page 635. Lastly, only one purely legal term has been left in the references: "certiorari," which is a request that a lower court be ordered to send the records of a case to a higher court for review.

Georgians' online access to state government may be found on the Internet at: www.georgia.gov/. The state Supreme Court and its rulings are online at: www.gasupreme.us/. The state Court of Appeals and its rulings are now online at: www.gaappeals.us/. A database of Georgia appellate rulings is available online at: caselaw.findlaw.com/court/ga-court-of-appeals/. Opinions of the U.S. Court of Appeals for the 11th Circuit, of which Georgia is a part, are at: www.ca11.uscourts.gov/opinions/index.php; and also at: www.findlaw.com/casecode/courts/11th.html.

The Official Code of Georgia (unannotated) is available at: www.lexis-nexis.com/hottopics/gacode/default.asp – for those interested in the specific wording of the statutes discussed herein, as is legislation introduced in the Georgia General Assembly, at: www.legis.state.ga.us/htdig/search.htm. Annual summaries of all recent Georgia statutes may be found online at: www.legis.ga.gov/Legislation/en-US/GeneralStatutes.aspx. The official Internet site of the Georgia state legislature is: www.legis.state.ga.us/.[1] Live webcam coverage of the General Assembly through the Georgia Legislative Network on the legislature's Internet site by the Georgia Technology Authority began with the 2000 legislative session.

Agency rules and regulations available through the Secretary of State are online at: sos.ga.gov/rules_regs.htm. Opinions of the state Attorney General are available through a link on that office's official site at: law.ga.gov/. Executive orders are available through a link on the governor's official site at: www.gov.state.ga.us/. Finally, the state's electronic, virtual library, GALILEO, is accessible to the public at: www.galileo.usg.edu/.

Other Internet-based resources with links to Georgia legal materials and information include:

- 50states.com's "Georgia" (2013) –
  www.50states.com/georgia.htm
- Administrative Office of the Courts of Georgia, "Courts of Georgia" (undated) –
  www.georgiacourts.org/courts/index.html
- AllLaw.com's "Georgia State Resources" (2013) –
  www.alllaw.com/state_resources/georgia/
- American Law Sources Online: Georgia (2013) –
  www.lawsource.com/also/usa.cgi?ga
- Atlanta Unfiltered (2013) – www.atlantaunfiltered.com/
- Bibb County Government, "Courts" (undated) –

---

1. For information about the legislative process in Georgia, see, "How a State Bill Becomes a Law," Atlanta Journal-Constitution, Jan. 10, 2010, B4.

www.co.bibb.ga.us/

- Burnett, Anne, "Georgia Legal Resources on the Internet" (2003) digitalcommons.law.uga.edu/cgi/viewcontent.cgi?article=1 018&context=speeches
- Chatham County Courts (2013) – www.chathamcourts.org
- Citizen Media Law Project's "Georgia Legal Guide" (2013) – www.citmedialaw.org/state-guide/Georgia
- Civil Process Division, Georgia Sheriff's Association, "Georgia – All Types of Information" (undated) – www.georgiacivilprocess.org/Georgia.htm
- Cobb County Superior Court Administration (undated) – sca.cobbcountyga.gov/
- Cobb County Superior Court Records (undated) – www.cobbsuperiorcourtclerk.org/
- Cornell University Law School Legal Information Institute's "Georgia Legal Materials" (undated) – www.law.cornell.edu/states/georgia.html
- Cornell University Law School Legal Information Institute's "Basic Legal Citation" (2013) – www.law.cornell.edu/citation/
- Courtroom View Network (2013) – www.courtroomview.com/
- Digital Library of Georgia, "GeorgiaInfo" (2013) – georgiainfo.galileo.usg.edu/
- Digital Library of Georgia, "Georgia's Administrative Rule-Making Process" (undated) – georgiainfo.galileo.usg.edu/pdf/adminruleprocess.pdf
- Digital Library of Georgia, "Passing a Law in the Georgia General Assembly" (2013) – georgiainfo.galileo.usg.edu/legchart/legchart.htm
- Duhaime's Legal Dictionary (undated) – www.duhaime.org/diction.htm

- Emory Law Library's Electronic Resources, "Georgia Law" (2009) – library.law.emory.edu/?id=6375#c21730
- FindLaw's Cases & Codes (2013) – www.findlaw.com/casecode/
- FindLaw's "Resources by Jurisdiction: Georgia" (2013) – www.findlaw.com/11stategov/ga/laws.html
- Fred Friendly Seminars (undated) – www.fredfriendly.org/
- Freedom Forum (undated) – www.freedomforum.org/
- Fulton County Courts, Atlanta (undated) – home.fultoncourt.org/
- Fulton County Law Library, Atlanta (undated) – fultoncourt.org/library/
- Fulton County *Daily Report* (2013) – www.dailyreportonline.com/
- Georgetown University's Law Library's "Georgia Resources" (September 2011) – www.ll.georgetown.edu/states/georgia.cfm
- Georgia City Websites and City Codes (undated) – law.justia.com/georgia/cities/
- Georgia Department of Community Affairs' "CityScapes" (undated) – www.dca.state.ga.us/cityscapes/default.asp
- Georgia Department of Community Affairs' "Georgia County Snapshots" (2006) – www.dca.state.ga.us/CountySnapshotsNet/
- Georgia First Amendment Foundation (2011) – www.gfaf.org/
- Georgia First Amendment Foundation's "Georgia Law Enforcement and the Open Records Act: A Law Enforcement Officer's Guide to Open Records in Georgia" (2005) – www.gfaf.org/resources/resourcesBlueBook.pdf
- Georgia First Amendment Foundation's "Georgia Public Schools and the Open Records Act: A Citizen's Guide To

Accessing School Records" (2007) –
www.gfaf.org/resources/greenBook.pdf
- Georgia First Amendment Foundation's "Georgia's 'Sunshine Laws' – A Citizen's Guide to Open Government" (2008) – www.gfaf.org/resources/sunshine_laws.pdf
- Georgia Press Association's "Georgia Law for Journalists" (23rd ed. 2012) – www.gapress.org/PDFs/2012Lawbook.pdf
- Georgia Press Association's "Georgia Newspaper Directory" (2013) – www.gapress.org/gpa_directory_2013/directory.html
- Georgia's Probate Courts (undated) – www.gaprobate.org/
- Georgia State University College of Law's "Free Legal Research Sources" (2012) – law.gsu.edu/library/4529.html?version=html
- Georgia State University College of Law's "Georgia Practice Material" (March 21, 2013) – libguides.law.gsu.edu/georgiapracticematerials
- Georgia State University College of Law's "Peach Sheets" (2013) – law.gsu.edu/lawreview/index/peach_sheets/; or law.gsu.edu/lawreview/peachsheets.htm
- Georgia State University College of Law's "Law Library Research Guides" (2013) – law.gsu.edu/library/research/
- "Getting To Know Georgia" (June 2003) – sos.georgia.gov/civicsday/Getting%20To%20Know%20Georgia.pdf
- Gwinnett Courts (undated) – www.gwinnettcourts.com/home.asp#home/
- Gwinnett Forum (2013) – www.gwinnettforum.com/
- InsiderAdvantage Georgia (2013) – insideradvantagegeorgia.com/
- Johnson, Nancy, "Winning Research Skills" (2009) –

lscontent.westlaw.com/images/banner/SurvivalGuide/PDF0 8/08WinningResearchSkills.pdf
- Judicial Branch of Georgia's "Self-Help Resources" (undated) – www.georgiacourts.org/aoc/selfhelp/
- Kennesaw State University's Public Journalism Network (2013) – pjnet.org/
- Kuesterlaw's "Georgia Law Resources" (undated) – www.kuesterlaw.com/kgalaw.htm
- Law.com (2013) – www.law.com/jsp/law/index.jsp
- Law & Legal Research (undated) – law.onecle.com/
- Law Librarians' Society of Washington, D.C., "Legislative Source Book" (2013) – www.llsdc.org/sourcebook/
- Law Library of Congress' "Research Help: Georgia" (Aug. 1, 2012) – www.loc.gov/law/help/guide/states/us-ga.php
- Law Professor Blogs Network (undated) – lawprofessors.typepad.com/
- Law Research Services' "Georgia Law & Government" (undated) – www.justlawlinks.com/STATE/csga.htm
- Lawyer.com's "Georgia Lawyers, Laws & Resources" (2013) – research.lawyers.com/Georgia/Georgia-Lawyers-Laws-and-Resources.html
- Lawyer.com's "Legal Dictionary" (2013) – research.lawyers.com/glossary/
- 'Lectric Law Legal Lexicon (2013) – www.lectlaw.com/def.htm
- Legal Law Help's "Georgia State Laws" (2013) – www.legallawhelp.com/state_law/Georgia/
- Libcat's "Georgia Libraries" (2010) – www.librarysites.info/states/ga.htm
- Media on Twitter (2013) – www.mediaontwitter.com/
- Mercer Law School's "Georgia Research" (undated) – www.law.mercer.edu/library/research/georgia

- Municode.com's "Georgia Ordinances & Minutes" (2013) www.municode.com/library/ClientListing.aspx?stateID=10
- Muscogee County's Office of the Clerk of Superior, State & Juvenile Courts (2011) – www.muscogeecourts.com/
- National Center for State Courts' "Privacy/Public Access to Court Records: Resource Guide" (undated) – www.ncsc.org/topics/access-and-fairness/privacy-public-access-to-court-records/resource-guide.aspx
- National Center for State Courts' "State Court Web Sites: Georgia" (2013) – www.ncsconline.org/Information-and-Resources/Browse-by-State/State-Court-Websites.aspx#georgia
- National Law Journal (2013) – www.law.com/jsp/nlj/index.jsp
- New Georgia Encyclopedia (2012) – www.georgiaencyclopedia.com/nge/Home.jsp
- NewsLink's "Georgia Newspapers" (undated) – newslink.org/ganews.html
- Nolo's "Plain-English Law Dictionary" (2013) – www.nolo.com/dictionary/
- Nolo's "Legal Research" (2013) – www.nolo.com/legal-research/
- Pew Center State & Consumer Initiatives: Georgia (2012) – www.pewstates.org/states/georgia-328017
- Reporter's Committee for Freedom of the Press (undated) – www.rcfp.org/
- Reynolds National Center for Courts & Media (2013) – courtsandmedia.org/
- Rominger Legal's "Georgia Legal Resources & Research" (2010) – www.romingerlegal.com/state/georgia.html
- RTNDA: The Association of Electronic Journalists, "Cameras in the Court Guide: Georgia" (2012) – www.rtdna.org/content/cameras_al_id

- SCOG Blog (undated) – scogblog.wordpress.com/
- Society of Professional Journalists, "Freedom of Information" (2013) – www.spj.org/foi.asp
- "State and Local Government on the Net: Georgia State and Local Government" (2010) – www.statelocalgov.net/state-ga.cfm
- State Bar of Georgia (2013) – www.gabar.org/
- Stone Mountain Judicial Circuit, DeKalb County, Georgia (undated) – web.co.dekalb.ga.us/superior/index.html
- Student Press Law Center (2013) – www.splc.org/
- Sunshine Review, Georgia Open Records Act (undated) – sunshinereview.org/index.php/Georgia_Open_Records_Act
- Superior Court of Fulton County's "Media Alert" (undated) fultoncourtinfo.blogspot.com/
- Supreme Court of the United States (2013) – www.supremecourtus.gov/
- Topix's "Georgia News" (2013) – www.topix.net/state/ga/
- University of Georgia School of Law's "Georgia Research Resources" (2013) – libguides.law.uga.edu/content.php?pid=51866&sid=27742 92
- U.S. Courts, The Federal Judiciary Court Locator (undated) – www.uscourts.gov/courtlinks/
- U.S. District Court, Middle District of Georgia (2006) – www.gamd.uscourts.gov/
- U.S. District Court, Northern District of Georgia (2013) – www.gand.uscourts.gov/
- U.S. District Court, Southern District of Georgia (undated) www.gasd.uscourts.gov/
- U.S. Law Libraries (2013) – www.hg.org/law-libraries.html
- USA.gov (undated) – www.usa.gov/
- USNPL's "Georgia Newspapers" (2013) –

www.usnpl.com/ganews.php
- University of Iowa College of Law Library's "Georgia" (2012) – libguides.law.uiowa.edu/georgia
- Washburn University School of Law's "Georgia Law & Government Resources" (undated) – www.washlaw.edu/uslaw/states/georgia.html

(Some of the page files listed above – those with a *.PDF suffix – require Adobe Reader to view. It is available to download free at: http://get.adobe.com/reader/.)

The best overall resource on Georgia law is still: Nancy P. Johnson, Nancy J. Adams & Elizabeth G. Adelman's "Researching Georgia Law (2006 Edition)," 22 Georgia State University Law Review 381 (2006). Their book, *Georgia Legal Research*, was published in 2007 by Carolina Academic Press.

Many students at Georgia State University have assisted with the preliminary research for the different editions of this project:

- First edition (1992) – Glynda Bennett, Katie Black, Carlos Campos, Tracey Crosby, Richard Daigle, Rob Fricks, Chuck Hamby, Marie Hardin, Kim Kline, Bob Knowles, Elfriede Kristwald, Rob Maynard, Maggie Meroney, and Faith Peppers.
- Second edition (1996) – Andrew Agustin, Harriet Bowen, Hugh Carver, Virginia Charles, Candy Crowe, Ann Cunningham, Joey Goddard, Mary Beth Holcomb, Mike Johnson, Linda Kelley, DeAnn Lee, Tom McCaskey, Louis Rom, Laurie Searle, Michelle Silvers, and Katherine Yancey.
- Third edition (2001) – Susan Adams, Sally Holmes Allen, Rosemary Anderson, Brian Back, Margarita Birger, Amber Bradley, Claire Brinsden, Cindi Brown, Marianne Chrisman, Kristin Davis, Darren Drevik, Stacey Evans,

Tomas Etzler, Cathy Fallon, Stacia Farrell, Susan Flowers, Mark Gulledge, Donia Halusky, Jonathon Hammond, Linda Harris, Adrienne Harton, Laura Ippoliti, Meg Jones, Betsy Jordan, Lucy Mayne, Cynthia Mitchell, Jennifer Muto, Josh Parish, Karri Parks, Denise Pasciuto, Rachel Tobin Ramos, Sheryl Riley, Tom Rogers, Martina Skockova, Karen Slay, Brian Smith, Chris Snider, Gail Snyder, Mwanawa Tarver, Tim Weaver, and Alex Wood.

- Fourth edition (2005) – Darwin Berman, Bryan Cardinale-Powell, Cynthia Curtin, Shonalee King, Kwaku Mawuena, Bryce McNeil, Jack Morris, Andrew Mosley, Judi Peterson, Tracye Poole, James Roland, Erin Ryan, Chris Taylor, and Willie Wilder.

- Fifth edition (2008) – Lyndel Abamonte, Clarissa Ampie, Anna Baranchuk, Courtney Barton, Veda Behfarshad, Tom Bevan, Matthew Blakely, Brandi Bragdon, Alicia Bruce, Jim Burress, Nathalie Carter, Jessica Chalmers, Zuzana Chovanova, Shirley Cruz, Bonnie Davies, Drew Dotson, Tabitha Dove, Jenna Finke, Meghan Gleason, Larkin Grant, Jodie Hair, Andy Hawley, Jamie Hayes, Leighton Hellem, Rick Herder, Steve Herro, Matheson Herron, Tiffany Hicks, Scott Higgs, Shana Holmes, Jory Holt, Jamie Howe, Ryan Jackson, Iyanna James, Ashlee Johnson, Jerel Johnson, Alexis Jones, Michael Kien, Pauline Kim, Gayla Kirkland, Mark Legrande, Marissa Levasseur, Brandon Marlow, Kaitlin Martinucci, Laura McMillan, Vincent Migliore, Brittany Miller, Lindsay Mills, Christina Montrois, Chika Oduah, Ese Okuma, Dan Pesavento, Kelly Petty, Cassandra Powell, Alejandra Puente, Jasmine Ragland, Michael Rahl, Karolina Regulska, Mirelys Rodriguez, Monica Roper, Anni Rust, Alaina Shapiro, Robyn Shortland, Sumitra Srinivasan, Charles Stanley, Joshua Stewart, Bethany Strotter, Joe Valenzano, Ashley Ware, Vittoria Williams, Fangjie Xu, and Cassie Yoder.

- Sixth edition (2011) – Drew Ayers, Manuel Barrigan, Jay Black, Carolyn Byers, Denise Chavous, Tyrus Collins, Eric Connelly, Michael Corcoran, Shirley Cox, Heather Croft, Shuhua Dai, Pam Dorsett, Matt Duffy, Tavia Holloway, Kendra Kelly, Jay Lakes, Nneka Logan, Chenelle Marshall, Sam Miller, Shannon Montgomery, Tami Morris, Karen Petruska, Jaleene Plummer, Miranda Sain, Drew Seals, Minla Shields, Ashley Strickland, and Jamin Whatley.
- Seventh edition (2014) – Jena Alford, Tamra Al-Kalil, Johnola Asberry, Porsha Campbell, Mica Critchfield, Arafa Crossley, Georgette Eva, Kyle Gammon, Megan Gill, Sheri Gray, Alecia Hammond, Kerri Hayes, Jenna Howard, Mary Jarrell, Almeera Jiwa, Kirsten Koroly, Sandra McGill, Kimberly Miller, Charles Murphy, Anna Norris, Jennifer Perez, Ivanka Skovardanova, Keri Storla, Niki Strickland, Chris Toula, Kayla Vigneaux, Brooke Wilder, Elizabeth Wilkes, and Morgan Wolkin.

All these deserve my sincere gratitude for their assistance, especially Minla Shields who this year volunteered to help with the research necessary for this new edition. Yet while this book obviously benefited from all their efforts, any errors remain solely my responsibility.

This work is dedicated to Professor Jere Hoar of the University of Mississippi, who first helped combine my passion for the law with my love of journalistic excellence, and also to my father, Carroll Edward Lisby (1931-2012), who first inspired that affection. My hope is that this book will also be a continual reminder to Melissa, Amanda, Madison, Paul, Shayne, and Alayna of my belief that all things are possible....

- Greg Lisby
November 15, 2013

1. Freedom of Expression in Georgia

The Georgia Constitution of 1983,[1] like the federal constitution, divides government into three branches of equal authority: the legislative - formally known as the General Assembly - executive, and judiciary. Yet while there has only been one U.S. Constitution (not counting the Articles of Confederation) and one First Amendment[2] - which Georgia belatedly and symbolically ratified in 1941 on the 150h anniversary of the Bill of Rights - there have been ten Georgia constitutions and eight different guarantees of free expression. Georgia's first, the Constitution of 1777 - which pre-dates the U.S. Constitution by twelve years - was "written in haste and contain[ed] only the minimum essentials" of governmental structure as the new state had yet to prove it could keep the independence it had declared.[3] Yet despite its "minimalist"

---

1. Effective July 1, 1983; revised and updated, January 2009. Available at: http://www.sos.ga.gov/elections/GAconstitution.pdf (last accessed Nov. 15, 2013).

2. The First Amendment to the U.S. Constitution states: "Congress shall make no law respecting an establishment of religion, or prohibiting the free exercise thereof; or abridging freedom of speech, or of the press; or the right of the people peaceably to assemble, and to petition the Government for a redress of grievances." The first ten amendments became part of the Constitution on Dec. 15, 1791, when Virginia became the eleventh state to ratify them. "No returns were made by the states of Massachusetts, Connecticut, Georgia, and Kentucky" (Documents Illustrative of the Formation of the Union of the American States, 1927, at 1065).

3. Ethel K. Ware, A Constitutional History of Georgia (1947) at 193. The Constitution of 1777 was completed Feb. 5, 1777, a bare seven months after the Declaration of Independence was signed.

nature, constitutional Article LXI of the 63 provisions still proclaimed:

Freedom of the press and trial by jury to remain inviolate forever.

Georgia's transformation from the last of the thirteen original colonies into a state of the Union - which involved the surrender of powers more properly belonging to a national government, such as the control of an army and the issuance of patents - required that a second constitution be adopted in 1789, patterned closely after the federal document which Georgians William Few and Abraham Baldwin had helped design. Of the eight miscellaneous provisions included in Article IV, §3 almost duplicated Georgia's previous guarantee of free expression, yet still did not impose any direct prohibition against government action, as the wording of the First Amendment to the U.S. Constitution had done. One word had been deleted from Georgia's previous guarantee; it now read:

Freedom of the press and trial by jury shall remain inviolate.

The Constitution only lasted nine years before being revised again, this time to meet the needs of a population settling the western regions of the state and to protect citizens from abuses of legislative power which resulted in the Yazoo land scandal.[4] As part of that revision, Article IV, §5 of the Constitution of 1798 was changed to read:

---

4. In 1795, the legislature sold 35 million acres of land in West Georgia to several land companies for $500,000. In apparent gratitude for their support, "every member of the legislature who voted for the measure got a share," with one exception (id. at 74).

Freedom of the press and trial by jury, as heretofore used in this State, shall remain inviolate; and no ex post facto law shall be passed.

Despite several attempts to revise the Constitution of 1798 - sometimes called "Georgia's greatest constitution"[5] - and the fact that until 1845 no supreme court existed in the state to interpret its provisions[6] - as the U.S. Supreme Court had claimed as its responsibility with regard to the U.S. Constitution[7] - Georgia did not see the need for a new charter until 1861, after its secession from the Union.[8] Interestingly, the Constitution of 1861, although a secessionist document,

---

5. Leah F. Chanin & Suzanne L. Cassidy, Guide to Georgia Legal Research and Legal History (1990) at 10.

6. "A constitutional amendment in 1835 provided the authority to establish a Supreme Court of Georgia, but the court was not actually created until December 1845. When finally established, the three supreme court judges sat in each of five judicial circuits or districts once a year" (id. at 66). The court was to consist of "not more than nine" members who were elected for six-year terms. At present, seven justices sit on the Supreme Court.

7. "It is emphatically the duty of the judiciary department to say what the law is," Chief Justice John Marshall wrote in Marbury v. Madison, 5 U.S. (1 Cranch) 137 (1803) at 177.

8. Georgia seceded from the Union on Jan. 21, 1861. The Constitution of the Confederate States of America was adopted on March 11. (A guarantee of free expression identical to the First Amendment to the U.S. Constitution may be found in Article I, §9, ¶12. For a side-by-side comparison of the two constitutions, see, J.L.M. Curry, Civil History of the Government of the Confederate States, Richmond, Va., 1901, at 274-309.) The Georgia legislature ratified the Confederate constitution unanimously on March 16 and submitted the states own new constitution to the people on March 23 - the first Georgia constitution to be ratified by a popular vote. Confederate troops in South Carolina fired on Fort Sumter on April 12, marking the beginning of the Civil War.

officially recognized the principle of judicial review of legislative acts and contained Georgia's first formal declaration of rights. Of these, Article I, §8 set forth a conservative approach toward freedom of expression, one that protected the freedom only from prior restraints:

> **Freedom of thought and opinion, freedom of speech, and freedom of the press, are inherent elements of political liberty. But while every citizen may freely speak, write and print, on any subject, he shall be responsible for the abuse of the liberty.**[9]

The end of the war four years later necessitated yet another constitution under which Georgia might be restored to the Union. Article I, §6 of the Constitution of 1865 declared:

> **Freedom of speech, and freedom of the press, are inherent elements of political liberty. But while every citizen may freely speak or write or print on any subject, he shall be responsible for the abuse of the liberty.**

In 1866, however, the U.S. Congress required that the former states of the Confederacy ratify the Fourteenth Amendment[10] as a condition for re-admission to the Union.

---

9. For an early application of this concept, see, Western Union Telegraph Co. v. Prichett, 108 Ga. 411, 34 S.E. 216 (1899).

10. Section I of the Fourteenth Amendment to the U.S. Constitution states: "All persons born or naturalized in the United States, and subject to the jurisdiction thereof, are citizens of the United States and of the State wherein they reside. No State shall make or enforce any law which shall

Georgia refused; its Constitution of 1865 was rejected and the state subjected to a military government under the Reconstruction Acts of 1867. The end of radical reconstruction (Georgia was the last of the former Confederate states to have its civil rights restored) required another constitution - the Constitution of 1868. In Article I, its Declaration of Fundamental Principles, Georgia accepted the three Civil War amendments to the U.S. Constitution, renouncing involuntary servitude and also forbidding legislation regarding the "social status" of any citizen.[11] For the first time, it made no change in the wording of its free expression guarantee.[12]

Between 1870 and 1876, "there was a good deal of agitation for a new convention to frame a Constitution whose terms would not be dictated by necessity or pressure,"[13] and which would not be "a carpetbag product."[14] The result was the Constitution of 1877, which "tried to meet all needs,"[15] and included yet another variation of the states free expression guarantee. In Article I, §I, ¶XV, "Liberty of Speech or of the Press Guaranteed," this constitution prohibited direct government action for the first time:[16]

---

abridge the privileges or immunities of citizens of the United States; nor shall any State deprive any person of life, liberty, or property, without due process of law, nor deny any person within its jurisdiction the equal protection of the laws."

11. Georgia Constitution of 1868, Article I, §11.

12. Georgia Constitution of 1868, Article I, §9.

13. Ware, A Constitutional History of Georgia at 149.

14. Id. at 159.

15. Id. at 168.

16. In Article I, §II, ¶I, it also provided: "In all prosecutions or indictments for libel, the truth may be given in evidence; and the jury in all criminal cases shall be the judges of the law and the facts. The power of judges to grant new trials in case of convictions is preserved."

No law shall ever be passed to curtail, or restrain the liberty of speech, or of the press; any person may speak, write, and publish his sentiments, on all subjects, being responsible for the abuse of that liberty.

The Constitution of 1877 served Georgia for 68 years - the record for Georgia constitutions. However, it also comprised a patchwork of 301 amendments by 1943 when a new constitution was proposed.[17] The Constitution of 1945 created a new office of lieutenant governor, but included no changes in Georgia's "first amendment."[18]

By 1972, the Constitution of 1945 had been amended 767 times and the need for constitutional revision was again obvious. Described by its supporters as an "editorial revision,"[19] the Constitution of 1976 was approved by "the largest vote ever cast on any state constitution in Georgia."[20] The protection it granted freedom of expression in Article I, §I, ¶IV, "Liberty of Speech and of the Press Guaranteed," was again changed slightly and now read:

No law shall ever be passed to curtail, or restrain the liberty of speech, or of the press;

---

17. Included in these amendments was one, ratified on Oct. 3, 1906, which authorized the creation of the Court of Appeals of Georgia. The Georgia Constitution of 1983 requires that the court "consist of not less than nine judges" (Article VI, §V, ¶I).

18. Georgia Constitution of 1945, Article I, §I, ¶XV, "Liberty of Speech or of the Press Guaranteed."

19. Merritt B. Pound & Albert B. Saye, Handbook on the Constitutions of the United States and Georgia (12th ed.) (1984) at 50. See also, Leah Chanin & Suzanne Cassidy, Guide to Georgia Legal Research and History (1990) at 17.

20. Pound & Saye, id. at 49.

any person may speak, write and publish his sentiments, on all subjects, being responsible for the abuse of that liberty.

Because the "Constitution remained excessively long and subject to numerous amendments as each biennial general elections,"[21] work began almost immediately on another revision. This effort resulted in the constitution under which Georgia is now governed - the Constitution of 1983. The wording of the state's guarantee of free expression was again edited slightly (see, Figure 1, below):

GEORGIA'S GUARANTEE OF FREE EXPRESSION
(Figure 1)

Freedom of Speech and of the Press Guaranteed
No law shall be passed to curtail or restrain the freedom of speech or of the press. Every person may speak, write, and publish sentiments on all subjects but shall be responsible for the abuse of that liberty.

> **- Article I, §I, ¶V**
> **Georgia Constitution of 1983**

---

21. Id. at 50.

Georgia Courts

Even amid constitutional revision, Georgia's court system has long resembled the federal system in that it has two basic types of courts - trial and appellate. The primary federal trial-level court is the U.S. District Court.[22] Each state is divided into 1-4 districts. Georgia has three districts: Northern, Middle, and Southern. These are courts of general jurisdiction. In civil matters, however, claims must either involve a federal question or involve parties of diverse citizenship and claims of a legislatively set minimum monetary amount. The two federal appellate courts are the U.S. Court of Appeals[23] - Georgia is part of the 11th Circuit - and the U.S. Supreme Court.[24]

Trial-level courts in Georgia include Probate, Juvenile, and Magistrate courts for each of Georgia's 159 counties; State courts organized into eight districts; and Superior courts organized into 49 circuits and 10 districts of varying size, which also have limited appellate jurisdiction over Magistrate courts, county Recorder's courts, and certain Municipal courts when new evidence is discovered.[25] Until adoption of the

---

22. See, U.S. District Court for the Northern District of Georgia (2013), available at: http://www.gand.uscourts.gov/ (last accessed Nov. 15, 2013); U.S. District Court, Middle District of Georgia (2006), available at: http://www.gamd.uscourts.gov/ (last accessed Nov. 15, 2013); U.S. District Court, Southern District of Georgia (undated), available at: http://www.gasd.uscourts.gov/ (last accessed Nov. 15, 2013).

23. The court for the 11th Circuit has jurisdiction over cases from Georgia, Alabama, and Florida. Previously, Georgia was part of the 5th Circuit. See, United States Court of Appeals: Eleventh Circuit (2010), available at: http://www.ca11.uscourts.gov/ (last accessed Nov. 15, 2013).

24. See, Supreme Court of the United States (2013), available at: http://www.supremecourtus.gov/ (last accessed Nov. 15, 2013).

25. See, Administrative Office of the Courts, Judicial Branch of Georgia (undated), available at: http://www.georgiacourts.org/courts/ (last accessed Nov. 15, 2013).

Constitution of 1983, Georgia had some 2,470 different trial courts. While constitutional revision reduced that number to approximately 600, its system is still "fairly complicated."[26]

Georgia's Superior courts are the state's most important trial court, because they decide the most serious criminal and civil damage cases, and have exclusive jurisdiction in felony criminal cases (except most crimes involving juveniles), as well as real estate, and family and domestic relations cases.[27] Superior court judges are "arguably the single most powerful figures in courthouses across the state."[28] They are chosen from at-large districts in non-partisan elections by majority vote to four-year terms - except in cases of death, retirement, or resignation, when a replacement is appointed by the governor, as are most all Georgia's judges.

In 1988, a federal lawsuit challenged the manner of election of these judges on the grounds that circuit-wide elections were racially discriminatory and diluted the voting power of minorities. In 1995, a three-judge federal panel concluded that Georgia's selection procedures were not discriminatory in purpose or effect; soon afterwards, the U.S. Department of Justice withdrew its challenge to the selection procedures, and the U.S. Supreme Court upheld the three-judge panel's decision.[29] After nine years of legal wrangling, all challenges

---

26. Ann Blum & R. Ernest Taylor (eds.), An Introduction to Law in Georgia (Athens, Ga., 1985) at 29.

27. Georgia Constitution of 1983, Article VI, §IV, ¶I. See, The Council of Superior Court Judges of Georgia, The Superior Court of Georgia (undated), available at: http://www.cscj.org/ (last accessed Nov. 15, 2013).

28. Steve Harvey & Rhonda Cook, "Settlement Seen in Judicial Suit," Atlanta Journal-Constitution, Sept. 28, 1991, B2.

29. "Feds Back Out of Judge Selection Case," Atlanta Journal-Constitution, June 8, 1995, E6. See also, Rhonda Cook, "Court Allows Vote on Georgia Judges," Atlanta Journal-Constitution, Dec. 12, 1995, D1.

were dropped in 1997.[30]

Below the level of Superior Court but with concurrent jurisdiction to conduct trials in misdemeanor cases and all civil actions are the State courts.[31] Created in 1970 to reduce the workload of the Superior courts, they also may conduct preliminary hearings in felony cases and decide most civil disputes, except those over which the superior courts have exclusive jurisdiction.[32]

Each of Georgia's 159 counties has a Probate, Juvenile, and Magistrate court.[33] Among the oldest courts in Georgia, Probate courts have the exclusive power to probate wills, administer estates, appoint guardians, issue marriage licenses and licenses to carry firearms, require involuntary hospitalization of incapacitated individuals, and - in some counties - to handle violations of game and fish laws, and traffic and truancy cases.[34] Juvenile courts have jurisdiction over delinquent and deprived children under the age of 17 (though the Superior courts now have jurisdiction over

---

30. "Judicial Election Fight Dropped," Atlanta Journal-Constitution, June 24, 1997, B5.

31. Georgia Constitution of 1983, Article VI, §III, ¶I.

32. See, Council of State Court Judges, Judicial Branch of Georgia: State Court (undated), available at: http://www.statecourt.georgiacourts.gov/ (last accessed Nov. 15, 2013).

33. Georgia Constitution of 1983, Article VI, §III, ¶I. See, Administrative Office of the Courts, Judicial Branch of Georgia (undated), available at: http://www.georgiacourts.org/courts/ (last accessed Nov. 15, 2013).

34. See, Council of Probate Courts, Judicial Branch of Georgia (undated), available at: http://w2.georgiacourts.org/probate/ (last accessed Nov. 15, 2013). See also, Georgia Probate Courts, Judicial Branch of Georgia (undated), available at: https://www.gaprobate.org/ (last accessed Nov. 15, 2013).

juveniles who commit certain violent felonies),[35] while Magistrate courts - formerly Justice of the Peace courts - deal primarily with minor civil claims (in which the amount in dispute does not exceed $15,000 and in which a jury trial is not required), landlord-tenant cases, and the like, as well as being charged with the issuance of summonses, and arrest and search warrants.[36]

Some 370 other special courts operate in Georgia, serving a various incorporated municipalities and with limited civil and criminal jurisdiction, including traffic violations, the issuance of warrants, and some marijuana possession cases, involving one ounce or less, and minor shoplifting cases. These include the City Court of Atlanta and Municipal courts throughout Georgia[37] which, before 1983, were known as Recorder's courts, Mayor's courts, and Police courts.

Georgia has two appellate-level courts - the Court of Appeals and the Supreme Court. The Georgia Court of Appeals has jurisdiction over all lower court cases involving personal injury, child custody, medical malpractice, criminal cases other than capital felonies, and contract law - except those in which the state's highest court has exclusive jurisdiction[38] - and reviews cases to correct legal errors and errors of law, not to

---

35. See, Council of Juvenile Court Judges of Georgia, Judicial Branch of Georgia (undated), available at: http://w2.georgiacourts.org/cjcj/ (last accessed Nov. 15, 2013).

36. See, Council of Magistrate Court Judges, Judicial Branch of Georgia (undated), available at: http://www.georgiacourts.org/councils/magistrate/index.html (last accessed Nov. 15, 2013).

37. See, Council of Municipal Court Judges, Judicial Branch of Georgia (undated), available at: http://www.georgiacourts.org/councils/municipal/index.html (last accessed Nov. 15, 2013).

38. Georgia Constitution of 1983, Article VI, §V, ¶¶I-V. See also, Court of Appeals of Georgia (2013), available at: http://www.gaappeals.us/ (last accessed Nov. 15, 2013).

alter trial outcomes. The Georgia Supreme Court has sole jurisdiction over cases involving constitutional issues, felony convictions for which the death penalty can be imposed, election contests, wills, land titles, divorce and alimony, and equity.[39] The Supreme Court may also answer any question of law – including those from both federal trial-level or appellate courts – and to hear an appeal of decisions made by the Court of Appeals "which are of gravity or great public importance."[40] (As noted earlier, the Superior Court also has limited appellate jurisdiction over Magistrate courts, Probate courts, county Recorder's courts, and certain Municipal courts. See, Figure 2, p. 13.)[41]

---

39. Georgia Constitution of 1983, Article VI, §VI, ¶¶II(1-2)-III(1-8). See also, Supreme Court of Georgia (undated), available at: http://www.gasupreme.us/ (last accessed Nov. 15, 2013).

40. Georgia Constitution of 1983, Article VI, §VI, ¶V.

41. See also, Legislator's Guide to the Judicial Branch (2007), available at: http://www.georgiacourts.org/aoc/publications/Guide_Judy_for_Web.pdf (last accessed Nov. 15, 2013).

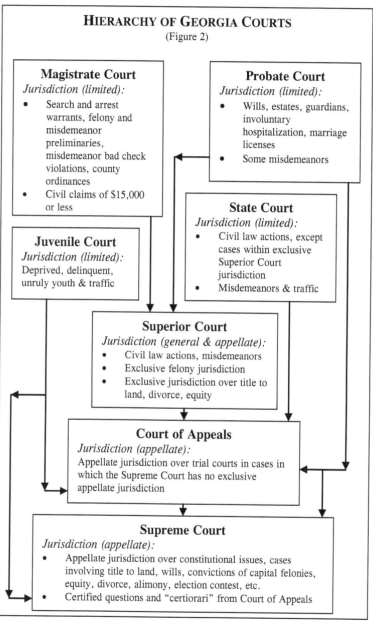

HIERARCHY OF GEORGIA COURTS
(Figure 2)

Magistrate Court
Jurisdiction (limited):
- Search and arrest warrants, felony and misdemeanor preliminaries, misdemeanor bad check violations, county ordinances
- Civil claims of $15,000 or less

Probate Court
Jurisdiction (limited):
- Wills, estates, guardians, involuntary hospitalization, marriage licenses
- Some misdemeanors

State Court
Jurisdiction (limited):
- Civil law actions, except cases within exclusive Superior Court jurisdiction
- Misdemeanors & traffic

Juvenile Court
Jurisdiction (limited):
Deprived, delinquent, unruly youth & traffic

Superior Court
Jurisdiction (general & appellate):
- Civil law actions, misdemeanors
- Exclusive felony jurisdiction
- Exclusive jurisdiction over title to land, divorce, equity

Court of Appeals
Jurisdiction (appellate):
Appellate jurisdiction over trial courts in cases in which the Supreme Court has no exclusive appellate jurisdiction

Supreme Court
Jurisdiction (appellate):
- Appellate jurisdiction over constitutional issues, cases involving title to land, wills, convictions of capital felonies, equity, divorce, alimony, election contest, etc.
- Certified questions and "certiorari" from Court of Appeals

Protected/Unprotected Expression

The First Amendment to the U.S. Constitution and Georgia's guarantee of free expression have been interpreted and applied in Georgia cases,[42] as protecting:

- pamphlets and leaflets;[43]
- the discussion of matters of public concern;[44]
- symbolic expression, such as the burning of the American flag;[45]
- commercial expression which concerns a lawful activity and is not misleading;[46]

---

42. For an overview, see, H.W. Divine, "Freedoms of the First Amendment in Georgia," 15 Georgia Bar Journal 405 (1953). Its speech and press clauses are among the "fundamental personal rights and liberties" protected from state restriction by the due process clause of the Fourteenth Amendment. See, Carr v. Georgia, 176 Ga. 55, 166 S.E. 827 (1932, later appeal, 176 Ga. 747, 169 S.E. 201 (1933); Lovell v. Griffin, 303 U.S. 444 (1938); Staub v. Baxley, 355 U.S. 313 (1958); 106 Forsyth Corp. v. Bishop, 362 F.Supp. 1389 (M.D. Ga. 1972), affirmed, 482 F.2d 280 (5th Cir. 1973), certiorari denied, 422 U.S. 1044 (1975); Walter v. Georgia, 131 Ga. App. 667, 206 S.E.2d 662 (1974), appeal dismissed, 233 Ga. 10, 209 S.E.2d 605 (1974). The U.S. Supreme Court first established this rule in Gitlow v. New York, 268 U.S. 652 (1925).

43. See, Lovell v. Griffin, 303 U.S. 444 (1938).

44. See, for example, Wood v. Georgia, 370 U.S. 375 (1962); Credit Bureau of Dalton v. CBS News, 332 F.Supp. 1291 (N.D. Ga. 1971); Lindsey v. Board of Regents, 607 F.2d 672 (5th Cir. 1979).

45. See, for example, Monroe v. State Court of Fulton County, 739 F.2d 568 (11th Cir. 1984), affirming 571 F.Supp. 1023 (N.D. Ga. 1983). For an earlier, contrary view, see, Monroe v. Georgia, 250 Ga. 30, 295 S.E.2d 512 (1982). The results of the U.S. Supreme Court's most recent attempts to deal with this issue may be found in Texas v. Johnson, 491 U.S. 397 (1989) and U.S. v. Eichman, 496 U.S. 310 (1990).

46. See, for example, Atlanta Co-Operative News Project v. U.S. Postal Service, 350 F.Supp. 234 (N.D. Ga. 1972); Daugherty v. East Point, 447 F.Supp. 290 (N.D. Ga. 1978); H&H Operations v. Peachtree City, 248 Ga.

- live theater;[47]
- the right to mail letters;[48]
- a limited right to gather news;[49]
- films;[50] and even
- provocative expression,[51]
- revolutionary expression,[52] and
- nude dancing.[53]

500, 283 S.E.2d 867 (1981), certiorari denied, 456 U.S. 961 (1982). This protection, however, is not absolute. See, for example, U.S. v. Bob Lawrence Realty, 474 F.2d 115 (5th Cir. 1973), certiorari denied, 414 U.S. 826 (1973). The U.S. Supreme Court first extended First Amendment protection narrowly to commercial expression in Bigelow v. Virginia, 421 U.S. 809 (1975), and, more broadly, in Virginia State Board of Pharmacy v. Virginia Citizens Consumer Council, 425 U.S. 748 (1976).

47. See, for example, Southeastern Productions v. Atlanta, 334 F.Supp. 634 (N.D. Ga. 1971).

48. See, for example, Anderson v. Dean, 354 F.Supp. 639 (N.D. Ga. 1973).

49. See, for example, Cable News Network v. American Broadcasting Co., 518 F.Supp. 1238 (N.D. Ga. 1981).

50. See, for example, K. Gordon Murray Productions v. Floyd, 217 Ga. 784, 125 S.E.2d 207 (1962). The U.S. Supreme Court first extended First Amendment protection to films in Joseph Burstyn, Inc. v. Wilson, 343 U.S. 495 (1952).

51. See, for example, Wilson v. Gooding, 303 F.Supp. 952 (N.D. Ga. 1969), appeal dismissed, 396 U.S. 112 (1969), affirmed, 431 F.2d 855 (5th Cir. 1970), 405 U.S. 518 (1972).

52. See, for example, High Ol' Times, Inc. v. Busbee, 456 F.Supp. 1035 (N.D. Ga. 1978), affirmed, 621 F.2d 141 (5th Cir. 1980).

53. See, for example, Harris v. Entertainment Systems, 259 Ga. 701, 386 S.E.2d 140 (1989). Sanitation laws, however, require that the dancers wear shoes. See, Gary Abramson, "Gold Club Lifts a Glass to High Court," Atlanta Journal-Constitution, Dec. 6, 1989, B1, B10. Accompanying the article is a full-color picture of a partially clothed dancer, with a wad of money stuffed beneath a leg garter, swirling to a musical beat. Justice Charles L. Weltner protested, "I cannot believe that our forebears, in [protecting free expression] intended to vest in each Georgian a constitutional right to dance

15

(Interestingly, the U.S. Supreme Court upheld a similar Indiana statute on the grounds that it was designed to protect morals and public order, and did not prohibit "nudity because of the erotic message conveyed by the dancers.... The perceived evil that Indiana [sought to prevent was] not erotic dancing, but public nudity ... whether it [was] combined with expressive activity.... Indiana's requirement that the dancers wear at least pasties and a G-string [was] modest, and the bare minimum necessary to achieve the states purpose."[54] The ruling led some to conclude that the protections of the Georgia Constitution are "substantially broader" than those of the U.S. Constitution.[55] Others suggested that such cases are an example of the "new federalism" and the rising supremacy of state law.[56])

---

naked for tips in a barroom" (259 Ga. at 705). The ruling overturned a 1988 state statute which prohibited partial nudity at clubs where alcoholic beverages were consumed (1988 Georgia Laws, 212, codified as O.C.G.A. 3-3-40 through O.C.G.A. 3-3-46). Subsequent cases limited this right in places where alcoholic beverages are served. See, Pel Asso, Inc. v. Joseph, 262 Ga. 904, 427 S.E.2d 264 (1993); Don Gravely v. Max Bacon, 263 Ga. 203, 429 S.E.2d 663 (1993). In 1994, Georgia voters amended the state constitution to allow the regulation of such activities by counties and municipalities. See, World Famous Dudley's Food & Spirits v. City of College Park, 265 Ga. 618, 458 S.E.2d 823 (1995).

54. Barnes v. Glen Theater, 501 U.S. 560 (1991) at 572.

55. Michael Hauptman, president of the Georgia chapter of the American Civil Liberties Union, quoted in Jim Yardley's article, "Nude Dancing: An Unclear Future," Atlanta Journal-Constitution, June 22, 1991, A1. For a different view, see, Lynn Hogue, "Assaying the Dross in the Gold Club Case: Some Thoughts on Substantive Due Process and Georgia's Barroom Sex Law," 27 Georgia State Bar Journal 170 (1991).

56. See, Charles N. Davis & Paul H. Gates, Jr., "Superseding the Federal Constitution: The New Federalism, State Constitutional Supremacy and First Amendment Jurisprudence," Communication and the Law (March 1995), 27; Nancy Bowman, "State Constitutions May Prove Best Libel Defense," The Quill (October 1992), 64; Bill Rankin, "Georgia Supreme Court: A Shift in Philosophy," Atlanta Journal-Constitution, Dec. 20, 1998,

Georgia's free expression guarantee, according to Chief Justice W.H. Duckworth, is "absolute as to what it protects," as long as the media violate no constitutional rights of others.[57] "All interference [with protected expression] is absolutely interdicted" by Georgia's constitution, "but it does not protect an abuse of that liberty."[58] Freedom of expression must be exercised responsibly.[59]

Thus,

- extortionate expression,[60]
- terroristic threats, including the online dissemination of information designed to encourage terroristic acts,[61]
- incitement to riot,[62]

H1, H5.

57. K. Gordon Murray Productions v. Floyd, 217 Ga. 784, 125 S.E.2d 207 (1962) at 791. See, for example, McGill v. Georgia, 209 Ga. 500, 74 S.E. 78 (1953). For instances where the freedom was not held to be absolute, see, for example, Wolfe v. Albany, 104 Ga. App. 264, 121 S.E.2d 331 (1961); Atlanta Co-Operative News Project v. U.S. Postal Service, 350 F.Supp. 234 (N.D. Ga. 1972); Airport Bookstore v. Jackson, 242 Ga. 214, 248 S.E.2d 623 (1978), certiorari denied, 441 U.S. 952 (1979); High Ol' Times v. Busbee, 456 F.Supp. 1035 (N.D. Ga. 1978), affirmed, 621 F.2d 141 (5th Cir. 1980); Walt Disney Productions v. Shannon, 247 Ga. 402, 276 S.E.2d 580 (1981); Department of Transportation v. Shiflett, 251 Ga. 873, 310 S.E.2d 509 (1984).

58. K. Gordon Murray Productions, 217 Ga. 784, 125 S.E.2d 207 (1962) at 792, 791.

59. See, for example, 106 Forsyth Corp. v. Bishop, 362 F.Supp. 1389 (M.D. Ga. 1972), affirmed, 482 F.2d 280 (5th Cir. 1973), certiorari denied, 422 U.S. 1044 (1975).

60. See, for example, U.S. v. Quinn, 514 F.2d 1250 (5th Cir. 1975), certiorari denied, 424 U.S. 955 (1976).

61. O.C.G.A. 16-11-37. See, 2010 Georgia Laws 999. See, for example, Lanthrip v. Georgia, 235 Ga. 10, 218 S.E.2d 771 (1975).

62. See, for example, Sumbry v. Land, 127 Ga. App. 786, 195 S.E.2d 228 (1972), certiorari denied, 414 U.S. 1079 (1973).

- expression which advocates the unlawful overthrow of government,[63]
- obscenity,[64]
- "fighting words,"[65]
- abusive language,[66]
- certain fraudulent or deceptive trade or telemarketing practices, including the promotion of illegal lotteries, especially when directed toward the elderly or disabled,[67] or even
- symbolic actions, such as draft card burning,[68]
- wearing a mask or hood (with the obvious exceptions of

---

63. See, for example, Carr v. Georgia, 176 Ga. 55, 166 S.E. 827 (1932), later appeal, 176 Ga. 747, 169 S.E. 201 (1933). See also, O.C.G.A. 16-11-4.

64. See, for example, S.S.W. Corp. v. Slaton, 231 Ga. 734, 204 S.E.2d 155 (1974). The private possession of obscene material, however, is protected. See, for example, Stanley v. Georgia, 394 U.S. 557 (1969); Gable v. Jenkins, 309 F.Supp. 998 (N.D. Ga. 1969), affirmed, 397 U.S. 592 (1970); U.S. v. Thevis, 320 F.Supp. 713 (N.D. Ga. 1970).

65. O.C.G.A. 16-11-39. See, for example, Bolden v. Georgia, 148 Ga. App. 315, 251 S.E.2d 165 (1978); Brooks v. Georgia, 166 Ga. App. 704, 305 S.E.2d 436 (1983); Evans v. Georgia, 188 Ga. App. 347, 373 S.E.2d 52 (1988).

66. O.C.G.A. 40-1-4. See, for example, Watts v. Six Flags Over Georgia, 140 Ga. App. 106, 230 S.E.2d 34 (1976). However, the Georgia Supreme Court ruled that a bumper sticker containing the words, "Shit Happens," was protected expression. See, Cunningham v. Georgia, 260 Ga. 827, 400 S.E.2d 916 (1991).

67. O.C.G.A. 10-1-851; O.C.G.A. 46-5-27; O.C.G.A. 10-1-393; O.C.G.A. 10-5B-2; O.C.G.A. 10-5B-4; O.C.G.A. 16-8-12. See, 2012 Georgia Laws 1136, Senate Bill 431, §1.

68. See, for example, U.S. v. Southern Motor Carriers Rate Conference, 467 F.Supp. 471 (N.D. Ga. 1979), reversed on other grounds, 471 U.S. 48 (1984). The U.S. Supreme Court first determined that this activity was not protected expression in U.S. v. O'Brien, 391 U.S. 367 (1968).

       holiday costumes and for safety reasons),[69] and
- hair length[70]

are not protected forms of expression in Georgia.

---

69. O.C.G.A. 16-11-38. Though not mentioned, the purpose of the 1951 statute was to reduce violence by the Ku Klux Klan while protected by the anonymity of the mask. The statute was upheld in Georgia v. Miller, 260 Ga. 669, 398 S.E.2d 547 (1990). See, Wayne R. Allen, Klan, Cloth and Constitution: Anti-Mask Laws and the First Amendment, 25 Georgia Law Review 819 (1991). See also, Daniels v. Georgia, 264 Ga. App. 460, 448 S.E.2d 185 (1994).

70. See, for example, Stevenson v. Wheeler County Board of Education, 306 F.Supp. 97 (S.D. Ga. 1969), affirmed, 426 F.2d 1154 (5th Cir. 1970), certiorari denied, 400 U.S. 957 (1970); Howell v. Wolf, 331 F.Supp. 1342 (N.D. Ga. 1971); Ashley v. Macon, 377 F.Supp. 540 (M.D. Ga. 1974), affirmed, 505 F.2d 868 (5th Cir. 1975); Nalley v. Douglas County, 498 F.Supp. 1228 (N.D. Ga. 1980).

Continuing Debates

Issues which may not yet be completely settled in Georgia generally include statutes which could be applied in a discriminatory manner, legal standards over which there appears to be increasing disagreement, and topics which may have an inherent appeal but which could infringe upon free expression guarantees. Some of these include:

- Whether economic development discussions between the state and private industry should be public;[71]
- Whether non-English signs threaten the public safety;[72]

---

71. See, "Jim Galloway, "Bill Trades Secrecy for Jobs," Atlanta Journal-Constitution, Feb. 5, 2005, A1, A8; "Secrecy Only Clouds Decision-Making," Atlanta Journal-Constitution, Feb. 6, 2005, E6; Walter Woods, "State's Secrets Haven't Spilled," Atlanta Journal-Constitution, Feb. 12, 2005, A1; Jim Wooten, "Secrecy Betrays the Real Georgia," Atlanta Journal-Constitution, Feb. 13, 2005, E6; Walter Woods, "N.C. Raises Caution Flags on Secrecy," Atlanta Journal-Constitution, Feb. 20, 2005, E1; Brandon Larrabee, "New Bid for Industrial Recruitment Secrecy Could Resurface in Georgia," Georgia FOI Access (Winter 2007), 2. With regard to the development of the Georgia Aquarium, see, Jim Tharpe, "Fishy Secrets Hush-Hush," Atlanta Journal-Constitution, July 24, 2005, D1. A legislative proposal to allow an economic development exemption to Georgia's open meeting and open records laws failed in 2005. See, "Legislature Recap," Atlanta Journal-Constitution, March 27, 2005, C5.

72. O.C.G.A. 50-3-100. See also, Sophia Lezin, "Fines Anger Latino Merchants," Atlanta Journal-Constitution, March 7, 1999, E1, E13; Sophia Lezin, "Latino Merchant Files Suit in Norcross Sign Dispute," Atlanta Journal-Constitution, March 10, 1999, C3; Milo Ippolito, "Norcross Says Adios to Ban on Non-English Signs," Atlanta Journal-Constitution, May 6, 1999, B1; Milo Ippolito, "Ethnic Sign Law Revision Explored," Atlanta Journal-Constitution, May 24, 1999, J1; Sophia Lezin, "Norcross Council To Consider Revamped Sign Law," Atlanta Journal-Constitution, May 26, 1999, J1; Peter J. Kent, "Revised Sign Ordinance Up for Vote Tonight," Atlanta Journal-Constitution, June 7, 1999, J1, J3; Rick Badie, "Language of Signs

- The extent to which the governor's personal finances are subject to public disclosure, as well as whether the Office of the Governor is subject to state open meetings and open records laws;[73]
- Whether city litter ordinances may be used to control the distribution of free publications;[74]
- The extent of billboard companies' free speech rights in communities that do not want them;[75]
- Whether concerns over property values and "quality of life" may be used to restrict the location of adult businesses;[76]
- The extent to which court records should be available on the Internet;[77]

Remains an Issue in Norcross," Atlanta Journal-Constitution, Dec. 23, 2001, J1.

73. Alan Judd, "Barnes Wants Limit on Data Public Sees About His Finances," Atlanta Journal-Constitution, April 26, 2000, B1, B5; Martha Ezzard, "Governor Is Right To Seek Clarification on Blind Trust," Atlanta Journal-Constitution, May 7, 2000, F7; Kathey Pruitt, "Barnes Says He'll Disclose All Finances," Atlanta Journal-Constitution, June 14, 2000, C1, C6. See also, Peter Canfield & Marcia Bull Stadeker, "The Chief Executive's Office: Open or Closed?" Georgia FOI Access (Fall 2000), 3-4.

74. Bill Rankin, "Papers Tossed in Yards Are Protected Speech, Court Says," Atlanta Journal-Constitution, May 18, 1999, C7.

75. Dana Tofig, "Bill(board) of Rights Challenged," Atlanta Journal-Constitution, Oct. 10, 2000, B1; Christopher Quinn, "Exurbs Send Message with Billboard Laws," Atlanta Journal-Constitution, Feb. 6, 2003, D3.

76. Carlos Campos, "Zoning Out Unwelcome Neighbors," Atlanta Journal-Constitution, June 1, 1997, F1; Duane Stanford, "Adult Videos on Sale at a Convenience Store Near You," Atlanta Journal-Constitution, May 28, 2000, J1.

77. Yolanda Rodriguez, "Cyber-court: Cobb Hears Case for Opening Records," Atlanta Journal-Constitution, May 11, 2000, D1, D6.

- Whether security restrictions on newspaper rack placement and newspaper delivery at Hartsfield International Airport may ever be justified;[78]
- The extent to which a mayor's appointment book and work schedule are public records;[79]
- The degree to which fraud may be prevented through restrictions on the unauthorized use of legally protected symbols on the Internet;[80]
- Whether allegations of ethics violations by legislators and subsequent investigations should be public;[81]
- Whether publicly available campaign donation information should also be available online;[82]

---

78. See, Atlanta Journal-Constitution v. Atlanta Dept. of Aviation, 6 F.Supp.2d 1359 (N.D.Ga.1998), 277 F.3d 1322 (11h Cir. 2002). See also, Reporters Committee for Freedom of the Press, "Airport Ban on News Distribution Enjoined Third Time," News Media Update, Aug. 12, 1996.

79. Julie B. Hairston, "Mayor's Work Schedule a Mystery," Atlanta Journal-Constitution, Sept. 28, 2000, C1, C4.

80. Reporters Committee for Freedom of the Press, "State Law Restricts Anonymity, Misrepresentation on Internet," News Media Update, July 15, 1996, page number unknown. See, O.C.G.A. 16-9-109.1. See also, David H. Rothman, "The Internet Police Law: The Day the Sites Went Out in Georgia" (undated), previously available at: http://www.clark.net/pub/rothman/ga.htm (copy on file with author); Art Kramer, "ACLU Sues the State Over Its Ban on Some Internet Communication," Atlanta Journal-Constitution, Sept. 25, 1996, D3; Art Kramer, "Special Order in the Court: Professor's Demo Explores Issue of Cyber-Anonymity," Atlanta Journal-Constitution, Jan. 31, 1997, F3.

81. See, Jim Galloway, "Ethics Bill Will Shut Out Public," Atlanta Journal-Constitution, April 2, 2005, A1.

82. See, Ty Tagami, "Campaign Donations Listed Online," Atlanta Journal-Constitution, June 14, 2005, B3; Ben Smith, "25 Big Donors You Didn't Know," Atlanta Journal-Constitution, July 24, 2005, J1. See also, Georgia Common Cause, Holding Power Accountable (undated), available at: http://moneywatch.commoncause.org/money.asp (last accessed Nov. 15, 2013).

- The extent to which records of monies paid state employees should be available online;[83]
- Whether membership cooperatives selling natural gas and electricity in Georgia, which by their nature are not regulated by the Public Service Commission, should be more open and transparent in their business dealings with their customers;[84]
- The degree to which secrecy in negotiations involving the commitment of taxpayer monies by local governments in such things as land purchases, which are being used to attract sports teams or sporting events or venues to re-locate in Georgia, can ever be appropriate;[85]
- Whether use of automobile license plate recognition software by the Georgia State Patrol and police departments in Sandy Springs, Atlanta, and Gwinnett County violates constitutional privacy rights or protections against unreasonable searches;[86] and

---

83. See, Dept. of Audits & Accounts, "Open Georgia: Transparency in Government" (2008), available at: http://www.open.ga.gov/index.html (last accessed Nov. 15, 2013). Privacy advocates contend that "at the very least, the Internet has made it far easier for anyone to obtain not only someone else's birth date or Social Security number but also, liens, lawsuits, divorces and other personal and potentially embarrassing – but technically public – information." Brian Bergstein, "Data-Mining Tools Fuel Concerns about Privacy," Atlanta Journal-Constitution, Jan. 4, 2004, C2.

84. See, Margaret Newkirk, "A Push for More Access at Co-Ops," Atlanta Journal-Constitution, Jan. 16, 2011, D1, D3; Tim Eberly & Margaret Newkirk, "Cobb EMC Board Works Outside Spotlight," Atlanta Journal-Constitution, Nov. 25, 2007, F1, F8.

85. "Gwinnett Back to Secret Deals" (editorial), Atlanta Journal-Constitution, Jan. 18, 2008, A14.

86. See, Rhonda Cook, "Tag Readers Raise Privacy Concerns," Atlanta Journal-Constitution, Dec. 1, 2012, B1, B8.

- Under what circumstances the act of promoting assisted suicide can be seen as constitutionally protected speech.[87]

Without doubt, other issues will also arise.

---

87. Final Exit Network v. Georgia, 290 Ga. 508; 722 S.E.2d 722 (2012). See, O.C.G.A. 16-5-5; 2012 Georgia Laws 637, House Bill 1114. See also, Kim Severson, "Georgia Court Rejects Law Aimed at Assisted Suicide," New York Times, Feb. 7, 2012, A19; Alyson Palmer, "Supreme Court Dumps Suicide Law," Daily Report, Feb. 7, 2012, 1, 4; Bill Rankin, "Ga. Supreme Court: Law on Assisted Suicide Rejected," Atlanta Journal-Constitution, Feb. 7, 2012, A1, A19.

QUESTIONS

1. Name Georgia's three appellate, law-interpreting courts.

2. Why was Georgia's Constitution of 1865 rejected by the federal government? What was the result of this rejection?

3. Which Georgia court was created to reduce the workload of the superior courts? What type of jurisdiction does it have?

4. Georgia is presently governed by which constitution?

5. Which is Georgia's most important trial-level, fact-finding court? Is it a court of limited or general jurisdiction?

6. What symbolic expression is prohibited in Georgia because of its association with the Ku Klux Klan's history of terrorism?

7. In what area of protected expression does Georgia's position seem to be most at odds with that of the U.S. Supreme Court?

8. Which of Georgia's three appellate courts has exclusive jurisdiction over cases involving freedom of expression?

9. What was the occasion for Georgia's symbolic ratification of the First Amendment to the U.S. Constitution?

Thought Question:

Why does the Georgia Supreme Court interpret the state constitution's free expression guarantee absolutely, when the U.S. Supreme Court has never interpreted the First Amendment similarly?

2. Libel in Georgia

Because Georgia was one of the original Thirteen Colonies, its laws of defamation are deeply rooted in English common law, based upon the maxim: "A good name is rather to be chosen than great riches...."[1] The two types of actions which redress injury to reputation are actions for slander,[2] which seek recovery for words spoken, and actions for libel, which seek recovery for defamation which is "written" and thus both more permanent and more pervasive. The tort of civil libel is particularly concerned with damage to one's reputation and the righting of that wrong - or at least the payment of compensation by the wrong-doer for the injury - because, in the words of Justice Joseph H. Lumpkin, "every man has the right to the enjoyment of a good reputation unassailed."[3] The law of criminal libel, on the other hand, is more concerned with exacting a penalty on behalf of the state - such as a fine or incarceration - from the guilty person or persons.

1. Proverbs 22:1, quoted in Spence v. Johnson, 142 Ga. 267, 82 S.E. 646 (1914) at 269. See also, American Broadcasting-Paramount Theatres v. Simpson, 106 Ga. App. 230, 126 S.E.2d 873 (1962); Eason Publications v. Atlanta Gazette, 141 Ga. App. 321, 233 S.E.2d 232 (1977).

2. See, for example, Strange v. Henderson, 223 Ga. App. 218, 477 S.E.2d 330 (1996). The statute of limitations for slander suits in Georgia is the same as it is for libel – one year. O.C.G.A. 9-3-33.

3. Spence v. Johnson, 142 Ga. 267, 82 S.E. 646 (1914) at 269.

Elements of Civil Libel

Lawsuits seeking compensation for damage to one's reputation under the requirements of civil libel[4] must establish three contentions: defamation which causes harm, publication, and identification.

First, and most importantly, the reputation of the person seeking damages must have been harmed.[5] The person must have been defamed - that is, the person must be a less productive, less valuable, less useful member of the community as a result of the defamation.[6] And central to any contention

---

4. In Georgia, libel is "actionable per se" and does not require proof of special damages; plaintiffs can recover by showing general damages alone. See, for example, Weatherholt v. Howard, 142 Ga. 41, 84 S.E. 119 (1915); Davis v. Macon Telegraph Publishing Co., 93 Ga. App. 633, 92 S.E.2d 619 (1956). Georgia's prohibition against oral defamation - slander - is codified in O.C.G.A. 51-5-4. As an example of a recent case involving accusations of fornication made in a religious assembly, see, Driver v. Fogarty, No. 2007-V-146-S, Amendment to the Amended and Recast Complaint for Damages, Superior Court of Twiggs County, Ga. (Oct. 8, 2008), available at: http://www.13wmaz.com/news/PDF/driver_complaint.pdf (last accessed Nov. 1, 2013).

5. Libel, according to Georgia law, is a false and defamatory statement which damages a person's reputation and which exposes him to "public hatred, contempt, or ridicule." See, for example, Hood v. Dun & Bradstreet, 335 F.Supp. 170 (N.D. Ga. 1971), quoting O.C.G.A. 51-5-1(a) and O.C.G.A. 51-5-2(a). The dead have no reputation and, thus, cannot be defamed through civil libel. See, for example, Saari v. Gillett Communications, 195 Ga. App. 451, 393 S.E.2d 736 (1990).

6. Georgia courts have held: that it was not defamatory to state that a racial minority group had endorsed a candidate for election, even though the endorsement resulted in the candidate's defeat - Watkins v. Augusta Chronicle, 49 Ga. App. 43, 174 S.E. 199 (1934); that a telegram containing the words, "Must have March payment immediately or legal action," did not charge the recipient with being a "dead beat" - Davis v. General Finance & Thrift Corp., 80 Ga. App. 708, 57 S.E.2d 225 (1950); that unfavorable commercial publicity lacked the necessary "element of personal disgrace" - Southard v. Forbes, Inc., 588 F.2d 140 (5th Cir. 1979); that a false obituary

that a person has been defamed in Georgia is that the defamation must both be "false and malicious."[7] Claims of libel by implication or libel by omission are not generally successful in Georgia.[8]

Malice, according to state statute, may be "inferred from the character of the charge"[9] and is "common law" malice - ill will, spite, hatred, or charges deliberately calculated to injure one's reputation.[10] Since 1964, defamed public officials and public figures can only collect damages by showing that the publisher or broadcaster acted with actual malice - defined as "knowledge that [the defamation] was false or [with] reckless disregard of whether it was false or not"[11] - established in a

---

stating that a funeral home which predominantly served black families was in charge of arrangements was not defamatory - Thomason v. Times-Journal, 190 Ga. App. 601, 379 S.E.2d 551 (1989); that the act of firing an employee is not the equivalent of defamation - Brewer v. Metropolitan Atlanta Rapid Transit Authority, 204 Ga. App. 241, 419 S.E.2d 60 (1992).

7. This is also known as "express malice." See, for example, Ajouelo v. Auto-Soler Co., 61 Ga. App. 216, 6 S.E.2d 415 (1940). From this, it may be inferred that truth is an absolute and complete defense in such cases.

8. For an example of claims alleging libel by implication, see, Mead v. The True Citizen, 203 Ga. App. 361, 417 S.E.2d 16 (1992). For an example of claims alleging libel by omission, see, Cox Enterprises v. Bakin, 206 Ga. App. 813, 426 S.E.2d 651 (1992), certiorari denied, 114 S.Ct. 193 (1993).

9. O.C.G.A. 51-5-5. See, for example, Straw v. Chase Revel, 813 F.2d 356 (11th Cir. 1987), certiorari denied, 484 U.S. 856 (1987), where the concept of inferring malice from the character of the charge was held to be constitutional, as long as the trial judge gives careful consideration to the distinction between "common law" malice and the constitutional standard of actual malice.

10. See, for example, Horton v. Georgian Co., 175 Ga. 261, 165 S.E. 443 (1932); Williams v. Trust Company of Georgia, 140 Ga. App. 49, 230 S.E.2d 45 (1976).

11. New York Times v. Sullivan, 376 U.S. 254 (1964) at 280.

clear and convincing manner.[12] Actual malice may be distinguished from "common law" malice in that actual malice "does not involve the motives of the speaker or publisher - but rather [his or her] awareness of actual or probable falsity or his reckless disregard" for it.[13]

Georgia recognizes four statutory origins or types of defamation:

1. Defamation by "newspaper, magazine, or periodical;"[14]
2. Defamation "expressed in print, writing, pictures, or signs;"[15]
3. Defamation by "the owner, licensee, or operator of a visual or sound broadcasting station or network of stations and [his or her] agents," also known as "defamacast";[16]

---

12. See, for example, Rosanova v. Playboy Enterprises, 411 F.Supp. 440 (S.D. Ga. 1976), affirmed, 580 F.2d 859 (5th Cir. 1978); Barber v. Perdue, 194 Ga. App. 287, 390 S.E.2d 234 (1989).

13. Williams v. Trust Company of Georgia, 140 Ga. App. 49, 230 S.E.2d 45 (1976) at 56.

14. O.C.G.A. 51-5-2. This is also known in Georgia as "newspaper libel." See, for example, Jim Walter Homes v. Strickland, 185 Ga. App. 306, 363 S.E.2d 834 (1987). This includes defamation on Internet websites. See, Milum v. Banks, 283 Ga. App. 864, 642 S.E.2d 892 (2007).

15. O.C.G.A. 51-5-1. See, for example, Mathews v. Atlanta Newspapers, 116 Ga. App. 337, 157 S.E.2d 300 (1967).

16. O.C.G.A. 51-5-10. See, for example, Georgia Communications v. Horne, 174 Ga. App. 69, 329 S.E.2d 192 (1985). See also, L. Lin Wood, "The Case of David v. Goliath: Jewell v. NBC and the Basics of Defamacast in Georgia," 7 Fordham Intellectual Property, Media & Entertainment Law Journal 673 (Spring 1997). In 2004 broadcasters were exempted from civil liability for defamatory errors associated with any abducted child alert, known in the state as "Levi's Call: Georgia's Amber Alert Program." See, O.C.G.A. 51-1-50.

4. "Willful disparagement" of Georgia agricultural products not based on "reasonable and reliable scientific inquiry, facts, or data."[17]

Interestingly, the statutes codifying the first two offenses read almost exactly the same; publishers in either situation must not be guilty of malicious defamation. It is not clear to what extent these differ, as Georgia courts in the past have held that the freedom to publish enjoyed by - and therefore the responsibility of - the news media is the same as that of ordinary citizens.[18] However, according to Georgia's statutory standards, broadcasters need only exercise "due care" for them not to be responsible for defamation.[19] Broadcasters enjoy absolute

---

17. O.C.G.A. 2-16-1, O.C.G.A. 2-16-2. See, Mark Sherman, "New Law Lets Farmers Sue for Product Defamation," Atlanta Journal-Constitution, April 29, 1993; D2. A challenge to the "banana bill" in 1994 by Action for a Clean Environment and Parents for Pesticide Alternatives failed. See, "'93 State Law Challenged," Atlanta Journal-Constitution, March 31, 1994, C6. See, generally, Jamison S. Prime, "Fruitfully Correct: Alar Incident Spurs States To Nip Critics in the Bud," The Quill (January/February 1995), 38-39; Anne Hawke, "Veggie Disparagement," The Quill (September 1998), 13-15; Melody Petersen, "Farmers' Right To Sue Grows, Raising Debate on Food Safety," New York Times, June 1, 1999, A1, C9.

18. See, for example, Lowe v. News Publishing, 9 Ga. App. 103, 70 S.E. 607 (1911). Charles and Cynthia Adams contend that the tort of newspaper libel, though diminished in significance by the "federalization" of libel law in 1964, has not been "completely eviscerated" (Georgia Law of Torts, 1998, at 476). For a post-1964 example of media liability, see, Western Broadcasting v. Wright, 182 Ga. App. 359, 356 S.E.2d 52 (1987).

19. O.C.G.A. 51-5-10(a). Broadcasters have even greater protection in libel suits involving public officials in that the public official must also prove actual malice before being able to collect damages. See, for example, Pierce v. Pacific & Southern Co., 166 Ga. App. 113, 303 S.E.2d 316 (1983).

immunity when broadcasting remarks made by or directly on behalf of candidates for public office.[20]

In addition, there are generally five types of defamation:

- False allegations of criminal activity.[21]

Thus, wrongfully accusing someone of arson,[22] bribery,[23] gambling,[24] adultery,[25] fornication,[26] thievery,[27] forgery,[28] swindling,[29] embezzlement,[30] prostitution,[31] perjury,[32] any

---

20. O.C.G.A. 51-5-10(b).

21. See, for example, Witham v. Atlanta Journal, 124 Ga. 688, 53 S.E. 105 (1906); Revco Discount Drug Centers v. Famble, 173 Ga. App. 330, 326 S.E.2d 532 (1985).

22. See, for example, Giddens v. Mirk, 4 Ga. 364 (1848).

23. See, for example, Atlanta News v. Medlock, 123 Ga. 714, 51 S.E. 756 (1905).

24. See, for example, Atlanta Journal v. Doyal, 82 Ga. App. 321, 60 S.E.2d 802 (1950).

25. See, for example, Barker v. Green, 34 Ga. App. 574, 130 S.E. 599 (1925); Freeman v. Busch Jewelry, 98 F.Supp. 963 (N.D. Ga. 1951). However, for a more recent attitude, see, for example, Meyer v. Ledford, 170 Ga. App. 245, 316 S.E.2d 804 (1984).

26. See, for example, Richardson v. Roberts, 23 Ga. 215 (1857). For a modern example, see, Driver v. Fogarty, No. 2007-V-146-S, Superior Court of Twiggs County (2010). See also, Katheryn Tucker, "Slander Costs Pentecostal Church $526K," Daily Report, July 15, 2012, 1, 9.

27. See, for example, Augusta Chronicle Publishing v. Arrington, 42 Ga. App. 746, 157 S.E. 394 (1931).

28. See, for example, Western Union Telegraph v. Vickers, 71 Ga. App. 204, 30 S.E.2d 440 (1944).

29. See, for example, Simpson v. Jacobs Pharmacy, 76 Ga. App. 232, 45 S.E.2d 678 (1948).

30. See, for example, Elsas v. Browne, 68 Ga. 117 (1881).

31. See, for example, Pledger v. Hathcock, 1 Ga. 550 (1846).

32. See, for example, Atlanta News Publishing v. Medlock, 123 Ga. 714, 51 S.E. 756 (1905).

"indictable" offense[33] - or even a misdemeanor[34] - is defamatory, as is language an "average and reasonable" reader,[35] drawing from all parts of the publication and considering the circumstances in which publication occurred,[36] would deem to impute criminality.[37]

- False accusations of an illness or affliction, such as venereal disease.[38]

However, following the U.S. Supreme Court's ruling in *Philadelphia Newspapers v. Hepps*,[39] if the person injured is unable to prove falsity, there is no defamation.[40]

- Words not charging a specific crime, but immorality or moral turpitude.[41]

---

33. See, for example, Zakas v. Mills, 148 Ga. App. 220, 251 S.E.2d 135 (1978).

34. See, for example, Davis v. Macon Telegraph Publishing, 93 Ga. App. 633, 92 S.E.2d 619 (1956).

35. See, for example, Ingram v. Atlanta Newspapers, 99 Ga. App. 246, 108 S.E.2d 151 (1959).

36. See, for example, Camp v. Maddox, 93 Ga. App. 646, 92 S.E.2d 581 (1956).

37. See, for example, Stancel v. Pryer, 25 Ga. 40 (1858).

38. See, for example, Watson v. McCarthy, 2 Ga. 57 (1847); Williams v. Equitable Credit, 33 Ga. App. 441, 126 S.E. 855 (1925); Kaplan v. Edmondson, 68 Ga. App. 151, 22 S.E.2d 343 (1942).

39. 475 U.S. 767 (1986).

40. See, for example, Cox Enterprises v. Thrasher, 264 Ga. 235, 442 S.E.2d 740 (1994), reversing 209 Ga. App. 716, 434 S.E.2d 497 (1993). See also, Trisha Renaud, "Reporter's Alleged Trickery Makes Libel a Jury Question," Daily Report, July 7, 1993, 1, 4; "Georgia High Court Affirms Paper's Summary Judgment," News Media & the Law (Summer 1994), 12. See also, Atlanta Journal-Constitution v. Jewell, 251 Ga. App. 808, 555 S.E.2d 175 (2001).

41. See, for example, Castleberry v. Kelly, 26 Ga. 606 (1858); Lewis v.

- "Words falsely spoken of one in reference to his trade, office, or profession," tending "directly to injure him in his vocation or occupation."[42]

However, a single mistake does not equate with a general lack of skill.[43]

- False complaints which are libelous *per se* - those libelous on their face without any proof of special damages.[44]

However, Judge Robert L. Russell noted that "mere billingsgate, insult, and contemptuous language are not

---

Hudson, 44 Ga. 568 (1872); Hardy v. Williamson, 86 Ga. 551, 12 S.E. 874 (1891); Shiver v. Valdosta Press, 82 Ga. App. 406, 61 S.E.2d 221 (1950).

42. Spence v. Johnson, 142 Ga. 267, 82 S.E. 646 (1914) at 273. See, for example, Aiken v. Constitution Publishing, 72 Ga. App. 250, 33 S.E.2d 555 (1945). Corporate entities may also be harmed by defamatory remarks, which could also result in criminal prosecution in Georgia when banks' financial integrity is questioned. See, Russell Grantham, "Bad-Mouthing Banks? Beware – False Statements Could Break Law," Atlanta Journal-Constitution, July 19, 2008, C1, C4.

43. See, for example, Holder Construction v. Ed Smith & Sons, 124 Ga. App. 89, 182 S.E.2d 919 (1971).

44. Georgia courts have held: that it was libelous per se for one falsely to accuse a local merchant of being "an itinerant trader of small responsibility and uncertain prospects" - Dun v. Weintraub, 111 Ga. 416, 36 S.E. 808 (1900); that it was libelous per se falsely to report that criminal charges were pending against another - Witham v. Atlanta Journal, 124 Ga. 688, 53 S.E. 105 (1906); that it was libelous per se to impute the crime of larceny to another - Harrison v. Pool, 24 Ga. App. 587, 101 S.E. 765 (1919); that it was libelous per se falsely to state that someone was gambling in violation of state law - Atlanta Journal v. Doyal/Nix v. Doyal, 82 Ga. App. 321, 60 S.E.2d 802 (1950); that it was libelous per se for a magazine article falsely to charge a university coach with fixing a football game - Curtis Publishing v. Butts, 351 F.2d 702 (1965), affirming 225 F.Supp. 916 (1964).

sufficient *alone* to state a cause of action."[45] Thus, neither issuing a false credit report that a person is divorced[46] nor stating that a legislator is unfairly allied with labor unions[47] is actionable, though making a person the butt of jokes and ridicule by accusing him of stealing another's false teeth is.[48]

Nevertheless, harmless words may become defamatory in light of extrinsic facts.[49] This concept is known as libel *per quod* or libel by innuendo. It is important to note here that Georgia does not follow the "Innocent Construction Rule," where words capable of being understood in two or more ways are assumed to have been used innocently. In such cases in Georgia, the jury must decide which meaning was intended.[50]

A second element of libel is that the defamation must have been published; that is, it must have been spread or disseminated to others.[51] Without this element, there is no libel,

---

45. Berry v. Baugh, 111 Ga. App. 813, 143 S.E.2d 489 (1965) at 816. Emphasis in original. A newspaper headline that a contractor had "raped" the land was not libelous. See, Lucas v. Cranshaw, 289 Ga. App. 510, 659 S.E.2d 612 (2008).

46. See, Duncan v. Credit Service Exchange, 56 Ga. App. 551, 193 S.E. 591 (1937).

47. See, Anderson v. Kennedy, 47 Ga. App. 380, 170 S.E. 555 (1933).

48. See, Augusta Chronicle Publishing v. Arrington, 42 Ga. App. 746, 157 S.E. 394 (1931).

49. See, for example, Warner Brothers Pictures v. Stanley, 56 Ga. App. 85, 192 S.E. 300 (1937); Macon Telegraph v. Elliott, 165 Ga. App. 719, 302 S.E.2d 692 (1983), certiorari denied, 466 U.S. 971 (1984).

50. See, for example, Southard v. Forbes, Inc., 588 F.2d 140 (5th Cir. 1979); Stalvey v. Atlanta Business Chronicle, 202 Ga. App. 597, 414 S.E.2d 898 (1992); Nix v. Cox Enterprises, 247 Ga. App. 689, 545 S.E.2d 319 (2001). (NOTE: The author served as an expert witness for the plaintiff in Stalvey v. Atlanta Business Chronicle.)

51. See, O.C.G.A. 51-5-1(b), O.C.G.A. 51-5-2(b). Publication takes place when defamation "is communicated to any person other than the party libeled" (O.C.G.A. 51-5-3). See, for example, McFarlan v. Manget, 179 Ga. 17, 174 S.E. 712 (1934); Ray v. Henco Electronics, 156 Ga. App. 394, 274

though in 1909 the Georgia Supreme Court held that the statement that one "did publish" was sufficient to establish this element.[52] Yet the manner in which it is published appears to be of little consequence, because even oral communication of written defamation has been held to constitute "publication."[53] The author and the communicator of the libel are equally responsible; "tale-bearers are as bad as tale-makers," according to Judge H.E. Nichols.[54]

However, publication does not take place when remarks are made to persons properly engaged in a "good-faith" investigation and with duty and authority to control that inquiry.[55] In addition, Georgia courts have protected

---

S.E.2d 602 (1980). Georgia adheres to the "Single Publication" Rule, which means that "one publication is only one libel ... but each new printing of the paper ... constitutes a libel actionable at law." Rives v. Atlanta Newspapers, 220 Ga. 485, 139 S.E.2d 395 (1964) at 487. See also, Cox Enterprises v. Gilreath, 142 Ga. App. 297, 235 S.E.2d 633 (1977). The rule was applied to Internet postings in McCandliss v. Cox Enterprises, 265 Ga. App. 377, 593 S.E.2d 856 (2004) at 379-380.

52. See, Morgan v. Black, 132 Ga. 67, 63 S.E. 821 (1909). However, the allegation that defamatory words were "generally circulated in the county" is not publication. See, Beck v. Oden, 64 Ga. App. 407, 13 S.E.2d 468 (1941). More recently, Georgia's appellate court said the defamatory words must also be understood. See, Sigmon v. Womack, 158 Ga. App. 47, 279 S.E.2d 254 (1981).

53. See, Garren v. Southland Corp., 235 Ga. 784, 221 S.E.2d 571 (1976), reversing 135 Ga. App. 77, 217 S.E.2d 347 (1975).

54. Davis v. Macon Telegraph Publishing, 93 Ga. App. 633, 92 S.E.2d 619 (1956) at 640.

55. See, for example, Melton v. Bow, 145 Ga. App. 272, 243 S.E.2d 590 (1978). This group apparently does not include ministers. See, for example, Lois Gibson, "Angela Driver's Case against Pastor Mark E. Fogarty," Spiritual Abuse, Aug. 9, 2012, available at: http://www.spiritualabuse.org/experiences/lawsuits/mark_fogarty.html (last accessed Nov. 1, 2013).

communication dealing with job-related concerns.[56] In *Kurtz v. Williams* (1988), the Georgia Court of Appeals held that publication did not exist where a hospital officer advised other hospital officials of an allegation that an employee was engaging in an extramarital affair on the job.[57] And the refusal to make a published statement or the failure to present the whole truth, even if that failure may be interpreted as damaging to a person's reputation, cannot be defined as "publication."[58]

Third, the person seeking damages for libel must have been identified[59] or, in the words of Justice Bond Almand of the Georgia Supreme Court: "The defamatory words must refer to some ascertained or ascertainable person...."[60] Where there is doubt, it is a question for the jury.[61] But to attribute harassment to "persons who for their own selfish reasons" wished to see a project fail is not identification, even if testimony is introduced that some knew to whom the statement referred.[62] Traditionally, identification of a person or small group of persons by name is enough to meet this requirement. It is not, however, the only

---

56. See, for example, Neal v. McCall, 134 Ga. App. 680, 215 S.E.2d 537 (1975).

57. "Where the communication is intra-corporate, or between members of unincorporated groups or associations, and is heard by one who, because of his/her duty or authority has reason to receive the information, there is no publication" (188 Ga. App. 14, 371 S.E.2d 878, at 15).

58. See, for example, Comer v. National Bank of Georgia, 184 Ga. App. 867, 363 S.E.2d 153 (1987).

59. For there to be identification, defamatory words must be understood as referring to the person claiming to be defamed, not just to someone with the same name. See, for example, Minday v. Constitution Publishing, 52 Ga. App. 51, 182 S.E. 53 (1935).

60. Ledger-Enquirer v. Brown, 214 Ga. 422, 105 S.E.2d 229 (1958) at 423.

61. See, for example, Walker v. Sheehan, 80 Ga. App. 606, 56 S.E.2d 628 (1949).

62. Fiske v. Stockton, 171 Ga. App. 601, 320 S.E.2d 590 (1984).

means of identification.[63] For example, a person can be identified when fiction is a little too close to reality, as was the case with the 2003 novel about Buckhead socialites, *The Red Hat Club* by Haywood Smith. A jury found some 30 similarities between an Atlanta woman and the book's "SuSu" character, a sexually promiscuous alcoholic, and concluded that a "reasonable person ... who reads the book [would] reasonably conclude that the character SuSu is" the plaintiff.[64]

If these three contentions are established, the newspaper or other mass medium is as guilty of libel as its reporter, based on the "Doctrine of Respondeat Superior," which provides that an employer is liable for an employee's conduct, within the scope of his or her employment.[65] However, Georgia does judicially recognize the so-called "wire service defense," in which the news media are not liable for republishing a release from a reputable news agency without substantial changes and without

---

63. Georgia courts have held: that a picture in an advertisement may identify a person as a contented holder of an insurance policy - Pavesich v. New England Life Insurance, 122 Ga. 191, 50 S.E. 68 (1905); that having formerly done business under the name of the company defamed could be sufficient to defame the former owner also - Weatherholt v. Howard, 143 Ga. 41, 84 S.E. 119 (1915).

64. Smith v. Stewart, 291 Ga. App. 86, 660 S.E.2d 822 (2008) at 90. See, Stephen Gurr, "Jury Rules for Plaintiff in Red Hat Club Trial," Gainesville Times, Nov. 9, 2009, available at: http://www.gainesvilletimes.com/archives/26196/ (last accessed June 19, 2013). The ruling was upheld by both the Georgia Court of Appeals and the Georgia Supreme Court.

65. See, for example, Ferguson v. Park Newspapers of Georgia, 148 Ga. App. 848, 253 S.E.2d 231 (1979). On the other hand, a corporation is not responsible for defamatory remarks made by its officers, unless it expressly directed them to make the remarks in question. See, for example, WMH v. Thomas, 260 Ga. 654, 398 S.E.2d 196 (1990).

actually knowing that the information contained therein is false.[66]

---

66. See, for example, Brown v. Courier Herald Publishing, 700 F.Supp. 534 (S.D. Ga. 1988). Otherwise, repetition of libel is still libel and makes the person repeating the defamation also liable. See, for example, McCracken v Gainesville Tribune, 146 Ga. App. 274, 246 S.E.2d 360 (1978).

Libel Defenses

In addition to the "wire service defense," Georgia also recognizes both truth and privilege as defenses in libel cases. Truth is an absolute and complete defense, recognized as such by both the state constitution (see, Figure 3, below) and state statute,[67] and by a long line of court rulings.[68] In addition, though the Georgia Supreme Court has not adopted such a rule, the Georgia Court of Appeals has held that "substantial" truth or accuracy is sufficient.[69]

TRUTH AS A CONSTITUTIONAL DEFENSE IN GEORGIA
(Figure 3)

Libel
In all civil or criminal actions for libel, the truth may be given in evidence; and, if it shall appear to the trier of fact that the matter charged as libelous is true, the party shall be discharged.

- Article I, §8, ¶VI
Georgia Constitution of 1983

---

67. O.C.G.A. 51-5-6.

68. See, for example, Henderson v. Fox, 83 Ga. 233, 9 S.E. 839 (1889); Tetrault v. Shelton, 179 Ga. App. 50, 329 S.E.2d 636 (1986).

69. See, for example, Jones v. Neighbor Newspapers, 142 Ga. App. 365, 236 S.E.2d 23 (1977); Stange v. Cox Enterprises, 211 Ga. App. 731, 440 S.E.2d 503 (1994). Compare, Western Broadcasting of Augusta v. Wright, 182 Ga. App. 359, 356 S.E.2d 53 (1987) at 360 (where the court concluded that a broadcast "could not be considered accurate or even substantially accurate"). In addition, "close resemblance" may not be enough to protect oneself from a defamation lawsuit. Alyson Palmer, "Art Imitates Life Too Closely, Says Atlanta Woman," Daily Report, April 1, 2008, 1, 8-9.

Absolute privilege, as codified by statute,[70] protects publication of all charges, allegations, affidavits, testimony, and pleadings on file in Georgia courts,[71] as well as separation notices filed with the state Department of Labor in connection with administration of the Employment Security Act of 1941[72] and all other records of the department.[73] Although not specifically mentioned by statute, Judge I.H. Sutton believed the defense protects "legislative and judicial proceedings and other acts of State, including, it is said, communications made in the discharge of a duty under express authority of law, by or to heads of executive departments of the State, and matters involving military affairs."[74]

Other types of communication - disseminated "in good faith and with good intentions"[75] - protected by statutory qualified or conditional privilege[76] include:

---

70. O.C.G.A. 51-5-8. "The remarks of a legislator in debate, the words of a judge in the course of a judicial proceeding, the averments in a pleading filed in a court of competent jurisdiction, which are pertinent and material to the relief sought, are instances of absolute privilege" (Bell v. Anderson, 194 Ga. App. 27, 389 S.E.2d 762 (1989) at 28).

71. See, for example, Rivers v. Goodson, 188 Ga. App. 661, 373 S.E.2d 843 (1983).

72. O.C.G.A. 34-8-122(a). See, for example, Cox v. Brazo, 165 Ga. App. 888, 303 S.E.2d 71 (1983), affirmed, 251 Ga. 491, 307 S.E.2d 474 (1983).

73. O.C.G.A. 34-8-122(a).

74. Lamb v. Fedderwitz, 68 Ga. App. 233, 22 S.E.2d 657 (1942) at 234, affirmed, 195 Ga. 691, 25 S.E.2d 414 (1943).

75. These are "necessary and essential ingredients of a conditionally privileged communication" (Cohen v. Hartlage, 179 Ga. App. 847, 348 S.E.2d 331 (1986) at 849). The claim of privilege may not be "used merely as a cloak for venting private malice" (O.C.G.A. 51-5-9). See, for example, Pearce v. Brewer, 72 Ga. 243 (1884). If malice is evident and may be established with "convincing clarity," a defense of qualified privilege will not be effective. See, for example, Edmonds v. Atlanta Newspapers, 92 Ga. App. 15, 87 S.E.2d 415 (1955); WSAV-TV v. Baxter, 119 Ga. App. 185, 166

- Statements made in good faith in the performance of a public duty;[77]
- Statements made in good faith in the performance of a legal or moral private duty;[78]
- Statements made with a good faith intent on the part of the speaker to protect his interest in a matter in which it is concerned;[79]

S.E.2d 416 (1969). Note that defamation does not become privileged simply by being published as news. See, for example, Atlanta News Publishing v. Medlock, 123 Ga. 714, 51 S.E. 756 (1905).

76. O.C.G.A. 51-5-7. See, for example, Horton v. Georgian Co., 175 Ga. 261, 165 S.E. 443 (1932). The elements of qualified privilege are: 1) good faith, 2) an interest to be upheld, 3) a statement properly limited in its scope, 4) a proper occasion, and 5) publication to proper persons. "The absence of any one or more of these constitutional elements will, as a general rule, prevent the party from relying on the privilege" (Duchess Chenilles, Inc. v. Master, 84 Ga. App. 822, 67 S.E.2d 600 (1951) at 829).

77. Georgia courts have held: that disbarment proceedings are privileged - James v. Brandon, 61 Ga. App. 719, 7 S.E.2d 305 (1940); that personnel investigations by a government official are privileged - McKinnon v. Trivett, 136 Ga. App. 59, 220 S.E.2d 63 (1975); that statements made in good faith pursuant to a police investigation are privileged - Cleveland v. Greengard, 162 Ga. App. 201, 290 S.E.2d 545 (1982).

78. Georgia courts have held: that communications relating to church matters are privileged - Etchison v. Perguson, 88 Ga. 620, 15 S.E. 680 (1892); that communications relating to family matters are privileged - Cochran v. Sears, Roebuck & Co., 72 Ga. App. 458, 34 S.E.2d 296 (1945); that a physician's erroneous statement that his patient had venereal disease is privileged, if he makes the statement in the performance of a private duty to disclose - Thomas v. Hillson, 184 Ga. App. 302, 361 S.E.2d 278 (1987).

79. Georgia courts have held: that statements made in furtherance of efforts to recover stolen property are privileged - Chapman v. Battle, 124 Ga. 574, 52 S.E. 812 (1905); that a workers' compensation report a physician sent to an insurance company is privileged when the doctor makes the report to protect his own interests in the matter - Auer v. Black, 163 Ga. App. 787, 294 S.E.2d 616 (1982); that statements made during an attempt to resolve a business dispute are privileged - Layfield v. Turner Advertising, 181 Ga.

- Fair and honest reports of the proceedings of legislative or judicial bodies;[80]
- Fair and honest reports of court proceedings;[81]
- Comments of counsel, fairly made, on the circumstances of a case in which he or she is involved and on the conduct of the parties connected with it;[82]
- Truthful reports of information received from any arresting officer or police authority;[83] and
- Comments upon the acts of public persons in their public capacity.[84]

App. 824, 354 S.E.2d 14 (1987); that telephone conversations between a person's past and future employers are conditionally privileged - Watkins v. Laser/Print Atlanta, 183 Ga. App. 172, 358 S.E.2d 477 (1987). However, listing someone as a delinquent debtor in a confidential report was not held to be privileged in Western Union Telegraph v. Pritchett, 108 Ga. 411, 34 S.E. 216 (1899).

80. See, for example, Reece v. Grissom, 154 Ga. App. 194, 267 S.E.2d 839 (1980). The fair and accurate reporting of administrative agency proceedings in Georgia is also protected by qualified privilege. See, for example, Morton v. Stewart, 153 Ga. App. 636, 266 S.E.2d 230 (1980). However, there is no privilege when a report is not true and correct. See, for example, Atlanta News v. Medlock, 123 Ga. 714, 51 S.E. 756 (1905); Wood v. Constitution Publishing, 57 Ga. App. 123, 194 S.E. 760 (1937).

81. See, for example, Western Broadcasting of Augusta v. Wright, 182 Ga. App. 359, 356 S.E.2d 53 (1987).

82. See, for example, Lester v. Thurmond, 51 Ga. 118 (1874).

83. False, inaccurate reports - or those based on a journalist's own investigation - are not protected by qualified privilege. See, for example, Minton v. Thomson Newspapers, 175 Ga. App. 525, 333 S.E.2d 913 (1985). In addition, false information disclosed by government investigators who cannot make arrests is not protected by privilege. See, Heard v. Neighbor Newspapers, 259 Ga. 458, 383 S.E.2d 553 (1989), reversing 190 Ga. App. 756, 380 S.E.2d 279 (1989).

84. See, for example, Barwick v. Wind, 203 Ga. 827, 48 S.E.2d 523 (1948). Public officials today can only recover damages by showing actual malice. See, for example, Murray v. Williams, 166 Ga. App. 865, 305 S.E.2d 502 (1983).

In *McCracken v. Gainesville Tribune*,[85] the Georgia Court of Appeals - citing *Edwards v. National Audubon Society*[86] as precedent - recognized the "neutral reporting defense," which may be defined as the public's qualified interest in being accurately informed by the media about public proceedings and public controversies without the media assuming any responsibility for any charges and counter-charges made. More recently, this same court has acknowledged that "the expression of opinion of 'matters with respect to which reasonable men might entertain differing opinions' ... is not libelous."[87]

Other, less complete - "technical" - defenses, serving primarily to limit monetary damages awarded, include:

- libel by invitation or consent;[88]

---

85. 146 Ga. App. 274, 246 S.E.2d 360 (1978).

86. 556 F.2d 113 (2nd Cir. 1977), certiorari denied, 434 U.S. 1002 (1977).

87. Bergen v. Martindale-Hubble, 176 Ga. App. 745, 337 S.E.2d 770 (1985) at 747, quoting, Grayson v. Savannah News-Press, 110 Ga. App. 561, 139 S.E.2d 347 (1964) at 568. Georgia courts have held: that the broadcast characterization of the taste of a restaurant's seafood gumbo as "yesterday's slop" is a protected expression of opinion - S&W Seafoods v. Jacor Broadcasting, 194 Ga. App. 233, 390 S.E.2d 228 (1989); that general negative expressions of opinion cannot be the basis of a libel claim - Elder v. Cardosa, 205 Ga. App. 163, 421 S.E.2d 753 (1992); that an assertion that a woman would be an unfit mother is merely opinion - Webster v. Wilkins, 217 Ga. App. 194, 456 S.E.2d 699 (1995); that the claim that a man did not live by the "ideals of Scouting" is also opinion – Gast v. Brittain, 277 Ga. 340, 589 S.E.2d 63 (2003). See also, David Hudson, "Letter to the Editor Not Libelous," GPA Bulletin, June 19, 1992, 9 (where a Toombs County judge held that, after paying a $750 wrecker fee, a truck owner who felt that he had been the "victim of not one but two counts of robbery" did not defame the wrecker service).

88. See for example, Sophiandoplis v. McCormick, 192 Ga. App. 583, 385 S.E.2d 682 (1989).

- expiration of the one-year statute of limitations for libel actions;[89] and
- publication of a retraction.[90]

If a retraction is published, it must be done within seven days and must be both conspicuous and public; in addition, an explanatory notice may also be required if requested by the injured person. After publication, damages are limited to compensation for actual injuries, unless evidence of malice is found.[91]

Since 1964, libel law nationwide has been "federalized" - the result of the U.S. Supreme Court's creation of a constitutional defense for libel in *New York Times v. Sullivan* and its progeny.[92] As a consequence, federal libel rulings have

---

89. O.C.G.A. 9-3-33.

90. O.C.G.A. 51-5-11 applies to the print media, while O.C.G.A. 51-5-12 applies to the broadcast media. They also apply to statements made in Internet chat rooms. See, Mathis v. Cannon, 276 Ga. 16, 573 S.E.2d 376 (2002). See also, Jonathan Ringel, "Net Insults, Libel Case Spur Court's Interest," Daily Report, May 6, 2002, 11, 8; Bill Rankin, "Cyber Libel Ruling Near," Atlanta Journal-Constitution, Sept. 15, 2002, D1, D8; Bill Rankin, "Court Backs Free Speech in Web Libel Suit," Atlanta Journal-Constitution, Nov. 27, 2002, B4; Jonathan Ringel & Richmond Eustis, "High Court Protects Internet Trash Talk," Daily Report, Dec. 2, 2002, 1, 6. (NOTE: The author worked as a law clerk – as part of a judicial externship in 2002 – for Justice Hugh P. Thompson of the Georgia Supreme Court and assisted with the research into the legal issues raised in Mathis v. Cannon.)

91. "It is unclear whether actual damages applies only to pecuniary damages or also to damages for hurt feelings" (Louise Hermanson, "Setting the Record Straight: A Proposal for Expanding the Role of Retraction in Libel Litigation," 133 Journalism Monographs, June 1992, at 37).

92. 376 U.S. 254 (1964). See also, Rosenblatt v. Baer, 383 U.S. 75 (1966); Curtis Publishing v. Butts/Associated Press v. Walker, 388 U.S. 130 (1967); St. Amant v. Thompson, 390 U.S. 727 (1968); Monitor-Patriot v. Roy, 401 U.S. 265 (1971); Rosenbloom v. Metromedia, 403 U.S. 29 (1971); Gertz v. Robert Welch, Inc., 418 U.S. 323 (1974); Time v. Firestone, 424 U.S. 448 (1976); Hutchinson v. Proxmire, 443 U.S. 111 (1979); Wolston v.

been superimposed on those of Georgia and every other state. State rules are still valid, as long as they do not conflict with the federal ones. Thus, as a general rule, in Georgia and elsewhere,

> defamed public officials and public figures can recover only upon a showing of [actual] malice, express or implied. Private individuals cannot recover unless the defamation is the result of fault or negligence on the part of the publisher. Recovery is restricted to actual or special damages.[93]

In at least one instance, Georgia courts have gone beyond the federal requirement and provided media with additional protection from liability. When its mayor was charged with criminal trespass, the Savannah News-Press erroneously reported that he was being accused of "cattle rustling" on another man's property. As the charge did not directly relate to his performance of his official duties, the Sullivan rule did not directly apply. However, Judge Harold R. Banke concluded that the charge "bears a close connection to his fitness for public office" and required the mayor to prove the newspaper acted with actual malice before he could collect damages.[94]

Reader's Digest, 443 U.S. 157 (1979); Dun & Bradstreet v. Greenmoss Builders, 472 U.S. 749 (1985); Hustler v. Falwell, 485 U.S. 46 (1988); Milkovich v. Lorain Journal, 497 U.S. 1 (1990); Masson v. New Yorker, 501 U.S. 496 (1991).

93. Rosanova v. Playboy Enterprises, 411 F.Supp. 440 (S.D. Ga. 1976) at 446. See, Lake Park Post v. Farmer, 264 Ga. App. 299, 590 S.E.2d 254 (2003). See also, Greg Land, "Experts: McKinney Libel Claims Face a Tough Road," Daily Report, July 31, 2007, 1, 9; Rhonda Cook, "McKinney Drops AJC Libel Lawsuit," Atlanta Journal-Constitution, Aug. 15, 2007, B6.

94. Savannah News-Press v. Whetsell, 149 Ga. App. 233, 254 S.E.2d 151 (1979) at 235.

Prior to 1964, Georgia courts were generally protective of those in the public eye. When a state official was accused of profiting from the construction of a bridge in Chatham County, the Georgia Court of Appeals reiterated the state supreme court's position that "the fact that one is in politics does not remove his humanity."[95] Since 1964, the U.S. Supreme Court has not negated the humanity of public officials and public figures, but it has indicated again and again that they need thicker skin than anyone previously thought necessary.

The Sullivan standard had only just been established by the U.S. Supreme Court when it was applied in a Georgia case, *Butts v. Curtis Publishing Co.*[96] Wally Butts, athletic director of the University of Georgia, had been accused by the *Saturday Evening Post* of conspiring to "fix" a football game between Georgia and the University of Alabama. The *Post* based its article on the affidavit of a man who claimed to have overheard a telephone conversation between Butts and Alabama head coach, Paul "Bear" Bryant, but "without substantial independent support."[97] The federal district court affirmed the Sullivan standard but concluded that Butts was not a public official, even though there was ample evidence to support the conclusion that the *Post* acted with reckless disregard for the article's falsity. The Fifth Circuit Court of Appeals agreed, but did not rule on Curtis Publishing's constitutional claims based on *Sullivan*, holding that the company should have seen "the handwriting on the wall" and raised the claims earlier.[98]

The U.S. Supreme Court concluded that, although Butts may not have been a public official, he was a public figure,

95. Savannah News-Press v. Grayson, 102 Ga. App. 59, 115 S.E.2d 762 (1960) at 65.

96. 242 F.Supp. 390 (N.D. Ga. 1964).

97. Curtis Publishing v. Butts/Associated Press v. Walker, 388 U.S. 130 (1967) at 157.

98. Curtis Publishing v. Butts, 351 F.2d 702 (5th Cir. 1965) at 734.

because of "the public interest in education in general, and in the conduct of the athletic affairs of educational institutions in particular."[99] He, therefore, could collect damages for libel "on a showing of highly unreasonable conduct constituting an extreme departure from the standards of investigation and reporting ordinarily adhered to by responsible publishers."[100] Later, taking their cue from the U.S. Supreme Court's ruling in *St. Amant v. Thompson*,[101] Georgia courts would conclude that it is sufficient to prove that a publisher had "serious doubts" about the truth of his or her statements.[102]

In 1974, the Georgia Court of Appeals incorporated the U.S. Supreme Court's *Monitor-Patriot v. Roy* decision[103] into Georgia law when it ruled in *Thibadeau v. Crane* that "one who is a public official or who is a candidate for public office must subject himself to the criticisms of both the press and the public for his conduct of the political campaign or for the office which he holds."[104] In the majority opinion, Judge Homer C. Eberhardt, referring to the lack of privacy public officials and public figures have, quoted the maxim: "If you can't stand the heat, get out of the kitchen."[105]

In Georgia, then, a person may be considered "public" by virtue of his or her position - a definition which includes such people as "artists, athletes, business people, dilettantes, anyone who is famous or infamous because of who he is or what he has done"[106] - or by commanding "a substantial amount of public

---

99. 388 U.S. 130 (1967) at 146.
100. Id. at 155.
101. 390 U.S. 727 (1968).
102. See, for example, Jackson v. Atlantic Monthly, 324 F.Supp. 1302 (N.D. Ga. 1971).
103. 401 U.S. 265 (1971).
104. 131 Ga. App. 591, 206 S.E.2d 609 (1974) at 593-594.
105. Id. at 594.
106. Rosanova v. Playboy Enterprises, 411 F.Supp. 440 (S.D. Ga.

interest."[107] As a federal district court stated, no one will ever be liable for publishing truthful statements about matters of legitimate public interest.[108] It is even possible for a person who is not a public figure for all purposes and in all contexts to be considered a "limited purpose" public figure with regard to a restricted range of issues.[109] And the responsibility for proving actual malice is always on the person filing the suit.[110]

Georgia courts have concluded that "defining a public figure is like trying to nail jellyfish to the wall"[111] and have begun with what seems like increasing frequency to decide that

---

1976), quoting Cepeda v. Cowles Magazines and Broadcasting, 392 F.2d 417 (9th Cir. 1968) at 419.

107. Williams v. Trust Company of Georgia, 140 Ga. App. 49, 230 S.E.2d 45 (1976) at 52. Georgia courts have held: that a person who injected himself into an election campaign in a foreign country is a public figure - Time v. McLaney, 406 F.2d 565 (5th Cir. 1969), certiorari denied, 395 U.S. 922 (1969); that a person reportedly involved in organized crime is a public figure - Rosanova v. Playboy Enterprises, 411 F.Supp. 440 (S.D. Ga. 1976), affirmed, 580 F.2d 859 (5th Cir. 1978); that the husband of a candidate for Congress is a public figure - Hemenway v. Blanchard, 163 Ga. App. 668, 294 S.E.2d 603 (1982); that an agent for an athlete who "used the media" during contract negotiations is a public figure - Woy v. Turner, 573 F.Supp. 35 (N.D. Ga. 1983).

108. See, for example, Pierson v. News Group Publications, 549 F.Supp. 635 (S.D. Ga. 1982). Among those things held to be matters of legitimate public interest are: exorbitant prices for accommodations during a major golf tournament - Bon Air Hotel v. Time, 295 F.Supp. 704 (S.D. Ga. 1969), affirmed, 426 F.2d 858 (5th Cir. 1970); a police chief's hiring practices - Sparks v. Thurmond, 171 Ga. App. 138, 319 S.E.2d 46 (1984).

109. See, for example, Byers v. Southern Newspaper, 161 Ga. App. 717, 288 S.E.2d 698 (1982); Holt v. Cox Enterprises, 590 F.Supp. 408 (N.D. Ga. 1984). See also, Greg Land, "Appeals Court Upholds Verdict Against Blogger," Daily Report, March 8, 2007, 1, 5.

110. See, for example, Blomberg v. Cox Enterprises, 228 Ga. App. 178, 491 S.E.2d 430 (1997).

111. Rosanova v. Playboy Enterprises, 411 F.Supp. 440 (S.D. Ga 1976) at 443.

more and more people are not public figures, even for limited purposes. For example, the publisher of a magazine with a limited circulation among a small segment of the business community is not a public figure,[112] nor are otolaryngologists involved in a "private struggle" chiefly of interest to plastic surgeons,[113] nor are attorneys who do not take advantage of opportunities to argue their clients' cases in the media,[114] nor is a man who is a candidate for re-election to the board of a property association,[115] nor is a high school principal,[116] nor is a college professor when discussing a public controversy in class.[117]

On the other hand, Richard Jewell - the former security guard who discovered the bomb in Centennial Olympic Park during the 1996 games in Atlanta - was determined to be a public figure and thus had to prove that the Atlanta newspapers either knew he was not the bomber himself or recklessly disregarded facts which pointed to that conclusion before he could collect monetary damages for their report that he was a suspect in the bombing. The Atlanta newspapers had initially relied upon truth as their defense to the libel suit, but relied on the constitutional actual malice defense after a Fulton County State Court judge ruled that in order to use truth as their defense they would have to identify the confidential sources

---

112. See, Straw v. Chase Revel, 813 F.2d 356 (11th Cir. 1987), certiorari denied, 484 U.S. 856 (1987).

113. See, Georgia Society of Plastic Surgeons v. Anderson, 257 Ga. 710, 363 S.E.2d 140 (1987).

114. See, Western Broadcasting of Augusta v. Wright, 182 Ga. App. 359, 356 S.E.2d 53 (1987).

115. See, Sewell v. Eubanks, 181 Ga. App. 545, 352 S.E.2d 802 (1987).

116. See, Ellerbee v. Mills, 262 Ga. 516, 422 S.E.2d 539 (1992), certiorari denied, 507 U.S. 1025 (1993).

117. See, Sewell v. Trib Publications, 276 Ga. App. 250, 630 S.E.2d 529 (2006).

who had told them that Jewell was a suspect, even though the sources had been promised anonymity.[118] As a public figure, he had to prove that the Atlanta newspapers acted with actual malice, a much more difficult standard of fault to prove than if he had been deemed a private individual.[119] With that determination, most of Jewell's claims were ruled not to be libelous.[120]

---

118. See, Alex Kuczynski, "2 Reporters Are Ordered to Jail over Suspect in Olympic Blast," New York Times, June 4, 1999, A20; Jay Croft, "Jewell Libel Case Focuses on Public Figure Question," Atlanta Journal-Constitution, July 27, 1999, B6; Ben Schmitt, "Appeals Court Will Consider Jewell Public Figure Ruling," Daily Report, Nov. 18, 1999, 1, 4. This requirement was subsequently reversed in Atlanta Journal-Constitution v. Jewell, 251 Ga. App. 808, 555 S.E.2d 175 (2001). There the appellate court ruled that the identity of anonymous sources does not have to be revealed when the plaintiff's rights will not be detrimentally affected. The Georgia Supreme Court and the U.S. Supreme Court both refused to hear his appeal. See, Bill Torpy, "Supreme Court refuses to Hear Jewell Libel Case," Atlanta Journal-Constitution, Oct. 8, 2002, B6.

119. See, Bryant v. Cox Enterprises, 311 Ga. App. 230, 715 S.E.2d 458 (2011). (G. Watson Bryant, Jr., served as executor of Jewell's estate after his 2007 death; Cox Enterprises is the parent company of the Journal-Constitution.) See also, Andria Simmons, "Georgia Court Upholds Ruling in Jewell Suit," Atlanta Journal-Constitution, Jan. 10, 2012, available at: http://www.ajc.com/news/ga-court-upholds-ruling-1297469.html (last accessed Jan. 10, 2012). The same challenges face Andrea Sneiderman. See, Greg Land, "Sneiderman Libel Suit Evokes Jewell Case," Daily News, June 27, 2012, 1, 2.

120. See, generally, Tonya Jones, "Richard Jewell's Court Battle against the AJC," Georgia State University Signal, April 12, 2005, 20. Richard Jewell died in August 2007. At the time of his death, one claim remained unresolved; it was subsequently dismissed in December 2007. See, "Georgia: Final Libel Claim in Olympic Bombing Case Is Dismissed," New York Times, Dec. 13, 2007, A24; Tim Eberly, "Judge Dismisses Last of Jewell's Libel Claims," Atlanta Journal-Constitution, Dec. 12, 2007, D1. See also, Robin McDonald, "Olympic Park Guard Jewell Dies at 44," Report, Aug. 30, 2007, 1, 9; Kevin Sack, "Richard A. Jewell, 44, Hero of Atlanta Bombing," New York Times, Aug. 30, 2007, A19; Jeffry Scott & Mike

With regard to non-public figures, Georgia adheres to the U.S. Supreme Court's ruling in *Gertz v. Robert Welch, Inc.*[121] Private individuals do not have to establish actual malice before being allowed to collect monetary damages, but "may recover if the [journalist] failed to use ordinary care [in other words, negligence] to determine the truth or falsity of the statement."[122] Factors to be considered by the jury include:

> 1) whether the material was topical and required prompt publication, or whether sufficient time was available for a thorough investigation of its contents; 2) the newsworthiness of the material and public interest in promoting its publication; 3) the extent of damage to the plaintiff's reputation should the publication prove to be false; ... 4) the reliability and truth-worthiness [sic] of the source.[123]

In some respects, many states seem to have missed the point of the *New York Times v. Sullivan* decision. The intent of the U.S. Supreme Court was to allow robust reporting by the media, even at the risk of a false report, to ensure the vigor of the media is not restrained where matters of public interest are

---

Morris, "Richard Jewell Found Dead at 44," Atlanta Journal-Constitution, Aug. 30, 2007, B1; Jeffry Scott, "Jewell Died of Heart Attack Linked to Diabetes, Experts Say," Atlanta Journal-Constitution, Aug. 31, 2007, E7.

121. 418 U.S. 323 (1974).

122. Diamond v. American Family, 186 Ga. App. 681, 368 S.E.2d 350 (1988) at 683-684. See also, Triangle Publications v. Chumley, 253 Ga. 179, 317 S.E.2d 534 (1984). According to the courts, the standard of care should be defined by reference to the procedures a reasonable publisher would have employed prior to publication of the defamatory material.

123. Triangle Publications v. Chumley, 253 Ga. 179, 317 S.E.2d 534 (1984) at 182.

concerned. This requires that courts agree that harnessing the media is more dangerous than unleashing them. Otherwise, by allowing themselves to become enmeshed in the gritty details of who is and who is not a public figure and what is and what is not an issue of public interest, they risk missing the overall purpose and intent of the rule while focusing on the details and nuances of its application.

This conclusion was illustrated by the 2006 Georgia Supreme Court ruling in *Berryhill v. Georgia Community Support & Solutions*,[124] which concluded that a woman complaining about the treatment of her disabled child could be sued for defamation by the care facility as her Internet postings and complaints to the state Department of Human Resources do not include – in fact, should the word "include" be construed to mean "to encompass" or "is the functional equivalent of"? – expression related to an "official proceeding," as required by the state's anti-SLAPP statute.[125] In dissent, Justice Robert

---

124. 281 Ga. 439, 638 S.E.2d 278 (2006). See, Alyson M. Palmer, "Justices Weigh Mom's Defense to E-Mail Suit," Daily Report, May 10, 2006, 1, 4; Alyson M. Palmer, "Split Court Rules for Defamation Plaintiff in Key Speech Case," Daily Report, Nov. 29, 2006; 1, 5; Jim Tharpe, "Court Allows Suit Over E-Mails," Atlanta Journal-Constitution, Nov. 29, 2006, B6.

125. O.C.G.A. 9-11-11.1. The law seeks to prevent companies, individuals or the government from using expensive defamation lawsuits to silence anyone who legitimately speaks out against others' decisions or actions. Such defamation suits are known as "strategic lawsuits against public participation" (SLAPP). See, generally, Sarah Staveley-O'Carroll, "Libel Tourism Laws: Spoiling the Holiday & Saving the First Amendment," 2009 New York University Journal of Law & Liberty 252. Statutes, such as Georgia's, are known as anti-SLAPP statutes. See, for example, Hagemann v. Marietta, 287 Ga. App. 1, 650 S.E.2d 363 (2007) (city's counterclaims violated the anti-SLAPP statute because the city's claims were shown to be false); Hagemann v. Berkman Wynhaven Associates, 290 Ga. App. 677, 660 S.E.2d 449 (2008) (sanctions required upon a finding of false verification); Lovett v. Capital Properties, 300 Ga. App. 799, 686 S.E.2d 411 (2009) (where a board's deliberations were an official proceeding as defined by the

Benham complained that the ruling was "undesirable as a matter of public policy," because it undermines the legislature's purpose in enacting the statute "by placing rigid restrictions on the scope of its protection."[126] Even though not included in any official proceeding, Justice Benham wrote, "it cannot be credibly argued that matters regulated by the government are not matters of public concern."[127]

The other conclusion illustrated by the *Berryhill* decision is simply this: the law treats Internet postings the same as it treats defamation in print, through broadcasting, by pictures or signs, or in other means of communication. If you cannot say something in any of these different media, you also likely cannot say it in cyberspace, even "hidden" by anonymity.[128]

---

statute); Hindu Temple v. Raghunathan, 311 Ga. App. 109, 714 S.E.2d 628 (2011) (where a religious institution's countersuit against those accusing it of fraud was covered by the statute); Jefferson v. Stripling, 316 Ga. App. 197, 728 S.E.2d 826 (2012) (where an attorney's claims against opposing parties in a property dispute were covered by the statute).

126. Berryhill v. Georgia Community Support & Solutions, 281 Ga. 439, 638 S.E.2d 278 (2006) at 445.

127. Id. at 446.

128. See, for example, Rhonda Cook, "Internet Privacy No So Private in Court," Atlanta Journal-Constitution, Jan. 20, 2011, available at: http://www.ajc.com/news/internet-privacy-not-so-809962.html (last accessed Jan. 20, 2011; Jerry Carnes, "Georgia Man Wins $404,000 in Internet Libel Lawsuit," Chicago Sun Times, Jan 22, 2011, available at: http://www.suntimes.com/news/nation/3430101-418/cooley-internet-404000-death-fiancee.html (last accessed Nov. 2, 2013); Katheryn Tucker, "Cop Wins Net Libel Case," Daily News, March 11, 2011, 1, 9; Eamon McNiff, "Innocent Man's Life Destroyed by Anonymous Topix Poster," ABC News, March 21, 2012, available at: http://abcnews.go.com/Technology/topix-innocent-mans-life-destroyed-anonymous-online-poster/story?id=15963310 (last accessed Nov. 1, 2013); Katheryn Tucker, "Flaming Can Be Defaming," Daily Report, March 12, 2012, 1, 4; Jim Galloway, "No-Holds-Barred Blogs Tested by Libel Lawsuit," Atlanta Journal-Constitution, May 6, 2012, B1, B2.

Criminal Libel

In the area of criminal libel, on the other hand, Georgia continues to cling to what many argue is an antiquated form of law.[129] Its elements are the same as those of civil libel - defamation,[130] identification,[131] and publication.[132] However, the alleged defamation need not be spread to any third party to constitute publication; dissemination to the intended party is enough.[133] Although not specifically required by state statute,[134] as is the case with civil libel, malice is also a necessary component of criminal libel and may be inferred from the character of the charge, based on the Georgia Supreme Court's ruling in *Taylor v. Georgia*.[135] Its presence is a question for the

---

129. See, for example, Gregory C. Lisby, No Place in the Law: The Ignominy of Criminal Libel in American Jurisprudence, 9 Communication Law & Policy 433 (2004). See also, Gregory C. Lisby, "Criminal Libel," First Amendment Center at Vanderbilt University (undated), available at: http://www.firstamendmentcenter.org/criminal-libel (last accessed Nov. 15, 2013).

130. See, for example, Giles v. Georgia, 6 Ga. 276 (1849). Only the words actually used - not innuendo - may be considered by the court. See, for example, Garland v. Georgia, 211 Ga. 44, 84 S.E.2d 9 (1954).

131. The tendency "to blacken the honesty, virtue, integrity, and reputation of the said [individual], and thereby to expose him to public hatred, ridicule, and contempt, in which said false, scandalous, malicious, and defamatory libel there were and are contained certain false, scandalous, malicious, defamatory, and libelous matters of and concerning the character, honesty, virtue, integrity, and reputation of the said [individual]" was a sufficient allegation that it identified the person in Taylor v. Georgia, 4 Ga. 14 (1848) at 15.

132. See, for example, Pledger v. Georgia, 77 Ga. 242, 3 S.E. 320 (1886).

133. See, for example, Lecroy v. Georgia, 89 Ga. 335, 15 S.E. 463 (1892).

134. O.C.G.A. 16-11-40 requires that criminal defamation be "with the intent to defame another," which would be understood similarly to the "common law" malice required in civil libel.

135. 4 Ga. 14 (1848).

jury.[136] For example, advising others not to rent from a certain real estate agent because of his racial prejudice and to leave "this old skunk to stink himself to death" was held to be malicious.[137] "Common law" defenses to a charge of criminal libel include truth[138] and privilege.[139]

On the federal level, the U.S. Supreme Court has pretty much eviscerated the concept by requiring that the same standards of fault be applied to criminal libel as to civil libel. Public officials involved in criminal libel suits must prove actual malice, just as public officials involved in civil libel suits must.[140] In addition, the U.S. Supreme Court ruled in 1966 that the "common law" of criminal libel, aimed at preventing breaches of the peace, was inconsistent with the provisions of the U.S. Constitution because it "makes a man a criminal simply because his neighbors have no self-control and cannot refrain from violence."[141]

---

136. See, for example, Graham v. Georgia, 7 Ga. App. 407, 66 S.E. 1038 (1910).

137. Pledger v. Georgia, 77 Ga. 242, 3 S.E. 320 (1886) at 245.

138. However, under "common law," truth was not a complete defense. The Georgia Constitution of 1877, §II, ¶I, made truth a constitutional defense: "In all prosecutions or indictments for libel, the truth may be given in evidence...." See also, the Georgia Constitution of 1983, Article I, §I, ¶VI.

139. Georgia courts have held: that a written accusation made in strict accordance with the rules and for the sole purpose of having the charges investigated was privileged (Graham v. Georgia, 7 Ga. App. 407, 66 S.E. 1038, 1910); and that an unsworn statement made before a municipal court was not privileged, unless relevant to the trial (Lecroy v. Georgia, 89 Ga. 335, 15 S.E. 463, 1892).

140. Garrison v. Louisiana, 379 U.S. 64 (1964).

141. Ashton v. Kentucky, 384 U.S. 195 (1966) at 200.

GEORGIA'S CRIMINAL LIBEL STATUTE
(Figure 4)

(a) A person commits the offense of criminal defamation when, without a privilege to do so and with intent to defame another, living or dead, he communicates false matter which tends to blacken the memory of one who is dead or which exposes one who is alive to hatred, contempt, or ridicule, and which tends to provoke a breach of the peace.
(b) A person who violates subsection (a) of this Code section is guilty of a misdemeanor.

- O.C.G.A. 16-11-40 (2013)

In 1982, the constitutionality of the state's criminal libel statute (see, Figure 4, above) was placed squarely before the Georgia Supreme Court. Two years earlier, "Happy" Howard Williamson, general manager of WVMG, Bleckley County's only radio station, had accused Jody Lucas, city manager of Cochran, of making

> so much money since he has been in City Hall that he's bought a big farm…. Now he's trying to buy a milk business in Cochran…. [It] must be nice to work for the city. It must be nice to make money over the table and under the table.[142]

The following day, Lucas swore out a warrant for Williamson's arrest on a charge of criminal libel; he also filed a civil libel suit against Williamson, seeking $500,000 in punitive damages.

---

142. Quoted in James Dodson, "The Trouble with Being Happy," *Atlanta Weekly*, April 18, 1982, 10-18, 25-26, at 18.

The trial court upheld the constitutionality of the statute but allowed Williamson to appeal its ruling before continuing with his trial. On appeal, Williamson claimed that the statute was so vague that no one could tell in advance what kind of conduct would be a violation of the law. As a result, he argued, it violated his First Amendment right of free expression.

The Georgia Supreme Court decided the case twice, focusing on the last of the elements of criminal libel - a tendency "to provoke a breach of the peace." First, it upheld the constitutionality of the statute (see, Figure 4, p. 57), holding that "even if the fourth element alone were too vague and overbroad to amount to a constitutionally acceptable crime, the specificity of the first three elements is such as to cause the statute to be valid."[143] However, less than three months later, it reconsidered its earlier ruling and reversed it by a 4-3 vote, determining that the phrase "tends to provoke a breach of the peace" was, after all, unconstitutionally vague under the First and Fourteenth amendments to the U.S. Constitution.[144] Nevertheless, the remainder of the statute "remains unchanged" and is, thus, still presumably valid.[145]

---

143. Williamson v. Georgia, 8 Media Law Reporter 2044 (1982) at 2045. Justice Harold G. Clarke wrote the majority opinion. Of the seven justices, only Justice Charles L. Weltner dissented, but without comment.

144. Williamson v. Georgia, 249 Ga. 851, 295 S.E.2d 305 (1982). Justice Weltner wrote the majority opinion, and Chief Justice Robert H. Jordon, along with Justices Clarke and George T. Smith, dissented.

145. Id. at 852.

QUESTIONS

1. Name the five kinds of defamation in Georgia.

   [handwritten: reputation, identification, publication, actual injury, legal fault]

2. How long is the statute of limitations for civil libel? What is the statute of limitations for product disparagement?

   [handwritten: 1 year, 2 years]

3. What libel defense is recognized both by the Georgia Constitution of 1983 and by state statute?

   [handwritten: Truth]

4. What part of the state's criminal libel statute was declared unconstitutional by the Georgia Supreme Court? To what extent does the crime of libel still exist in Georgia today?

   [handwritten: tends to provoke a breach of peace]

5. What is the "Innocent Construction" Rule? Does Georgia follow it or not? Why?

   [handwritten: Has to be direct libel, not meanings]

6. Name the four types of civil libel statutes in Georgia.

7. Name the legal doctrine that, as applied in Georgia, makes the mass media responsible for the acts of their employees.

   [handwritten: respondent superior]

8. If a defamatory statement is retracted within seven days, what kind of monetary damages are allowed?

   [handwritten: actual damages]

9. In Georgia, a person may be considered "public" in either of two ways. What are they?

   [handwritten: position; what they have done]

Thought Question:

The types of expression are protected by the defense of conditional privilege in Georgia all have what in common? What prerequisite must be established before the defense is valid? Why?

3. Invasion of Privacy in Georgia

lthough the right of privacy was first expounded in 1890[1] and then legislated into existence by the state of New York in 1903,[2] the Georgia Supreme Court was the first court of last resort to recognize the right of privacy judicially, the result of its 1905 decision in *Pavesich v. New England Life Insurance Company*.[3] In this landmark case, Paolo Pavesich brought suit against the New England Life Insurance Company for publishing his picture in an advertisement in the November 15, 1903, edition of the *Atlanta Constitution* above a quotation asserting, "In my healthy and productive period of life I bought insurance in the New England Mutual Life Insurance Company of Boston, Mass., and today my family is protected and I am drawing an annual dividend on my paid-up policies."[4] The picture was taken from a negative obtained by Thomas B. Lumpkin, the insurance company's general agent in Atlanta, from photographer J. Quinton Adams, without Pavesich's consent. Moreover, Pavesich never made the statement attributed to him nor had he purchased insurance from the company. Pavesich sued on two counts, one for libel

---

1. See, Samuel Warren & Louis Brandeis, "The Right to Privacy," 4 Harvard Law Review 193 (Dec. 15, 1890), available at: http://www-swiss.ai.mit.edu/6805/articles/privacy/Privacy_brand_warr2.html (last accessed Nov. 15, 2013).

2. The New York statute was a direct result of the outcome of Roberson v. Rochester Folding Box Co., 171 New York Reports 538, 64 Northeastern Reporter 442 (1902).

3. 122 Ga. 190, 50 S.E. 68.

4. Id. at 192.

and the other for a violation of his right of privacy. He sought $25,000 in damages.

The Georgia Supreme Court reversed a lower court's decision to dismiss Pavesich's suit and in doing so, legally recognized the right to privacy in the state. From that advertisement "has grown a whole field of law and ... Georgia [has] led the way."[5] Justice Andrew J. Cobb, the author of the court's "brilliant" unanimous opinion,[6] declared:

First, the absence - for centuries or even for all time - of a precedent for an asserted right "is not conclusive of the question as to the existence of the right."[7]

Second, the right to privacy, which is "derived from natural law"[8] and "recognized by municipal law, embraces far more than freedom from physical restraint."[9] One's

> right of privacy is embraced within the absolute
> rights of personal security and personal liberty.
> Personal security includes the right to exist and
> the right to the enjoyment of life while existing,
> and is invaded not only by a deprivation of life,
> but also by a deprivation of those things which
> are necessary to the enjoyment of life according
> to the nature, temperament, and lawful desires
> of the individual. Personal liberty includes not

---

5. Jefferson J. Davis, "An Enforceable Right of Privacy: Enduring Legacy of the Georgia Supreme Court," 3 Journal of Southern Legal History 111 (1994) at 120.

6. Quoting appellate Judge H. Sol Clark in Hines v. Columbus Bank & Trust Co., 137 Ga. App. 268, 223 S.E.2d 468 (1976) at 269.

7. Pavesich v. New England Life Insurance Co., 122 Ga. 190, 50 S.E. 68 (1905) at 193.

8. Id. at 194.

9. Id. at 195.

only freedom from physical restraint, but also
the right "to be let alone," to determine one's
mode of life, whether it shall be a life of
publicity or of privacy, and to order one's life
and manage one's affairs in a manner that may
be most agreeable to him so long as he does not
violate the rights of others or of the public.[10]

Third, the right of privacy gives an individual the "right to
enjoy life in any way that may be most agreeable and pleasant
to him ... provided that in such enjoyment he does not invade
the rights of his neighbor or violate public law or policy."[11] It
also includes the "right to withdraw from the public gaze in
such times as a person may see fit, when his presence in public
is not demanded by any rule of law"[12] - the right to be left
alone.

Fourth, "the right of privacy is unquestionably limited by
the right to speak and print,"[13] when exercised within the limits
of constitutional guarantees.

Fifth, the Georgia constitution forbids the abuse of freedom
of speech and of the press; yet "the law considers that the
welfare of the public is better [served] by maintaining the
liberty of speech and of the press than by allowing an individual
to assert his right of privacy in such a way as to interfere with
the free expression of one's sentiments and the publication of
every matter in which the public may be legitimately
interested."[14] Thus, anyone who seeks public office or anyone
who claims public approval or patronage of his efforts waives

---

10. Id. at 190-191.
11. Id. at 195.
12. Id. at 196.
13. Id. at 204.
14. Id.

his right of privacy to the extent that he cannot obstruct the public in any proper investigation into the conduct of his private life.

Sixth, one's right of privacy may be waived, except in those matters which law or policy demand be kept private. The problem, of course, is defining exactly what constitutes matters that must be kept private and what constitutes a legal waiver. Just how difficult this can be perhaps is best illustrated by the decision in *Multimedia WMAZ v. Kubach*, in which a badly divided state Court of Appeals reversed itself twice before upholding a jury verdict against a Macon television station for agreeing and then failing to obscure the face of a man suffering from the AIDS virus on a television call-in show.[15] The television station had contended that the man had waived his right to privacy by disclosing his condition to other friends and relatives.[16]

However, it must be noted that something offensive to an overly sensitive person does not constitute an invasion of privacy under modern privacy law; for there to be an actionable invasion of privacy, it must be disgusting to a person of "ordinary sensibilities," because "there are some shocks, inconveniences, and annoyances which members of society in the nature of things must absorb without the right of redress."[17]

---

15. 212 Ga. App. 707, 443 S.E. 2d 491 (1994). See, Ken Goodall, "Late Consolation for AIDS Plaintiff: Court Again Re-thinks Case, But Patient Doesn't Live To See It," Fulton County Daily Report, March 23, 1994, 1, 2.

16. Had the court upheld the television station, it would have been "the first official recognition in Georgia that the right to privacy can be waived through a person's actions" ("Court Reverses Decision in AIDS Case," Atlanta Journal-Constitution, Dec. 24, 1993, C2).

17. Davis v. General Financial & Thrift Corp., 80 Ga. App. 708, 57 S.E.2d 225 (1950) at 711. See, for example, Thomason v. Times-Journal, 190 Ga. App. 601, 379 S.E.2d 551 (1989).

In addition, a two-year statute of limitations applies to all actions for invasion of privacy in Georgia.[18]

One's right of privacy may extend as far as to include one's family. In *Pavesich*, the person who sued was the person whose picture was published. In *Bazemore v. Savannah Hospital*, the Georgia Supreme Court established the rule that others may also be harmed and thus have a cause of action when one's right of privacy is violated.[19] In this case, a couple sought damages for the unauthorized publication of a picture of their physically deformed, deceased child, arguing that publication of the picture harmed them, causing "chagrin, mortification, humiliation, insult, and injury."[20] Yet publication of photographs depicting a young girl who had been abducted and killed in a particularly gruesome manner did not harm her parents' privacy rights the Georgia Supreme Court ruled in *Waters v. Fleetwood*.[21] Even though the pictures showed the decomposition of part of the girl's body, which had been wrapped in chains, the court reiterated its position in *Pavesich* and concluded that "where an incident is a matter of public interest, or the subject matter of a public investigation, a publication in connection therewith can be a violation of no one's legal right of privacy."[22] And until the murderer is apprehended and brought to justice, the court ruled, "the matter will continue to be one of public interest, and the dissemination of information pertaining thereto would not amount to a violation of the petitioner's right of privacy."[23]

---

18. O.C.G.A. 9-3-33.
19. 171 Ga. 257, 155 S.E. 194 (1930).
20. Id. at 262.
21. 212 Ga. 160, 91 S.E.2d 344 (1956).
22. Pavesich, 122 Ga. at 167.
23. Waters, 212 Ga. at 160.

Newsworthy matters of public interest, such as an investigation of criminal activity, are thus exempted from Georgia's right of privacy.

Pavesich remained the privacy standard in Georgia for sixty-two years. However, in 1966, Judge Homer C. Eberhardt of the Georgia Court of Appeals incorporated new dimensions into the right of privacy with his majority opinion in *Cabaniss v. Hipsley*.[24] Lillian Hipsley, an exotic dancer, brought suit against C.B. Cabaniss, publisher of *Gay Atlanta* magazine, claiming that Cabaniss had obtained a copy of a provocative photograph of her and, without her knowledge or consent, had published it as part of an advertisement for Atlanta's Playboy Club. Billed as "Dawn Darling - Provocative and Exciting Exotic Dancer," she appeared in the photograph wearing only "two tantalizing, titillating tassels and a scanty G-string."[25] Below the picture was the assertion, "She's terrific." The case reporter agreed: "In naked truth she was, as advertised, utterly terrific!"[26] The problem was that while it was her picture, it was not her name; nor had she ever appeared at the Atlanta Playboy Club. The trial court awarded Ms. Hipsley $15,000 in damages.

On appeal, Judge Eberhardt relied not just on *Pavesich* but also on Dean William L. Prosser's four-part formulation of the right of privacy.[27] Prosser suggested that the right of privacy is in reality a combination of four loosely related torts, or private wrongful acts - an approach which has generally been followed by Georgia courts in subsequent privacy cases, including those in which the mass media are involved. These may be described as:

---

24. 114 Ga. App. 367, 151 S.E.2d 496.

25. Id. at 369.

26. Id.

27. See, "Privacy," 48 California Law Review 383 (1960).

- Intrusion upon a person's seclusion or physical solitude, or into his or her private affairs - a wrong similar to trespass;

- Public disclosure of embarrassing private facts about a person so as to offend a reasonable person of ordinary sensibilities;[28]

- Publicity which places a person in a false light in the public eye or publication of false information which publicly depicts a person as something or someone he or she is not, which is highly offensive to a reasonable person[29] - a wrong similar to libel;[30]

- Appropriation of the property right a person has in his or her name, image, or likeness for another's economic or commercial advantage.

Applying the facts at hand, Judge Eberhardt found no evidence that Ms. Hipsley's physical solitude had been violated. With regard to the second type of invasion of privacy, the publication of embarrassing private facts, he concluded that Ms. Hipsley "was what is commonly referred to as a strip-tease, and, by the very nature of her occupation, the facts

---

28. This offense extends only to unnecessary and illegitimate public scrutiny of one's private affairs. See, Multimedia WMAZ v. Kubach, 212 Ga. App. 707, 443 S.E.2d 491 (1994).

29. Falsity or fiction is an essential element of this offense. There can be no recovery of damages unless "knowing falsehood or reckless disregard for the truth" is established, following the rule set by the U.S. Supreme Court in Time v. Hill, 385 U.S. 374 (1967) at 390.

30. However, "while libel redresses an injury caused by the effect of false publicity on one's standing in the community, false light redresses the mental suffering caused by the publicity, irrespective of any harm to reputation" (Kenneth Franklin, "Invasion of Privacy: False Light Offers False Hope," 8 Loyola Entertainment Law Journal 411 (1988) at 417).

disclosed were neither private nor embarrassing to her."[31] As to the false light charge, the judge decided that simply incorrectly identifying someone could not justify a verdict for damages. And with regard to appropriation, "it is clear from the record that plaintiff's photograph was appropriated (mistakenly or otherwise) for commercial exploitation without her consent."[32] However, he declined to award damages and reversed the lower court's judgment because Ms. Hipsley had not offered evidence of a monetary injury, only damage to her feelings and sensibilities.

The introduction of Prosser's categories in 1966 gave future judges and juries a more tangible basis on which to decide privacy cases. However, how an individual's right of privacy would be balanced against competing interests remains unclear:

- To what extent should a "reasonable person" and his "ordinary sensibilities" affect the point at which intrusion into one's physical solitude is invaded? A department store's desire to keep its restrooms crime-free through surveillance activity conducted within toilet stalls was not held to be intrusive by the Georgia Court of Appeals.[33]

- When is the publication of embarrassing private facts unnecessary public scrutiny and when is it legitimate public concern? With this tort, three elements are involved: a public disclosure, private facts, and the disclosure must be offensive to a reasonable person of ordinary sensibilities. Yet it is understood that the act of filing a lawsuit may waive one's right to protect such

---

31. 114 Ga. App. 367, 151 S.E.2d 496 (1966) at 374.

32. Id. at 379.

33. See, Elmore v. Atlantic Zayre, 178 Ga. App. 25, 341 S.E.2d 905 (1986).

information from public disclosure. And even the improper release of results of an employment-related drug test might not be an embarrassing public disclosure.[34]

- To what extent must someone be presented as something he or she is not, how false or outrageous or fictitious must something be for it to constitute false light invasion of privacy? Because this privacy tort is so similar to libel, Georgia courts have held that there can be no recovery without knowing or reckless falsehood also being established.[35]

- When is the property right that one has in his or her image or likeness appropriated? Must financial gain be involved?[36] After all, Paolo Pavesich was an artist by profession.[37]

Subsequent decisions after *Hipsley* have attempted to establish the balance between an individual's right of privacy and competing interests and to find congruity between the individual's right to privacy and freedom of expression, the necessities of commerce, testimonial privilege, and legitimate public interests. In each instance, with one exception – which was subsequently overturned by the U.S. Supreme Court – the right of privacy in Georgia was held to be of lesser value than the opposing interest.

---

34. See, King v. Georgia, 276 Ga. 126, 577 S.E.2d 764 (2003); Foster v. Swinney, 263 Ga. App. 510, 588 S.E.2d 307 (2003).

35. See, Brewer v. Rogers, 211 Ga. App. 343, 439 S.E.2d 77 (1993).

36. See, Whisper Wear v. Morgan, 277 Ga. App. 607, 627 S.E.2d 178 (2006) (where a woman's likeness was used in breast pump ads without her consent).

37. Pavesich v. New England Life Insurance Co., 122 Ga. 190, 50 S.E. 68 (1905).

The first of these four "balancing" cases is *Cox Broadcasting Corporation v. Cohn.*[38] In this case, the owner of Atlanta's WSB-TV was sued for broadcasting the name of a deceased rape victim, during a news report about the trial of the six suspects. Cox Broadcasting claimed that it was "privileged under both state law and the First and Fourteenth Amendments."[39] At first, on appeal,[40] the Georgia Supreme Court found it unnecessary to consider the constitutionality of the state statue that forbids the publication of the names of victims of sexual assault,[41] concluding that the young woman's father did have a valid claim for invasion of his own privacy by reason of the broadcasting of his daughter's name. The U.S. Supreme Court, however, disagreed. (The Georgia Supreme Court would eventually agree with the U.S. Supreme Court's position in *Dye v. Wallace* and overturn the state's rape shield law.)[42]

Justice Byron White, writing for an 8-1 majority, declared the Georgia statute unconstitutional and ruled in favor of Cox Broadcasting, because the reporter "based his televised report upon notes taken during the court proceedings an obtained the name of the victim from the indictments handed to him at his request during a recess in the hearing. [The Cohn family] has

---

38. 420 U.S. 469 (1974).

39. Id. at 474.

40. Cox Broadcasting Corp. v. Cohn, 231 Ga. 60, 200 S.E.2d 127 (1973).

41. 1911 Georgia Laws 179. 1968 Georgia Laws 1249, made it a misdemeanor to publish or broadcast the name or identity of a rape victim. O.C.G.A. 16-6-23 – Georgia's rape confidentiality statute – which made it a crime to identify rape victims in the media, unless the information was obtained "in public court documents open to public inspection," was subsequently declared unconstitutional by the Georgia Supreme Court in Dye v. Wallace, 274 Ga. 257, 553 S.E.2d 561 (2001).

42. Id.

not contended that the name was obtained in an improper fashion or that it was not an official court document open to public inspection."[43]

Quoting Justice William O. Douglas in *Craig v. Harney*,[44] Justice White wrote, "A trial is a public event. What transpires in the court room is public property.... Those who see and hear what transpired can report it with impunity."[45] A person's right of privacy is, thus, curtailed when information is available in public records; reporters may relate such information protected by the defense of qualified privilege.

(Several other state criminal statutes beyond the scope of this treatise deal with physical invasions of privacy, encompassing prohibitions against eavesdropping, wiretapping, peeping toms, improper surveillance - including the use of hidden cameras - and the intentional interception of a cellular telephone signal or dissemination of its contents without the consent of at least one party to the conversation.)[46]

The next judicial attempt to balance the right of privacy with a competing social interest, this time the necessities of

---

43. 420 U.S. 469 (1974).

44. 331 U.S. 367 (1947).

45. Id. at 374. Quoted in Cox Broadcasting Corp. v. Cohn, 420 U.S. 469 (1974) at 492.

46. See, O.C.G.A. 16-11-60 through O.C.G.A. 16-11-66.1. This last section was added in 1993 and nullified a court of appeals' holding that over-the-air interception of cellular telephone calls was not an invasion of privacy. See, Salmon v. Georgia, 206 Ga. App. 469, 426 S.E.2d 160 (1992) at 471. In Georgia, the consent of all parties is required before a conversation in a private place may be recorded, though a party to the conversation may record it. See, O.C.G.A. 16-11-62, O.C.G.A. 16-11-66(d). See also, Malone v. Georgia, 246 Ga. App. 882, 541 S.E.2d 431 (2000). The law does not prohibit parents from monitoring conversations of their minor children. See, Bishop v. Georgia, 252 Ga. App. 211, 555 S.E.2d 504 (2001). However, the use of hidden cameras to record conversations in a private place requires the consent of all parties. See, O.C.G.A. 16-11-62(2).

commerce, was *Hines v. Columbus Bank & Trust Company.*[47] In this case, a bank official wrote a letter to the American ambassador of Costa Rica seeking "business information" - such as annual salary, employment, ownership and value of stock - concerning a U.S. citizen residing there. Mr. Hines claimed an invasion of his privacy. The appellate court's 6-3 majority opinion concluded that "law, logic, and the practicalities of modern commerce require a negative answer."[48] Judge H. Sol Clark stated that "the only category relevant to the instant case is the first classification, namely, that of intrusion into private affairs."[49] Using Judge Eberhardt's classifications, "under this theory 'the Georgia cases require that the intrusion must be physical, analogous to a trespass;'"[50] the "single letter of business inquiry" did not constitute and invasion of privacy.

Dennis v. Adcock,[51] the third case, involved the right of privacy being balanced against the concept of testimonial privilege. In this case, Michael Dennis was permanently injured while diving into a swimming pool owned by Adcock Morris Corporation. He sued for invasion of privacy when the company introduced confidential hospital records in evidence against him, which contained a statement to the effect that he "had been drinking beer all day."[52] Although he had never given the hospital authority to share his medical records with anyone other than his own attorneys, their introduction at the trial resulted in his being denied the claim for damages. The

---

47. 137 Ga. App. 268, 223 S.E.2d 468 (1976).

48. Id.

49. Id. at 269.

50. Id., quoting Peacock v. Retail Credit Co., 302 F.Supp. 418 (N.D. Ga. 1969) at 422.

51. 138 Ga. App. 425, 226 S.E.2d 292 (1976).

52. Id. at 427.

appellate court, however, unanimously concluded that "there is no privileged communications immunity in Georgia between hospital and patient."[53] Even if there were, the court said the use of such information "in a relevant court proceeding" is not an invasion of privacy. On the other hand, medical records in Georgia are traditionally confidential,[54] though the courts have not been inclined to award damages for their improper release.[55]

The last of these cases is *Ramsey v. Georgia Gazette Publishing Company.*[56] Ramsey is more or less a modern-day *Waters v. Fleetwood*,[57] in that it attempts to balance the right of privacy with legitimate public interests.[58] In *Ramsey*, the plaintiff was a Savannah dentist who was the primary suspect in a murder case. Although police had made no public statement of this nature, investigators had confirmed that he was their chief suspect. In conjunction with its reporting of the murder, the *Georgia Gazette* also reported that police were investigating complaints by the dentist's female patients that he had sexually harassed them and that he had tried to get other patients to obtain prescription drugs for his personal use. The basis of Dr. Ramsey's complaint was that matters published in the newspaper constituted public disclosure of private information.

---

53. Id. at 429.

54. See, Ussery v. Healthcare, Inc., 289 Ga. App. 255, 656 S.E.2d 882 (2008); King v. Georgia, 276 Ga. 126, 577 S.E.2d 764 (2003).

55. See, Foster v. Swinney, 263 Ga. App. 510, 588 S.E.2d 307 (2003).

56. 164 Ga. App. 693, 297 S.E.2d 94 (1982).

57. 212 Ga. 160, 91 S.E.2d 344 (1956).

58. See also, Tucker v. News Publishing Co., 197 Ga. App. 85, 397 S.E.2d 499 (1990) (where a student who had been viciously attacked by other students and identified in newspaper reports could not claim a right to privacy because, willingly or not, he had become involved in a matter of public interest).

Although appellate Judge William L. McMurray, Jr., found that this case was a "publication of embarrassing private facts" type of invasion of privacy, he concluded that "in Georgia it seems clear that this cause of action is limited by an acknowledgment of a public interest in the investigation of criminal activity."[59] Therefore, he ruled that the trial court had been correct in granting the newspaper's motion for the claim to be dismissed.

More recently illustrative of the problem of determining the extent of a person's privacy rights when involved in a legitimate issue of public interest is *Macon Telegraph Publishing Company v. Tatum*,[60] in which a woman killed her attacker during an attempted sexual assault. When her name and address were published, she sued claiming that the articles violated her right to privacy because she was an intended rape victim. The Georgia Supreme Court disagreed:

> Tatum, [when she] committed a homicide, however justified, lost her right to keep her name private. When she shot [her attacker], Tatum became the object of a legitimate public interest and the newspaper had the right under federal and state constitutions to accurately report the facts regarding the incident, including her name.[61]

---

59. 164 Ga. App. 693, 297 S.E.2d 94 (1982) at 695.

60. 263 Ga. 678, 436 S.E.2d 655 (1993). See, Katie Wood, "Privacy Suit Appeal Focuses on Scope of Rape Shield Law," Daily Report, June 28, 1993, 1, 10.

61. Quoted in Peter Mantius, "Justices Affirm Newspaper in Right-to-Privacy Case," Atlanta Journal-Constitution, Dec. 4, 1993, B3. See also, Eric Velasco, "Ga. Supreme Court Rules Telegraph Had Right to Publish Woman's Name," Macon Telegraph, Dec. 3, 1993, A1; David Hudson,

As Justice Cobb stated in *Pavesich*,[62] "We are thoroughly satisfied ... that the law recognizes within proper limits ... the right of privacy...."[63] Yet "it must be kept within its proper limits, [especially] in the matters which are claimed to be of purely private concern."[64] The "proper limits" of privacy are at the core of *Bullard v. MRA Holding*,[65] where the issue involves a 14-year-old Georgia minor's ability to consent to the commercial use of her partially nude "image in one of the infamous 'Girls Gone Wild' series" of videos and DVDs, while on spring break in Panama City, Florida.[66] As of this writing,[67] a trial date has not yet been scheduled.

"Liability for News Article Concerning Assault," Georgia Press Bulletin, March 1, 1993, 3.

62. 122 Ga. 190, 50 S.E. 68 (1905).

63. Id. at 220.

64. Id. at 221. Of undoubted importance but beyond the scope of this work are the privacy concerns created by the growing use of data-mining tools by government and private entities – and the resulting societal surveillance mentality – which have access to information which is "technically public." Brian Bergstein, "Data-Mining Tools Fuel Concerns about Privacy," Atlanta Journal-Constitution, Jan. 4, 2004, C2. See, for example, Dan Sewell, "Data Mining Used in Kroger Coupon Program," Atlanta Journal-Constitution, Jan. 8, 2009, B1, B5.

65. 890 F.Supp.2d 1323 (N.D.Ga. 2012) (where the federal trial-level court asked the Georgia Supreme Court if a legitimate cause of action exists in Georgia); 292 Ga. 748, 740 S.E.2d 622 (2013) (where the Georgia Supreme Court concluded that an appropriation of likeness claim does exist). See, Amy Viteri, "Court Ruling Allows Woman to Sue 'Girls Gone Wild' over Picture," WSB-TV, March 28, 2013, available at: http://www.wsbtv.com/news/news/local/court-ruling-allows-woman-sue-girls-gone-wild-over/nW675/ (last accessed Nov. 1, 2013).

66. 890 F.Supp.2d 1323 (N.D.Ga. 2012) at 1325.

67. The research in this work is current through Nov. 15, 2013.

The Right of Publicity

Related to the privacy tort of appropriation – yet distinct from it – is the right of publicity, which was also first acknowledged in Georgia as a result of the state appellate court's ruling in *Cabaniss v. Hipsley*.[68] Defined as a person's right to profit economically from his name or likeness,[69] it differs from appropriation in that appropriation only prohibits others from profiting from a person's name or likeness without his or her consent. The right of publicity also may be assigned to others and, like most property rights, may be inherited by others after the person's death.

The so-called newsworthiness exception or defense to invasions of privacy suits, which so regularly undermines many privacy claims, was also at the center of a recent right of publicity case, *Toffoloni v. LFP Publishing Group*.[70] The issue

---

68. 114 Ga. App. 367, 151 S.E.2d 496 (1966) at 377-378. The U.S. Supreme Court recognized this right in Zacchini v. Scripps-Howard Broadcasting Co., 433 U.S. 562 (1977).

69. For the leading Georgia case, see Martin Luther King, Jr., Center for Social Change v. American Heritage Products, Inc., 250 Ga. 135, 296 S.E.2d 697 (1982).

70. 572 F. 3d 1201 (11th Cir. 2009) (where the federal appellate court held that the nude photos were not newsworthy); 38 Media Law Reporter 2589 (N.D.Ga. 2010) (where the trial-level court agreed that the photos were not newsworthy); 483 Federal Appendix 561 (11th Cir. 2012) (where the appellate court limited the punitive damages award). See, Megan Matteucci, "Hustler Could Appeal Ruling on Nude Photos of Benoit's Wife," Atlanta Journal-Constitution, June 25, 2009, available at: http://www.ajc.com/news/hustler-could-appeal-ruling-77480.html (last accessed June 18, 2011); Cristina Abello, "Supreme Court Declines to Hear Right-of-Publicity Case: Lawsuit Filed Against Hustler by Deceased Model's Mother Can Go Forward," The News Media & the Law (Winter 2010), p.20; Megan Matteucci, "Judge: Hustler Owes Family for Nude Photos of Wrestler's Wife," Atlanta Journal-Constitution, Nov. 25, 2010, C2; Greg Bluestein, "Judge Penalizes Hustler over Dead Woman's Photos," Atlanta Journal-Constitution, June 17, 2011, available at:

involved whether the publication in *Hustler* magazine of 20-year-old nude photographs of Nancy Benoit, a former model and professional wrestler, qualified as "news" in the year following the woman's murder by her husband or whether the pictures violated her estate's interest in controlling and limiting her right of publicity. Though her estate had a legal interest in protecting her right of publicity based on the appellate court's determination that the *Hustler* photographs were not "newsworthy," the estate won only $125,000 in compensatory damages and $250,000 in punitive damages – after an initial jury punitive damages award of $19.6 million - because of the "overwhelming evidence that [the magazine] reasonably and honestly (albeit mistakenly) believed that the photographs were ... part of a legitimate news story."[71] A larger, unanswered issue for the media is whether or to what extent courts should be involved in determining what is and is not newsworthy in this modern age of celebrity and entertainment "news" coverage.

---

http://www.ajc.com/news/nation-world/judge-panalizes-hustler-over-980047.html (last accessed June 18, 2011); Christian Boone, "Judge Lowers Hustler's Penalty for Benoit Pics," Atlanta Journal-Constitution, June 18, 2011, B6; Alyson Palmer, "Nudes as News Draws No Penalty," Daily Report, May 4, 2012, 1, 2. (NOTE: The author served as a consultant/expert witness for the defense in Toffoloni v. LFP Publishing Group.)

71. Toffoloni v. LFP Publishing, 483 Federal Appendix 561 (11th Cir. 2012) at 564.

QUESTIONS

1. What type of matters are exempted from the right of privacy, as it is recognized in Georgia?

2. The right of publicity was established in Georgia as the result of the court decision in what case?

3. What common law defense for invasions of privacy was in effect "constitutionalized" as the result of the U.S. Supreme Court decision in Cox Broadcasting v. Cohn (1975)?

4. The right of privacy, as recognized in Georgia, is derived from what type of law?

5. For there to be an actionable invasion of privacy, the invasion must be offensive and disgusting to whom?

6. The four-part formulation of the right of privacy was incorporated into Georgia law as the result of the court decision in what case?

7. What three criteria are required to create a valid false light invasion of privacy claim?

8. How does appropriation of one's likeness differ from the right of publicity in *Toffoloni v. LFP Publishing* (2012)?

Thought Question:
How has Georgia balanced the conflicting demands of the individual's right of privacy and the public's interest in freedom of expression when the identity of a victim of sexual assault is involved? Are there better ways to resolve this dilemma?

4. Advertising Regulation in Georgia

V ery few Georgia laws regulate what kinds of advertising content may or may not appear in the mass media[1] and, even in those which do, the media are usually not legally liable for publication or broadcast, as long as they act "in good faith without knowledge of [the advertisement's] false or fraudulent character."[2] Nevertheless, a state's ability to regulate advertising - despite its First Amendment protection[3] - has been upheld by the U.S. Supreme

---

1. In 1994, for example, the legislature made it a crime "for anyone to advertise or openly offer to assist in a suicide" (Rhonda Cook, "211 New Laws Take Effect in State Today," Atlanta Journal-Constitution, July 1, 1994, G6). But see, Final Exit Network v. Georgia, 290 Ga. 508; 722 S.E.2d 722 (2012). See also, Kim Severson, "Georgia Court Rejects Law Aimed at Assisted Suicide," New York Times, Feb. 7, 2012, A19. See also, O.C.G.A. 16-5-5; 2012 Georgia Laws 637, House Bill 1114.

2. O.C.G.A. 10-1-426. See, O.C.G.A. 10-1-421 (b), and O.C.G.A. 44-3-11. O.C.G.A. 26-2-24 protects the media from liability in the publication of false food advertisements, unless they refuse "to furnish ... the name and post office address of the manufacturer, packer, distributor, seller, or advertising agency who caused [them] to disseminate such advertis[ing]." Similarly, O.C.G.A. 44-3-185 shields the media from liability for the false advertising of time-shares, "unless the publisher, employee, or printer has actual knowledge of the falsity thereof or has an interest either as an owner or agent in the time-share project so advertised."

3. See, Bigelow v. Virginia, 421 U.S. 809 (1975), involving the advertising of abortions; Virginia Board of Pharmacy v. Virginia Citizen Consumers Council, 425 U.S. 748 (1976), involving the advertising of prescription drug prices. See also, Atlanta Co-Operative News Project v. U.S. Postal Service, 350 F.Supp. 234 (N.D. Ga. 1972), where a federal district court ruled that the advertising of abortions was protected expression.

Court,[4] as long as the requirements of the four-part test set forth in *Central Hudson Gas & Electric Corporation v. Public Service Commission*[5] warrant regulation. First, the advertisement in question must be scrutinized to determine whether it is protected by the First Amendment - it must promote a legal activity and not be misleading or "materially deceptive."[6] Second, the regulation must be examined to ascertain whether a "substantial" governmental interest is implicated. Third, it must be examined to see whether it "directly advances" that interest in the, fourth, least restrictive manner.[7]

In Georgia, advertising must "be accurate, truthful, and not misleading in fact or by implication."[8] Advertising "which is untrue or fraudulent and which is known or which by the exercise of reasonable care should be known to be untrue of fraudulent" is unfair and deceptive, and is, therefore, prohibited.[9] The "guiding principle" used in measuring the extent of an advertisement's unfairness is the "least sophisticated consumer" or "idiot" standard.[10]

---

4. See, Condado Holiday Inn v. Tourism Company of Puerto Rico, 478 U.S. 328 (1986).

5. 447 U.S. 551 (1980).

6. For an example of an advertisement containing fraudulent misrepresentation, see, Federal Trade commission v. Colgate-Palmolive, 380 U.S. 374 (1965).

7. Central Hudson Gas & Electric Corp. v. Public Service Commission, 447 U.S. 551 (1980) at 566.

8. See, for example, O.C.G.A. 33-59-8 (advertising by life settlement brokers).

9. O.C.G.A. 10-1-421. See, David B. Baldwin, "False Advertising in Georgia," 12 Mercer Law Review 260 (1960); David B. Baldwin, "False Advertising in Georgia – Prima Facie Violations – Proposed Statutes," 12 Mercer Law Review 360 (1961).

10. David E. Hudson, "Interpreting Acceptable Automobile Advertising," The GPA Bulletin, Oct. 11, 1991, 2.

For example, confusion deliberately generated by Associated Telephone Directory Publishers in the marketing and design of its "Atlanta Yellow Pages" was held to be deceitful.[11] Similarly, deception may result from assertions which are not literally false but which are still likely to mislead consumers,[12] as when the labels of a shipment of medicinal salt bore statements that the crystals were from Warm Springs, Georgia, "America's most famous health resort."[13] On the other hand, the promotion and sale of a substitute for creamery butter was not held to be misleading, unless it was so improperly labeled that it would deceive purchasers or so contaminated that the purchasers would be injured by its use.[14] And the statement that "a contribution from your order [for a bust of Martin Luther King, Jr.] goes to the King Center for Social Change," when, in fact , only three percent - ninety cents - of the $29.95 purchase price was contributed, was not misleading enough to be illegal.[15]

However, some types of promotional practices are strictly forbidden, such as, advertising without intending to sell an item or service according to the terms contained in the ad,[16] the

---

11. See, Southern Bell Telephone & Telegraph Co. v. Associated Telephone Directory Publishers, 756 F.2d 801 (11th Cir. 1985).

12. O.C.G.A. 26-2-21(a)(7). See, for example, O.C.G.A. 38-3-142 (where the name of the Georgia Emergency Management Agency or its acronym may not be used in an advertisement "reasonably calculated to convey the impression" of GEMA approval).

13. See, for example, Taylor v. U.S., 80 F.2d 604 (5th Cir. 1936), certiorari denied, 297 U.S. 708 (1936).

14. See, Baltimore Butterine Co. v. Talmadge, 32 F.2d 904 (S.D. Ga. 1929), affirmed, 37 F.2d 1014 (5th Cir. 1930).

15. See, The Martin Luther King, Jr., Center for Social Change v. American Heritage Products, Inc., 508 F.Supp. 854 (N.D. Ga. 1981).

16. O.C.G.A. 10-1-420. A properly sized disclaimer may diminish liability in such a situation.

advertising and sale of odometer altering devices,[17] advertising by or for an unlicensed insurance company[18] or an adoption agency not licensed by the Georgia Department of Human Resources,[19] the advertisement of any account or financial instrument as insured when it is not,[20] and advertising stating that retailers will "take care of the taxes" for customers, unless the retailer takes specific responsibility for paying the purchaser's sales tax and offers written evidence that the retailer is legally liable for paying such tax.[21]

Discriminatory housing[22] and employment[23] advertisements are also illegal.

Before passage of the Lottery for Education Act of 1992, Georgia had chosen to restrict lottery activities, as well as advertisements for lotteries - defined as "any scheme or procedure whereby one or more prizes are distributed by chance among persons who have paid or promised consideration for a chance to win such prize"[24] - unless they

---

17. O.C.G.A. 40-8-5(e).

18. O.C.G.A. 33-5-2(b). See also, Chatham County Hospital Authority v. John Hancock Mutual Life Insurance Co., 325 F.Supp. 614 (S.D. Ga. 1971); American Druggist Insurance Co. v. Georgia Power Co., 145 Ga. App. 104, 243 S.E.2d 319 (1978).

19. O.C.G.A. 19-8-19.

20. O.C.G.A. 7-1-133(a).

21. O.C.G.A. 48-8-36.

22. O.C.G.A. 8-3-202(3).

23. O.C.G.A. 45-19-31.

24. O.C.G.A. 16-12-20(4). See also, 2012 Georgia Laws 1136, Senate Bill 431 §2. According to Georgia courts, the crime of commercial gambling consists of three elements: prize, chance, and consideration. See, Grant v. Georgia, 75 Ga. App. 784, 44 S.E.2s 513 (1947); Monte Carlo Parties, Ltd. v. Webb, 253 Ga. 508, 322 S.E.2d 246 (1984). Lotteries also contain the same elements. See, Barker v. Georgia, 56 Ga. App. 705, 193 S.E.2d 605 (1937).

clearly contained the words, "Void in Georgia."[25] With the ratification of a constitutional amendment legalizing a state-sponsored lottery in November 1992, the rules have changed somewhat.[26] Now, advertisers may promote the Georgia Lottery, as well as state-sponsored lotteries elsewhere.[27]

However, advertising of "lotteries designed to benefit non-profit organizations," such as the Scouts, are still prohibited. The prohibition does not encompass "advertisements for promotional contests or giveaways, so long as the contest does not require any purchase to be included in a drawing."[28]

For example, "flexible participation" schemes,[29] "Pot O' Gold" sales promotions[30] and "sweepstakes" where players used newspaper advertising inserts to determine if they had a winning number by calling a "dial-it" (1-900-) telephone number were all held to constitute lotteries and advertisements for player/participants were illegal.[31] The publication or broadcast of news stories about winning lottery numbers,

---

25. O.C.G.A. 16-12-27.

26. See, "Lottery Advertising: Recent Changes in Georgia Law," Georgia Press Bulletin, April 15, 1993, 3.

27. Beer and wine retailers, such as convenience and grocery stores, may advertise the availability of lottery tickets in the media, but not retailers of alcohol and distilled spirits, such as liquor and package stores. "These stores may advertise their association with the Georgia Lottery on their own property, but they are not authorized under Department of Revenue regulations to advertise in newspapers or other media outlets" (James B. Ellington, "Watch Lottery Advertising by Liquor/Package Stores," Georgia Press Bulletin, Sept. 6, 1993, 3). See, O.C.G.A. 3-4-3.

28. David E. Hudson & James B. Ellington, "Georgia Law Prohibits Any Lottery Advertising," Georgia Press Association Editor's Forum (Summer 1990), 5.

29. See, Barker v. Georgia, 56 Ga. App. 705, 193 S.E.2d 605 (1937).

30. See, Boyd v. Piggly-Wiggly Southern, Inc., 115 Ga. App. 628, 155 S.E.2d 630 (1967).

31. 1984 Opinions of the Attorney General, No. 84-83, 182.

lottery jackpots, or lottery winners, however, is not considered advertising. Yet because of the potential legal liability associated with the public dissemination of incorrect information, the Georgia Press Association has recommended publishing a disclaimer.[32]

Georgia law still prohibits the advertising of casino gambling, sports pools, and pari-mutuel betting.[33] Anyone convicted of advertising commercial gambling is guilty of a high and aggravated misdemeanor.[34]

The Georgia Fair Business Practices Act of 1975[35] prohibits all "unfair or deceptive acts or practices in the conduct of consumer transactions and consumer acts or practices in trade or commerce,"[36] including misleading advertising.[37] Regulated actions must take place in the context of the consumer marketplace[38] and one-time, isolated actions which have no

---

32. "[Media Name] publishes unofficial winning numbers from the Georgia Lottery as a service to its readers. We do not certify these numbers as official winning numbers and are not responsible for any loss suffered by the holder of a lottery ticket should these reported numbers contain any errors or omissions or should they not be the official winning numbers. The reader should confirm any winning numbers with the Georgia Lottery Corporation." James Ellington, "Lawsuit Lottery," Georgia Press Bulletin, March 1994, 6.

33. O.C.G.A. 50-27-3.

34. O.C.G.A. 16-12-26.

35. 1975 Georgia Laws 376.

36. O.C.G.A. 10-1-393(a). See, 2010 Georgia Laws 302, Senate Bill 368 §1.

37. O.C.G.A. 10-1-393(b)(9) defines "trade" and "commerce" to include advertising. See, for example, Atlanta Gas Light Co. v. Semaphore Advertising, Inc., 747 F.Supp. 715 (S.D. Ga. 1990).

38. See, Pryor v. CCEC, 257 Ga. App. 450, 571 S.E.2d 454 (2000) (where a students' dismissal from a private school did not occur in a commercial context). On the other hand, see, Catrett v. Landmark Dodge, 253 Ga. App. 639, 560 S.E.2d 104 (2002) (where a claim regarding the condition of a car was within the scope of the statute).

impact on the general consuming public are beyond the scope of the statute,[39] as are private transactions.[40]

"By way of illustration only and without limiting the scope" of the act,[41] illegal practices include:

- The misrepresentation of goods and services as another's;[42]
- The creation of confusion or misunderstanding regarding the "source, sponsorship, approval, or certification of goods or services" or their "affiliation, connection, or association with or certification by another;[43]
- The use of "deceptive representations or designations of geographic origin in connection with goods and services," specifically the advertisement of a local telephone number for a non-local business without the inclusion of a non-local address.[44]
- The misrepresentation of a product or service's "sponsorship, approval, characteristics, ingredients, uses, benefits;" condition; quality, model, or style; or a

---

39. See, Davis v. Rich's Department Stores, 248 Ga. App. 116, 545 S.E.2d 661 (2001) (a one-time deviation from company policy was an isolated event).

40. See, Zeeman v. Black, 156 Ga. App. 82, 273 S.E.2d 910 (1980); Henderson v. Gandy, 280 Ga. 95, 623 S.E.2d 465 (2005).

41. O.C.G.A. 10-1-393(b). O.C.G.A. 10-1-393.1 applies similar rules to the practices of office supply companies.

42. O.C.G.A. 10-1-393(b)(1).

43. O.C.G.A. 10-1-393(b)(2-3).

44. O.C.G.A. 10-1-393(b)(4). See, for example, Taylor v. U.S., 80 F.2d 604 (5th Cir. 1936), certiorari denied, 297 U.W. 708 (1936); Blum v. General Motors Acceptance Corp., 185 Ga. App. 714, 365 S.E.2d 474 (1988). See also, David Hudson, "Interpreting Acceptable Automobile Advertising," The GPA Bulletin, Oct. 11, 1991, 2.

person's "sponsorship, approval, status, affiliation, or connection;"[45]

- The criticism of another's goods, services, or business "by false or misleading representation;"[46]

- The advertisement of any product or service "with intent not to sell them as advertised" or "with intent not to supply reasonably expectable public demand," unless quantity limitations are included in the advertisement;[47]

- The misrepresentation of "the reasons for, existence of, or amounts of price reductions;"[48]

- The failure to abide by the provisions of the Georgia code concerning health spas,[49] career consulting firms,[50] or "promotional giveaways;"[51]

- Any violation of federal law relating to the

---

45. O.C.G.A. 10-1-393(b)(5-7). Georgia law also prohibits "selling non-kosher foods labeled as kosher when done with fraudulent intent. They do not bar non-kosher food from being advertised as 'kosher-style' or 'kosher-type'." Elizabeth Lee, "Ruling on Kosher Label May Affect Laws in Georgia," Atlanta Journal-Constitution, Feb. 25, 2003, E4. For an example of "mere" sales exaggeration, see, Hill v. Jay Pontiac, Inc., 191 Ga. App. 258, 381 S.E.2d 417 (1989). But what if different sects of the same religious group have different definitions of "kosher"? See, Bill Rankin & Christopher Quinn, "Rabbi's Suit Challenges State Law on Kosher Food," Atlanta Journal-Constitution, Aug. 7, 2009, B1; Rosalind Bentley, "Suit Seeks To Clarify What's 'Kosher'," Atlanta Journal-Constitution, Aug. 23, 2009, C3. See, O.C.G.A. 10-1-393.11, O.C.G.A. 26-2-22.

46. O.C.G.A. 10-1-393(b)(8).

47. O.C.G.A. 10-1-393(b)(9-10).

48. O.C.G.A. 10-1-393(b)(11).

49. O.C.G.A. 10-1-393(b)(12). See also O.C.G.A. 10-1-393.2; Georgia Receivables v. Welch, 242 Ga. App. 146, 529 S.E.2d 164 (2000).

50. O.C.G.A. 10-1-393(b)(A-C).

51. O.C.G.A. 10-1-393(b)(16)(A-P). See, for example, Lamb v. United States Sales Corp., 194 Ga. App. 333, 390 S.E.2d 440 (1990).

advertisement of odometer altering devices;[52]

- The failure to notify buyers of campground or marine memberships of their right to cancel their purchase within seven days;[53]
- The misrepresentation or false advertisement of a vacation or holiday[54] or of an organization's intent to assist debtors;[55]
- The advertising of 976- telephone prefix numbers, unless the responsible parties are clearly identified;[56]
- The requirement that additional goods or services be purchased to qualify for any promotional giveaway;[57]
- The promotion or holding of any going-out-of-business sale for more than ninety days;[58]
- The improper distribution of real estate settlement proceeds;[59]
- Advertising by persons not legally licensed to provide personal care service;[60]
- Any "prize notification" that does not "conspicuously identify on its face" that its contents are a commercial solicitation and include the odds of winning;[61]

---

52. O.C.G.A. 10-1-393(b)(15). See also, 15 U.S. Code 1983 and O.C.G.A. 40-8-5(e).
53. O.C.G.A. 10-1-393(b)(17-19).
54. O.C.G.A. 10-1-393 (b)(22)(A-B).
55. O.C.G.A. 10-1-393(b)(20)(A-D).
56. O.C.G.A. 10-1-393(b)(21).
57. O.C.G.A. 10-1-393(b)(23), except as provided in O.C.G.A. 10-1-393(b)(16).
58. O.C.G.A. 10-1-393(b)(24)(A-C).
59. O.C.G.A. 10-1-393(b)(25).
60. O.C.G.A. 10-1-393(b)(26).
61. O.C.G.A. 10-1-393(b)(27).

- Any improper marketing of DUI alcohol or drug use risk reduction programs regulated by the Department of Human Resources;[62]
- Knowingly obtaining information under false pretenses from a consumer reporting agency;[63]
- The marketing of a service as a "home health agency," if it has not been duly licensed as such;[64]
- The use of recording devices by telemarketers to induce the purchase of goods or to collect amounts claimed as being owed;[65]
- The misrepresentation of health service discounts as insurance;[66]
- The sale of gift cards without expiration dates or notice of the cards' terms and conditions of use;[67] and
- The charging of exorbitant fees by Internet websites to remove publicly available arrest photographs.[68]

Since 1989, automobile dealers must also sell vehicles at or below advertised prices, have a sufficient supply of advertised vehicles on hand or disclose the limited quantity, advertise selling prices which represent the "actual total purchase price" of the vehicle, and not continue to advertise a vehicle for sale

---

62. O.C.G.A. 10-1-393(b)(28). See also, O.C.G.A. 40-5-81(c), for permissible advertising.

63. O.C.G.A. 10-1-393(b)(29).

64. O.C.G.A. 10-1-393(b)(30).

65. O.C.G.A. 10-1-393(b)(31).

66. O.C.G.A. 10-1-393(b)(32).

67. O.C.G.A. 10-1-393(b)(33).

68. O.C.G.A. 10-1-393.5(b.1). See, 2013 Georgia Laws 613, House Bill 150.

after it has been sold.[69] This last prohibition includes not indicating to telephone customers that an advertised vehicle is still available when it is not.

Prohibited practices also include: any display including Social Security numbers;[70] the use of police or fire department names or symbols;[71] the use of state police symbols or nomenclature;[72] the unauthorized use of a person's name for the purpose of soliciting charitable donations;[73] and the unauthorized use of the terms "M.D.," "Doctor," etc.[74] The Governor's Office of Consumer Affairs is usually Georgia consumers' first resource for complaints about such practices.[75]

In addition, there are also set requirements for advertising and solicitation by attorneys;[76] financial institutions;[77] legal services;[78] investment advisors;[79] telephone solicitors;[80]

---

69. "1975 Law Prohibits Deceptive Tactics," Atlanta Journal-Constitution, Dec. 6, 1993, E9. See also, Shelley Emling, "Did Car Dealer Pull bait and Switch? Ad Raises Questions," Atlanta Journal-Constitution, Dec. 6, 1993, E9.

70. O.C.G.A. 10-1-393.8 (a) & (b).

71. O.C.G.A. 25-13-4, 5, 6.

72. O.C.G.A. 35-2-82 through O.C.G.A. 35-2-84. See also, O.C.G.A. 35-2-102 through O.C.G.A. 35-2-104.

73. O.C.G.A. 43-17-12.

74. O.C.G.A. 43-34-26. See also, O.C.G.A. 43-34-44.

75. See, Governor's Office of Consumer Affairs (undated), at: http://consumer.georgia.gov (last accessed Nov. 15, 2013).

76. For the Georgia Bar rules 7.1-7.5 regulating advertising and communication of services by attorneys, see Part IV, Georgia Rules of Professional Conduct, Part Seven: Information about Legal Services, at: http://www.gabar.org/barrules/georgia-rules-of-professional-conduct.cfm (last accessed Nov. 15, 2013). See also, O.C.G.A. 15-19-54, O.C.G.A. 15-19-55.

77. O.C.G.A. 7-1-7, O.C.G.A. 7-1-68, O.C.G.A. 7-1-198, O.C.G.A. 7-1-552.

78. O.C.G.A. 10-1-427.

79. O.C.G.A. 10-5-2.

corporations, partnerships, and associations;[81] insurance companies;[82] pre-paid legal service insurance plans;[83] health care service providers;[84] certified public accountants;[85] providers of agricultural services;[86] chiropractors;[87] massage therapists;[88] notaries public;[89] monopolies, such as electric membership corporations,[90] gas utilities,[91] telephone cooperatives,[92] and railroads,[93] landscape architects;[94] optometrists;[95] opticians;[96] and pawnbrokers.[97] Advertising by

---

80. O.C.G.A. 10-5B-3.

81. O.C.G.A. 14-2-201, O.C.G.A. 14-2-201.1, O.C.G.A. 14-2-1006.1, O.C.G.A. 14-2-1105.1, O.C.G.A. 14-2-1403.1, O.C.G.A. 14-3-141(b), O.C.G.A. 14-3-303(b), O.C.G.A. 14-3-1005.1, O.C.G.A. 14-3-1104(a), O.C.G.A. 14-3-1404.1(b), O.C.G.A. 14-3-1408, O.C.G.A. 14-3-1433(b). See also, 2010 Georgia Laws 863, Senate Bill 296 §2.

82. O.C.G.A. 33-3-16, O.C.G.A. 33-5-2, O.C.G.A. 33-6-4, O.C.G.A. 33-6-5, O.C.G.A. 33-9-20, O.C.G.A. 33-12-14, O.C.G.A. 33-14-5, O.C.G.A. 33-14-8. See also, O.C.G.A. 33-59-10(d-p).

83. O.C.G.A. 33-35-12.

84. O.C.G.A. 43-1-19.1.

85. O.C.G.A. 43-3-35.

86. O.C.G.A. 43-4-10.

87. O.C.G.A. 43-9-19.

88. O.C.G.A. 43-24A-15(a-b). See, 2010 Georgia Laws 401, Senate Bill 364 §3.

89. O.C.G.A. 45-17-8.2(b).

90. O.C.G.A. 46-3-322, O.C.G.A. 46-3-363, O.C.G.A. 46-3-382, O.C.G.A. 48-3-383, O.C.G.A. 46-3-401, O.C.G.A. 46-3-420, O.C.G.A. 46-3-423, O.C.G.A. 46-3-503.

91. O.C.G.A. 46-4-22 and O.C.G.A. 46-4-53.

92. O.C.G.A. 46-5-43, O.C.G.A. 46-5-71, O.C.G.A. 46-5-72, O.C.G.A. 46-5-86, O.C.G.A. 46-5-87, O.C.G.A. 46-5-88, O.C.G.A. 46-5-91.

93. O.C.G.A. 46-8-70, O.C.G.A. 46-8-74, O.C.G.A. 46-8-232, O.C.G.A. 46-9-190.

94. O.C.G.A. 43-23-7.1.

95. O.C.G.A. 43-30-5.1.

dentists is regulated minimally.[98] Even the General Assembly is required to advertise the introduction of local legislation in "the locality affected."[99]

Aside from statutory remedies, consumers may also have tort remedies for fraud or misrepresentation through their reliance on advertising.

To be actually fraudulent, advertising must be: 1) a false representation, 2) the advertiser must know of the misrepresentation, 3) the advertiser must intend to induce reliance on the advertisement, 4) there must be actual, justifiable reliance, and 5) damage.[100] In order to be fraudulent, statements must misrepresent facts known to the advertiser and not be an opinion. "Puffing" and "dealer talk" are non-fraudulent statements of opinion.[101]

To constitute negligent misrepresentation, 1) the advertiser must be aware of the use to which the information will be put and intend that it be used in that way, 2) it must be foreseeable that a consumer would receive the advertisement, and 3) the consumer must show his misplaced reliance on the advertisement. The only real distinction between the two torts is knowledge of the falsity of the information disclosed. Due diligence is required before consumers may make claims for either tort.

A state's police power gives it even greater control over

---

96. O.C.G.A. 43-29-15.

97. O.C.G.A. 44-12-138.

98. O.C.G.A. 43-11-18.

99. Georgia Constitution of 1983, Article III, §V, ¶IX. For the implementing statute, see, O.C.G.A. 28-1-14.

100. See, GLW International v. Yao, 243 Ga. App. 38, 532 S.E.2d 151 (2000). See also, O.C.G.A. 51-6-2.

101. See, Anderson v. Atlanta Committee for the Olympic Games, 261 Ga. App. 895, 584 S.E.2d 16 (2003).

outdoor advertising and billboards as long as the requirements of the four-part *Central Hudson* test are met.[102] "Reasonable" sign ordinances are permissible as a proper exercise of the state's police power interest in the public's safety and welfare – including the state's interest in promoting aesthetics.[103] Thus, "for sale" signs with improper racial messages may be banned,[104] while a homeowner's protest sign may not be, "notwithstanding the trial court's designation of [it] as an unlawful interference with the enjoyment of the [developer's] property."[105]

However, the Georgia Supreme Court concluded that a Peachtree City ordinance prohibiting commercial signs with prices posted on them was unconstitutional.[106] Presiding Justice Harold N. Hill, Jr., wrote that the city had "no substantial governmental interest in permitting commercial signs yet

---

102. The U.S. Supreme Court applied the test to billboards in Metromedia, Inc. v. San Diego, 453 U.S. 490 (1981).

103. The Georgia Supreme Court has held that "aesthetics is within the public welfare aspect of police power." Parking Association of Georgia v. Atlanta, 264 Ga. 764, 450 S.E.2d 202 (1994) at 765-766. See, O.C.G.A. 32-6-75.3 See also, for example, Doraville v. Turner Communications Corp., 236 Ga. 385, 233 S.E.2d 798 (1976); Thomas v. Marietta, 245 Ga. 485, 265 S.E.2d 775 (1980); Department of Transportation v. Shiflett, 251 Ga. 873, 310 S.E.2d 509 (1984). Georgia's regulation of such signs may be found in O.C.G.A. 32-6-95. For an example of an "unreasonable" ordinance, see, Dills v. Cobb County, 755 F.2d 1473 (11th Cir. 1985); Adams Outdoor Advertising of Atlanta, Inc. v. Fulton County, 738 F.Supp. 1431 (N.D. Ga. 1990).

104. U.S. v. Bob Lawrence Realty Co., 474 F.2d 115 (11th Cir. 1973), certoirari denied, 414 U.S. 826 (1973).

105. Pittman v. Cohn Communities, Inc., 240 Ga. 106, 239 S.E.2d 526 (1977) at 108. See also, Organization for a Better Austin v. Keefe, 402 U.S. 415 (1971).

106. See, H&H Operations, Inc. v. Peachtree City, 248 Ga. 500, 283 S.E.2d 867 (1981).

prohibiting the posting of prices. Numbers ... are not aesthetically inferior to letters of the alphabet forming words...."[107]

This problem of discrimination against different forms of protected speech also resulted in an Atlanta Olympic advertising ordinance being declared unconstitutional. In 1994, the City Council approved a "mega-sign" ordinance that would have allowed corporate sponsors of the 1996 Olympic Games to erect 25-50 signs, 90 feet tall and 40 feet wide, through December 31, 1996. The ordinance was quickly challenged by companies who were not official Olympic sponsors. It was struck down when a federal judge ruled that it would "single out particular forms of expression for special treatment. A qualifying sign [would be] thus able to enjoy a benefit unavailable to a general advertising sign."[108] The District Court found that the Olympic sign ordinance "violates the First Amendment of the United States Constitution, and thus the City of Atlanta is permanently enjoined from enforcing it."[109]

Recently, a law providing that no outdoor advertising depicting obscene material be allowed and restricting outdoor advertising of commercial establishments where nudity is

---

107. Id. at 503.

108. U.S. District Court Judge William O'Kelley, quoted in Lyle v. Harris, "Law Permitting '96 'Mega-Signs' Knocked Down," Atlanta Journal-Constitution, May 4, 1995, A1. See also, Michelle Hiskey, "City Council Oks Strict Sign Statute," Atlanta Journal-Constitution, Aug. 16, 1994, C1; Michelle Hiskey, "'Super Signs' Get Thumbs Up," Atlanta Journal-Constitution, Sept. 1, 1994, F1; Michelle Hiskey & Melissa Turner, "ACOG Wins with New Ordinance," Atlanta Journal-Constitution, Sept. 1, 1994, F4; Michelle Hiskey & Lyle Harris, "Up with Olympic Signs: Council Set To OK Controversial Mega-Billboard Law," Atlanta Journal-Constitution, Sept. 5, 1994, C1, C4.

109. Outdoor Systems Inc. v. City of Atlanta, 885 F.Supp. 1572 (N.D. Ga. 1995).

exhibited was overturned.[110] Georgia courts have not given communities wide latitude in determining what constitutes acceptable billboard advertising,[111] yet complaints about billboards and community attempts to regulate them are on-going.[112]

The most contentious advertising debate in recent years revolves around campaign advertisements in judicial elections.[113] Historically, judicial elections in Georgia were low-key, civil, and largely uncontested. This changed completely with the federal appellate ruling in *Weaver v. Bonner*,[114] which forced the Georgia Supreme Court to amend the state's rules governing judicial conduct and issue new

---

110. O.C.G.A. 32-6-75; Georgia v. Café Erotica, 276 Ga. 97, 507 S.E.2d 732 (1998). Peter Mantius, "Court Overturns Law Prohibiting Signs for Nudes," Atlanta Journal-Constitution, March 5, 1996, C2; Bill Rankin, "High Court Gives OK to Nude Club Billboards," Atlanta Journal-Constitution, Nov. 3, 1998, B1.

111. See, Georgia v. Hartrampf, 273 Ga. 522, 544 S.E.2d 130 (2001); City of Walnut Grove v. Questco, 275 Ga. 266, 564 S.E.2d 445 (2002);

112. See, Christopher Quinn, "Exurbs Send Message with Billboard Laws," Atlanta Journal-Constitution, Feb. 6, 2003, D3; Doug Moore, "A Sign It Will Fight," Atlanta Journal-Constitution, Sept. 1, 2007, B1, B5.

113. Some contend that judges should not be elected at all, as the practice gives the appearance of justice being somehow based on current, popular opinion of the electoral majority. See, Adam Liptak, "Rendering Justice, with One Eye on Re-election," New York Times, May 25, 2008, A1, A13; John Schwartz, "Effort Begun To Abolish the Election of Judges," New York Times, Dec. 24, 2009, A12; A.G. Sulzberger, "Ouster of Iowa Judges Sends Signal to Bench," New York Times, Nov. 4, 2010, A1, P7.

114. 309 F.3d 1312 (11th Cir. 2002) (which established that judicial candidates have First Amendment rights). See, Jonathan Ringel, "Weaver Wins as 11th Circuit Kills Judicial Campaign Curbs," Daily Report, Oct. 22, 2002, 1, 3; and Bill Rankin, "Court Eases Judicial Campaign Rules," Atlanta Journal-Constitution, Oct. 23, 2002, B1.

judicial election rules.[115] The resulting campaign advertising raises questions about the degree to which partisanship, mudslinging, and "politics" are appropriate in judicial races, where candidates are supposedly valued for their nonpartisan behavior and elected based on their expertise and impartiality.[116] Whatever the answer, Georgia's judicial elections have not been the same since.[117]

---

115. Jonathan Ringel, "Georgia Justices Adopt JQC's Rule Changes for Campaigns," Daily Report, Jan. 9, 2004, page number unknown. See also, Georgia Code of Judicial Conduct (Jan. 7, 2004), available at: http://www.georgiacourts.org/files/ GEORGIA%20CODE%20OF%20JUDICIAL%20CONDUCT%20- %202009_23_11.pdf (last accessed Nov. 15, 2013).

116. See, for example, R. William Ide, "Beware Even the Appearance of Justice for Sale," Daily Report, July 2, 2004, 7; L. Lynn Hogue, "Lifting Bans on Speech Opens New World to Judicial Challengers," Daily Report, July 12, 2004, 9; Alyson Palmer, "Elect or Appoint? Court Races Pose Query," Daily Report, Sept. 20, 2006, 1, 8; Jay Cook, No Room for Special-Interest Politics in Judicial Elections," Atlanta Journal-Constitution, Oct. 10, 2006, page number unknown; Shannon L. Goessling, "Free Speech: Keep Politics in High Court Race," Atlanta Journal-Constitution, Oct. 26, 2006, page number unknown; Edward H. Lindsey, "Enough Is Enough," Daily Report, Nov. 11, 2006, page number unknown; Christopher J. McFadden, "Partisan Election Counters Rule of Law," Daily Report, Nov. 29, 2006, page number unknown; Irwin W. Stolz, Jr., "Is Justice for Sale in Georgia?" Daily Report, Dec. 18, 2006, page number unknown; Amanda Bronstad, "States Seek End to Ugly Judicial Races," Daily Report, April 14, 2008, 1, 10.

117. See, for example, Tom Baxter & Jim Galloway, "Perdue Takes Aim at Justice Sears," Atlanta Journal-Constitution, Feb. 2, 2004, page number unknown; Jonathan Ringel, "Hard-Hitting Campaigner Joins Race for Appeals Court," Daily Report, Feb. 27, 2004, 1, 6; Ernie Suggs, "Claims of Sexism Mar Race," Atlanta Journal-Constitution, July 15, 2004, C1; Nancy Badertscher, "High Court Race as Hot as Partisan Battle," Atlanta Journal-Constitution, July 17, 2004, A1, A8; Jonathan Ringel, "Brantley, Sears Swap Barbs in Court Race," Daily Report, July 19, 2004, 1, 5; Don Plummer, "Judges' Ace: Incumbency," Atlanta Journal-Constitution, July 25, 2004, C5; Greg Bluestein, "Mead Injects More Cash into COA Bid," Daily Report,

Nov. 23, 2004, 1, 2; Tom Baxter & Jim Galloway, "Legislator Alarmed at Judicial Politics," Atlanta Journal-Constitution, Nov. 24, 2004, D2; Jonathan Ringel, "No Pollyanna," Daily Report, Dec. 27, 2004, 15-17; Andy Peters & Alyson Palmer, "Business Lobby Takes Aim at Three Justices of High Court," Daily Report, June 20, 2006, 1, 4-5; Alyson Palmer, "Christian Group's Survey Tackles Abortion, Taxes," Daily Report, July 25, 2006, 1, 4-5; Jill Miller, "Supreme Court: Justice's TV Ad a Hard Hitter," Atlanta Journal-Constitution, Oct. 27, 2006, D1, D5; Jim Wooten, "Hunstein's Attack Ad Opens Pandora's Box," Atlanta Journal-Constitution, Oct. 29, 2006, page number unknown; Jill Miller & Jeremy Redmon, "Supreme Court: Foes in Judicial Contest Go Dirty," Atlanta Journal-Constitution, Oct. 31, 2006, A1, A4; Alyson Palmer, "Bar President Blasts Judicial Races' Price Tags," Daily Report, Nov. 7, 2006, 1, 11; Alyson Palmer, "Tough Race, Tougher Tactics," Daily Report, Dec. 20, 2006, 1, 8-9; Robin McDonald, "School Group Faults Judge's GOP Links," Daily Report, Sept. 22, 2008, 1, 10; Bill Rankin, "Judicial Opening Draws Six Hopefuls," Atlanta Journal-Constitution, Oct. 27, 2010, B2; Alyson Palmer, "Wilson: Nahmias Raises 'Phony' Voting Issue,' Daily Report, Oct. 27, 2010, page number unknown; Alyson Palmer, "After Near Silence, Adkins Will Campaign," Daily Report, Nov. 4, 2010, page number unknown; Alyson Palmer, "Race Heats Up as Adkins Gains Key Backers," Daily Report, Nov. 15, 2010, 1, 20; Alyson Palmer, "Judges Make Plans for 2012 Election," Daily Report, May 9, 2011, page number unknown; Andria Simmons, "Sign Theft Probed in Judicial Race," Atlanta Journal-Constitution, Aug. 3, 2012, B6.

Legal Notices

While Georgia has many other laws regulating advertising, the vast majority of these deal with the specifics of how and what government documents and announcements, known as legal notices, must be published in order to be enforceable.[118] Generally, this requires publication in "the official organ of [a] county."[119] If a county has no newspaper which qualifies,

---

118. For a synopsis of these, see, Georgia Press Association's Georgia Law for Journalists (23rd ed.) (2012), available at: http://www.gapress.org/PDFs/2012Lawbook.pdf (last accessed Nov. 15, 2013).

119. This may be defined as a newspaper which has been "continuously published and mailed to a list of bona fide subscribers in that county for a period of one year or is the direct successor of such a journal or newspaper" and which has a paid circulation of at least eighty-five percent of the total number of copies it distributes and has been paid, as established by an independent audit, for a period of 12 months prior to the newspaper's being declared or made the official organ - for 30 days before the notice becomes legally binding. See, O.C.G.A. 9-13-142. See, for example, McGity v. Chambers, 182 Ga. 341, 185 S.E. 513 (1936). For the reasoning behind these requirements, see, Williams v. Athens Newspapers, Inc., 241Ga. 274, 244 S.E.2d 822 (1978). However, its "bona fide subscribers" do not all have to be county residents. See, Community Newspapers, Inc. v. Baker, 198 Ga. App. 680, 402 S.E.2s 545 (1991). And a county's "official organ" does not lose its standing because it is printed elsewhere. See, Dooty v. Gates, 194 Ga. 787, 22 S.E.2d 730 (1942); Southeastern Newspapers Corp. v. Griffin, 245 Ga. 748, 267 S.E.2d 21 (1980). For an earlier, contrary view, see Carter v. Land, 174 Ga. 811, 164 S.E. 205 (1932). See also, O.C.G.A. 9-13-141. Failure to meet this 30-day requirement nullifies the legal action taken or proposed. See, for example, Richmond Country Business Association v. Richmond Country, 223 Ga. 337, 155 S.E.2d 395 (1967). News items published for more than 30 days prior to an election do not constitute the required "legal notice" (id.). Prior to 1910, the sheriff of each county selected the "official medium." See, for example, Coffee v. Ragsdale, 112 Ga. 705, 37 S.E. 968 (1901). By legislative act, the power was conferred jointly upon the county sheriff, court clerk, and ordinary (1910 Georgia Laws 87). For a case applying this rule, see, Dollar v. Wind, 135 Ga. 760 70 S.E.

notices may be published "in the nearest newspaper having the largest general circulation" in the county in question.[120] Advertising rates are set by statute.[121] Complete files of all newspapers containing legal advertisements must be preserved "for public inspection" for at least fifty years.[122]

---

335 (1911). There is no provision for two "official" organs. See, Rish v. Clements, 21 Ga. App. 287, 94 S.E. 318 (1917).

120. O.C.G.A. 9-13-140.

121. O.C.G.A. 9-13-143. For a different type of insertion, see, O.C.G.A. 46-3-503. However, the alternative placement of notices in another newspaper "having the largest general circulation in the county" or "at the courthouse and in a public place in each militia district" is provided for when rates cannot be agreed upon. O.C.G.A. 9-13-144. See, for example, Braddy v. Whiteley, 113 Ga. 746, 39 S.E. 317 (1901). Public officials who demand or receive legal advertising fees other than those provided by law are guilty of extortion. See, O.C.G.A. 45-11-6 through O.C.G.A. 45-11-7.

122. O.C.G.A. 15-6-74(a-b) (superior courts), O.C.G.A. 15-9-43(a) (probate courts) and O.C.G.A. 15-16-10(a)(4) (sheriffs). See also, 2012 Georgia Laws 173, House Bill 665 §§1-16.

QUESTIONS

1. What Georgia law regulating a type of advertising was void as a result of the 1992 general election?

2. What is the "guiding principle" in Georgia when assessing an advertisement's unfairness?

3. Reasonable sign regulations are permissible as a proper exercise of Georgia's exercise of what and its interest in what?

4. In what case did the Georgia Supreme Court conclude that words and numbers have equal aesthetic value in advertising?

5. Under what circumstances may Georgia media be liable for an advertisement published or broadcast?

6. Georgia law still prohibits the advertising of what three types of gambling activities?

7. The ruling in what case has resulted in a revision and reinterpretation of the rules governing state judicial elections?

8. What are the elements of negligent misrepresentation? How do they differ from the elements of fraudulent advertising?

Thought Question:
What types of advertising and promotional practices are prohibited in Georgia? To what extent should the state be involved in setting standards for the commercial exchange of goods and services? What argument may be made that the state should not be involved in this type of activity at all?

5. Free Press/Fair Trial in Georgia

I n 1981, using court-approved wiretaps, Georgia police uncovered a large gambling operation involving betting on the volume of stocks and bonds traded on the New York Stock Exchange. Guy Waller and 36 others were arrested and charged with commercial gambling and with violating Georgia's Racketeer Influenced and Corrupt Organizations (RICO) Act of 1980. When Waller asked the trial court to suppress the telephone wiretaps, prosecutors requested that any hearing on his request to suppress evidence be closed to the public. They argued that "in order to validate the seizure of evidence derived from the wiretaps, the State would have to introduce evidence 'which [might] involve a reasonable expectation of privacy of persons other than' the defendants."[1]

After a jury had been chosen, it was excused while the trial judge heard arguments on the motion to close the suppression hearing. Because the wiretaps involved conversations between Waller and some persons who had been indicted but who were not then on trial and others who had not yet been indicted, prosecutors argued that holding an open hearing would "taint" the evidence, making it unusable or inadmissible in future prosecutions. Over Waller's objections, the court ordered the suppression hearing closed to everyone except witnesses, court personnel, defendants and attorneys.

The suppression hearing lasted seven days, of which two and a half hours were devoted to the playing of the intercepted telephone conversations. According to a transcript of the

---

1. Waller v. Georgia, 467 U.S. 39 (1984) at 41.

hearing released after the trial, the remainder of the time was spent discussing procedural matters and allegations of police and prosecutorial misconduct. When the case was tried in open court, Waller was convicted of commercial gambling, but acquitted of the charges brought under the Georgia RICO statute. The Georgia Supreme Court affirmed Waller's conviction. Justice Harold G. Clarke agreed that information was revealed in the hearing "which was potentially harmful to others, and might prejudice other potential defendants. Under these circumstances, the court balanced [Waller's] rights to a public hearing on the motion against the privacy rights of others and closed the hearing,"[2] based on its responsibility "to protect the rights of parties and witnesses, and generally to further the administration of justice."[3]

The U.S. Supreme Court disagreed. Justice Lewis Powell, writing for a unanimous court, determined that the Sixth Amendment's guarantee of a public trial[4] extends beyond the trial itself and applied the four-part rule just developed by the court in *Press-Enterprise Co. v. Superior Court of California.*[5] Although the right to openness is not absolute, it should be presumed and Powell wrote in *Waller v. Georgia* that "there can be little doubt that the explicit Sixth Amendment right of the accused is not less protective of a public trial than the implicit First Amendment right of the press and public."[6] As a

2. Waller v. Georgia, 251 Ga. 124, 303 S.E.2d 437 (1983) at 126-127.

3. Lowe v. Georgia, 141 Ga. App. 433, 233 S.E.2d 807 (1977) at 435.

4. The Sixth Amendment to the U.S. Constitution states: "In all criminal prosecutions, the accused shall enjoy the right to a speedy and public trial...." Georgia's Constitution of 1983 provides for the right to "a public and speedy trial..." (Article I, §I, ¶XI).

5. 464 U.S. 501 (1984). In this case, the court extended the right to include jury selection proceedings.

6. Waller v. Georgia, 467 U.S. 39 (1984) at 46. For a recent application of this test, see, for example, Moody v. U.S., 17 Media Law Reporter 2096

result, pre-trial proceedings are presumptively open, unless the elements of a four-part test (see, Figure 5, below) are met.

THE WALLER TEST
(Figure 5)

- The party seeking to close the hearing must advance an overriding interest that is likely to be prejudiced;
- The closure must be no broader than necessary to protect that interest;
- The trial court must consider reasonable alternatives to closing the proceeding; and
- It must make findings adequate to support the closure.

- *Waller v. Georgia*, **467 U.S. 39 (1984) at 48**

The case was sent back to Georgia for state courts to decide what parts, if any, of a new suppression hearing should be closed.[7]

Yet this national commitment to assuring the fairness of trials through public access to courtrooms has not been without its problems. In 2010, for example, the U.S. Supreme Court summarily reversed a drug trafficking conviction based on a Georgia judge's decision to order spectators (including members of the defendant's family) to be excluded from the courtroom during pre-trial questioning of potential jurors, because of the courtroom's small size.[8] The Supreme Court agreed with Chief Justice Leah Sears of the Georgia Supreme Court who, contending that the closure was not required by space considerations, stated that "a room that is too small that it

---

(1990). See also, "Suit Over Seizure Not Investigation, Not Secret," The News Media & the Law (fall 1990), 4-5.

7. See, Waller v. Georgia, 253 Ga. 146, 319 S.E.2d 11 (1984).

8. Presley v. Georgia, 558 U.S. 209 (2010).

cannot accommodate the public is a room that is too small to accommodate a constitutional criminal trial."[9] The U.S. Supreme Court stated:

> The public has a right to be present whether or not any party has asserted the right.... Trial courts are obligated to take every reasonable measure to accommodate public attendance at criminal trials. Nothing in the record shows that the trial court could not have accommodated the public at Presley's trial.[10]

The issue may not yet be fully resolved, as less than three weeks later, the Georgia Supreme Court upheld the temporary closing of another courtroom to spectators during a felony murder trial, because of apprehension for the safety of two

---

9. Presley v. Georgia, 285 Ga. 270, 674 S.E.2d 909 (2009) at 274 (Sears, C.J., dissenting). The state Court of Appeals had also held that control of the courtroom was within the trial court's "sound discretion." Presley v. Georgia, 290 Ga. App. 99, 658 S.E.2d 773 (2008). See also, Alyson Palmer, "High Court OKs Closed Courtroom," Daily Report, March 24,2009, 1; Robin McDonald, "U.S. Justices Asked To Review Voir Dire Closing," Daily Report, Aug. 19, 2009, 1, 8; Rory Eastburg, "Taking Secrecy to Extremes: Judges Push Court Closure to the Limits, But Appeals Await," News Media & the Law, Fall 2009, 20-21; Alyson Palmer, "Justices Make Fast Work of Ga. Cases," Daily Report, Jan. 20, 2010, 1, 8; Adam Liptak, "Trial Conduct in Georgia Is Subject of 2 Rulings," New York Times, Jan. 20, 2010, A13; Mara Zimmerman, "Pushing Back on Court Closure: Supreme Court Clarifies the Right To View Jury Selection," News Media & the Law, Winter 2010, 11; Edward Tolley & Devin Smith, "The Case Against Closure: Open Courtrooms After Presley v. Georgia," Georgia Bar Journal, October 2010, 10-17.

10. Presley v. Georgia, 558 U.S. 209 (2010) at 214-215.

witnesses and concerns for security in the courtroom.[11] A year later, the Supreme Court ruled that a defendant's right to a fair trial was violated when his sibling was excluded from the courtroom.[12] Yet in 2013, the Supreme Court ruled that grand jury indictments must be announced in open court.[13]

It's clear that without a secure courtroom there can be no fair trial assured. The issue is control and balance. How can a fair trial and public access both be assured at the same time?[14] What is less clear at the moment is how these competing interests can be reconciled.

---

11. See, Reid v. Georgia, 286 Ga. 484, 690 S.E.2d 177 (2010). See also, Alyson Palmer, "Justices Favor Closing Court in Another Case," Daily Report, Feb. 9, 2010, 1, 8.

12. See, Purvis v. Georgia, 288 Ga. 865, 708 S.E.2d 283 (2011).

13. See, Georgia v. Brown, 293 Ga. 493, ___ S.E.2d ___ (2013); 315 Ga. App. 282, 726 S.E.2d 764 (2012). See also, Kathleen Joyner, "Justices Weigh In on Open Courts," Daily Report, Sept. 10, 2013, available at: http://www.dailyreportonline.com/PubArticleDRO.jsp?id=1202618642362 (last accessed Nov. 4, 2013).

14. As an illustration of electronic technology's potential benefits and potential problems, see, for example, Greg Land, "Judge Allows Witness to Testify via Skype," Daily Report, Feb. 17, 2011, 1, 10; "Juror Sent Texts to Victim's Kin," Atlanta Journal-Constitution, Dec. 3, 2012, B3.

The Problem of Prejudicial Publicity

Georgia's current concern with guaranteeing an accused person a fair trial in the face of potentially prejudicial media coverage - through the use of gag orders, closure of hearings, orders that the trial be postponed, changes in the trial's location, jury sequestration, and the like - seems to be a delicate balance between a trial's costs and the view that public access helps protect the rights of the accused.[15] As a result, Georgia historically has had a strong legal tradition in which motions for continuance or venue changes based on prejudicial

---

15. "Public access helps protect the defendant's rights, ensuring that the accused has adequate counsel and is not discriminated against because of race or economic status. Public scrutiny also helps safeguard the rights of the victim, ensuring that justice is done" ("Keeping the Courts Open," Atlanta Constitution, March 4, 1995, A18). The use of gag orders was rejected in Atlanta Journal-Constitution v. Georgia, 266 Ga. App. 168, 596 S.E.2d 694 (2004). But see, Tasgola K. Bruner, "Gwinnett Judge Eases Gag Order in Corbin Case," Atlanta Journal-Constitution, March 29, 2005, B1; and David Simpson, "Judge Orders Gag on Parents in Murder Case," Atlanta Journal-Constitution, March 31, 2005, C1. See also the news coverage of the arrest and trial of Brian Nichols, accused of killing four people, beginning at the Fulton County Courthouse in 2005: Steven Pollak, "Nichols' Lawyer Seeks Gag Order," Daily Report, April 11, 2005, page number unknown; Rhonda Cook, "Nichols Report Statements Kept Sealed," Atlanta Journal-Constitution, April 13, 2005, B1; Steven Pollak, "Court Safety Key in Debate Over Nichols Gag Order," Daily Report, April 15, 2005, 1; Greg Land, "News Media, Defense Spar in Nichols Case," Daily Report, April 6, 2006, 1, 5; Greg Land, "Courthouse Readies for Nichols Media Blitz," Daily Report, Nov. 17, 2006, 1, 5; Beth Warren, "Fuller: Quote Off the Record," Atlanta Journal-Constitution, Jan. 30, 2008, page number unknown; Bill Rankin, "Paper Asks Judge to Open Nichols Affidavit," Atlanta Journal-Constitution, June 18, 2008, page number unknown; Steve Visser, "Private Jury Pick Sought for Nichols," Atlanta Journal-Constitution, July 31, 2008, D1, D3; Jeffry Scott, "Media Welcome To Watch: Reporters Stay, Nichols Judge Rules," Atlanta Journal-Constitution, Aug. 1, 2008, F4.

publicity and public excitement were generally denied.[16] The test is: whether the setting of the trial is inherently prejudicial or "whether the jurors summoned to try the case have formed fixed opinions as to the guilt or innocence of the accused from reading such unfavorable newspaper publicity."[17]

The difficulty with the test, of course, lies with its application. A prime example of this difficulty was the trial of those involved in "modern Georgia's biggest mass murder" - the 1973 killing of six members of the Ned Alday family in Seminole County.[18] Despite evidence which overwhelmingly showed that Carl Isaacs, Wayne Coleman and George Dungee committed the murders, the Eleventh Circuit Court of Appeals ordered new trials in 1985 on the grounds that the men did not receive fair trials as a result of prejudicial pretrial publicity. Yet the Georgia Supreme Court had upheld the Seminole County verdicts with the following comment:

> To restrict the right of the press ... would be inconsistent with the First Amendment and with the right of the public to a free flow of information. This right of the media, however, must not be allowed to interfere with the judicial calm which must surround a trial free

---

16. See, Sandra Eckstein, "Changes of Venue Rare in Georgia," Atlanta Journal-Constitution, March 9, 1995, B3.

17. Krist v. Caldwell, 230 Ga. 536, 198 S.E.2d 161 (1973) at 537. See, Williams v. Georgia, 272 Ga. 335, 528 S.E.2d 518 (2000); Wilbanks v. Georgia, 251 Ga. App. 248, 554 S.E.2d 248 (2001).

18. Bill Montgomery, "Alday's Grisly Anniversary: Justice Eludes Family 20 Years After 6 Loved Ones Were Slain," Atlanta Journal-Constitution, May 14, 1993, D1, D4, at D1; Bill Montgomery, "The Alday Murders: Killer Has Date To Die Tuesday," Atlanta Journal-Constitution, May 4, 2003, E1, E4; Bill Montgomery, "Sounds of Grief Endure in Alday Case," Atlanta Journal-Constitution, June 1, 2003, C1, C8.

from emotionalism and sensationalism.... An important case draws public attention through "swift, widespread and diverse means of communication" and hardly any prospective juror "will not have formed some impression or opinion as to the merits of the case." The proper test is whether the prospective juror "can lay aside his impression or opinion and render a verdict based on the evidence presented in court."[19]

Obviously, the state Supreme Court felt the Alday jurors could do this, while the federal court of appeals disagreed.[20] However, appellate courts generally defer to trial courts' findings with regard to the need for a change of venue due to prejudicial publicity.[21]

Coupled with the U.S. Supreme Court's 1984 *Press-Enterprise Company v. Superior Court of California* ruling[22] and its 1986 *Press-Enterprise Company v. Superior Court of California* holding,[23] the decision in *Waller*[24] has, for the most

---

19. Coleman v. Georgia, 237 Ga. 84, 226 S.E.2d 911 (1976) at 87. See also, Isaacs v. Georgia, 237 Ga. 105, 226 S.E.2d 922 (1976); Dungee v. Georgia, 237 Ga. 218, 227 S.E.2d 746 (1976).

20. See, Coleman v. Kemp, 778 F.2d 1487 (11th Cir. 1985).

21. See, for example, Gissendaner v. Georgia, 272 Ga. 704, 532 S.E.2d 677 (2000); Miller v. Georgia, 275 Ga. 730, 571 S.E.2d 788 (2002); Morgan v. Georgia, 276 Ga. 72, 575 S.E.2d 468 (2003); Putnam v. Georgia, 245 Ga. App. 95, 537 S.E.2d 384 (2000); Warren v. Georgia, 245 Ga. App. 768, 538 S.E.2d 840 (2000); Brown v. Georgia, 246 Ga. App. 60, 539 S.E.2d 545 (2000); Williams v. Georgia, 253 Ga. App. 458, 559 S.E.2d 516 (2002).

22. 464 U.S. 501.

23. 478 U.S. 1.

24. 467 U.S. 39 (1984).

part, opened all parts of a criminal trial to the public.[25]

However, as the four-part Press-Enterprise/Waller test indicates, the right of access to Georgia courtrooms is not absolute. Courts generally have broad powers to preserve order and to prevent disruption of their proceedings[26] - including the control of streets and sidewalks adjacent to the courthouse[27] - because the public's right of access is inferior to the

---

25. According to the Georgia Supreme Court, state constitutional provisions requiring public criminal trials are applicable to pretrial, mid-trial, and post-trial proceedings, as well as to the trial itself. See, R.W. Page Corp. v. Lumpkin, 249 Ga. 576, 292 S.E.2d 815 (1982); Rockdale Citizen v. Georgia, 266 Ga. 579, 468 S.E.2d 764 (1996). If a motion is made to close a court proceeding, the Georgia Press Association recommends that a journalist raise his or her hand, stand, and respond in the following manner:

> You honor, I am ___, a reporter for the ___. I respectfully request the opportunity to register on the record an objection to the motion to close this proceeding to the public, including the press. Our legal counsel has advised us that standards set forth in recent state and federal court decisions give us the opportunity for a hearing before the courtroom is closed. Accordingly, I respectfully request such a hearing and a brief continuance so our counsel can be present to make the appropriate arguments. Thank you.

"Legal Survival Kit for Georgia Reporters and Editors," [1989], 7.

26. See, O.C.G.A. 15-1-3. See also, for example, Perryman v. Georgia, 114 Ga. 545, 40 S.E.2d 746 (1902), where the court stated: "It is a well-recognized principle of our law that the judges of superior and city courts are invested with a wide discretion in the management of the business before them, and this discretion will not be controlled unless it is shown to have been manifestly abused' (id. at 546).

27. See, for example, Atlanta Newspapers, Inc. v. Grimes, 216 Ga. 74, 114 S.E.2d 421 (1960). For a discussion of this case, see, T. Raworth Williamson, Jr., "Constitutional Law - Freedom of Speech and Press - Validity of Court Order Barring Newspapers from Court House Area," 23 Georgia Bar Journal 406 (1961).

independence of the judiciary and to the proper administration of justice.[28] Any obstruction of the administration of justice may be punished as a contempt of court.[29] A defendant's right to compel a reporter to testify in his defense against a murder charge was, for example, more important than the reporter's First Amendment interests.[30] However, a court order prohibiting a newspaper "from disclosing any information obtained [about a suspect in a murder case] without following a procedure of notification of intent to disclose and obtaining permission of the court" was improper.[31]

Nevertheless, the interior of a courtroom, during the conduct of a trial, is almost absolutely controlled by the judge. For example, in cases "in which the evidence is vulgar and obscene or relates to the improper acts of the sexes, and tends to debauch the morals of the young," Georgia judges may clear the courtroom "of all or any portion of the audience,"[32]

---

28. See, for example, McGill v. Georgia, 209 Ga. 500, 74 S.E.2d 78 (1953); Atlanta Newspapers, Inc. v. Georgia, 216 Ga. 399, 116 S.E.2d 580 (1960). For a discussion of the appellate court's decision in Atlanta Newspapers, Inc. v. Georgia, 101 Ga. App. 105, 113 S.E.2d 148 (1960), see, Larry Bryant, "Georgia - Constitutional Law - Contempt of Court - Freedom of the Press - Right to Public and Speedy Trial Before an Impartial Jury," 12 Mercer Law Review 284 (1960).

29. See, for example, Henry Farber, "Rockdale Reporter Released in Camera Flash Incident," Atlanta Journal-Constitution, Oct. 27, 2000, D14.

30. See, for example, Hurst v. Georgia, 160 Ga. App. 830, 287 S.E.2d 677 (1982). Conversely, in a criminal case involving a less serious offense, the Georgia Court of Appeals reached a different conclusion. See, Carver v. Georgia, 185 Ga. App. 436, 364 S.E.2d 877 (1987), affirmed, 258 Ga. 385, 369 S.E.2d 471 (1988).

31. Georgia Gazette Publishing Co. v. Ramsey, 248 Ga. 528, 284 S.E.2d 386 (1981) at 529.

32. O.C.G.A. 17-8-53. See, for example, Lancaster v. Georgia, 168 Ga. 470, 148 S.E. 139 (1929); Lowe v. Georgia, 141 Ga. App. 433, 233 S.E.2d 807 (1977); Babb v. Georgia, 157 Ga. App. 757, 278 S.E.2d 495 (1981).

especially juveniles.[33] In addition, judges are required to clear the courtroom "of all persons," except parties to the cause and their immediate families or guardians, attorneys and their secretaries, victims assistance personnel, officers of the court, jurors, newspaper reporters or broadcasters, and court reporters when a minor under the age of sixteen testifies about a sexual offense.[34] Even more broadly, judges for any "special reason" - such as the fear of possible harm because of testimony to be given[35] - may exclude "certain" spectators from the court-room,[36] along with all spectators during part of a rape trial, if the alleged victim is unable to testify.[37]

In Georgia courts today, there is a "strong presumption favoring the general rule, which is that in Georgia, the criminal trial itself and all consequent hearings on motions (pre-trial, mid-trial and post-trial) shall be open to the press and public on equal terms unless the defendant ... is able to demonstrate on the record by 'clear and convincing proof' that closing the hearing to the press and public is the only means by which a

---

33. See, for example, Parker v. Georgia, 162 Ga. App. 271, 290 S.E.2d 518 (1982).

34. O.C.G.A. 17-8-54. See, 2013 Georgia Laws 891, House Bill 480. See, for example, Moore v. Georgia, 151 Ga. 648, 108 S.E. 47 (1921); Lowe v. Georgia, 141 Ga. App. 433, 233 S.E.2d 807 (1977); Craven v. Georgia, 292 Ga. App. 592, 664 S.E.2d 921 (2008); Clark v. Georgia, 309 Ga. App. 749, 711 S.E.2d 339 (2011); Pate v. Georgia, 315 Ga. App. 205, 726 S.E.2d 691 (2012). In Mullis v. Georgia, 292 Ga. App. 218, 664 S.E.2d 271 (2008), a courtroom was allowed to be closed, even though the victim was 17 years old, because of the severe psychological effect the event had on the victim.

35. See, for example, Lowe v. Georgia, 141 Ga. App. 433, 233 S.E.2d 807 (1977).

36. See, for example, Tilton v. Georgia, 5 Ga App. 59, 62 S.E. 651 (1908).

37. See, for example, Moore v. Georgia, 151 Ga. 648, 108 S.E. 47 (1921), appeal dismissed, 260 U.S. 702 (1922).

'clear and present danger' to his right to a fair trial ... can be avoided."[38] For example, there is no right of access to communication between opposing counsel and the court, whether at the judge's bench or in his chambers, when the admissibility of evidence is involved.[39] Similarly, access is likely to be barred from hearings where the defendant requests expert assistance or discloses defense strategy,[40] or were crimes against children are involved.[41]

Journalists have greater rights of access to Georgia courtrooms and, thus, a greater responsibility to aid and promote the proper administration of justice than do members of the public at large. Concluding that Georgia law is more protective of the concept of openness than federal law in that the "state constitution point-blankly states that criminal trials *shall* be public,"[42] Chief Justice Robert H. Jordan noted that the presence of journalists in a courtroom from which some spectators had been excluded "usually will assure that the proceedings will be conducted fairly to all concerned, and discourage perjury and other misconduct by participants, including decisions based on secret bias and partiality."[43] Upholding this commitment has not been easy and some seem regularly to claim that "Georgia may be on the verge of

---

38. R.W. Page Corp. v. Lumpkin, 249 Ga. 576, 292 S.E.2d 815 (1982) at 579.

39. See, for example, U.S. v. Moody, 746 F.Supp. 1090 (M.D. Ga. 1990).

40. See, for example, Brooks v. Georgia, 259 Ga. 562, 385 S.E.2d 81 (1989). For a discussion of this case, see, "Hudson Comments on Court Decisions," The GPA Bulletin, Jan. 18, 1990, 1.

41. See, for example, Glover v. Georgia, 292 Ga. App. 22 (2008) (where a courtroom was closed during a child victim's testimony).

42. R.W. Page Corp. v. Lumpkin, 249 Ga. 576, 292 S.E.2d 815 (1982) at 578. Emphasis in original.

43. Id. at 581.

surrendering its reputation for maintaining one of the nation's most open criminal court systems."[44] In February 1995, a divided Georgia Supreme Court upheld the closing of a pretrial hearing in a Liberty County death penalty case to prevent prejudicial publicity.[45] But the following year, the Supreme Court overturned a Rockdale County judge's order which barred the public from pretrial hearings and sealed much of the court's record in a death penalty case, ruling that the order was based on speculation and not proof.[46]

Whether there appears to have been any wholesale change in Georgia's attitudes towards trial fairness and public openness depends upon one's reaction to recent courtroom closures in situations, such as, *Presley v. Georgia*,[47] and also to jurors' gifts to court officials in situations, such as, *Wellons v. Hall*.[48]

---

44. Peter Mantius & Bill Rankin, "Closed Hearings Cloud Georgia's Open Court Rule," Atlanta Journal-Constitution, April 16, 1995, G4.

45. See, Southeastern Newspapers Corp. v. Georgia, 265 Ga. 233, 454 S.E.2d 452 (1995). In his majority opinion, Justice George Carley wrote that "further publicity of the issue posed a 'clear and present danger' to the defendants right to a fair trial. He said the only way to keep other 'sensitive and prejudicial publicity' from tainting the jury pool was closing the hearing" (id.) See also, Bill Rankin, "Supreme Court Upholds Closing Hearing in Death Penalty Case," Atlanta Journal-Constitution, Feb. 28, 1995, C6; "Closure of Pre-Trial Hearings in Death Penalty Case Upheld," The News Media & the Law (Spring 1995), 15-16.

46. Rockdale Citizen v. Georgia, 266 Ga. 579, 468 S.E.2d 764 (1996).

47. 558 U.S. 209 (2010). See, Edward Tolley & Devin Smith, "The Case against Closure: Open Courtrooms after Presley v. Georgia," Georgia Bar Journal, October 2010, at 10.

48. 558 U.S. 220 (2010). There, jurors' gift of chocolate to a judge – shaped in the form of male genitalia – and to a bailiff - a shaped in the form of female breasts – were deemed by the U.S. Supreme Court to be "unusual facts [which] raise a serious question about the fairness of a capital trial" (id., at 225). For the earlier Georgia Supreme Court ruling, see, Wellons v. Georgia, 266 Ga. 77, 463 S. E. 2d 868 (1995). For the subsequent, federal appellate ruling, see, Wellons v. Hall, 554 F.3d 923 (11th Cir. 2009). See

Are such events evidence of impropriety or just naïveté of an earlier time? Are closed proceedings becoming the norm?[49] The Georgia Judicial Qualifications Commission believes so and states that "the systematic exclusion of the public" from court proceedings violates state law.[50] In response to a lawsuit filed by the Southern Center for Human Rights, several Middle Georgia judges have agreed to a settlement aimed at providing greater public access to their courts.[51]

---

also, Alyson Palmer, "Justices Make Fast Work of Ga. Cases," Daily Report, Jan. 20, 2010, 1, 8; Adam Liptak, "Trial Conduct in Georgia Is Subject of 2 Rulings," New York Times, Jan. 20, 2010, A13; Bill Torpy & Bill Rankin, "Juror's Candy Sparks Appeal," Atlanta Journal-Constitution, Feb. 14, 2010, B1, B5; Alyson Palmer, "Former Chief Justice Weighs in on Court Reporter Gift Ruling," Daily Report, March 22, 2010, 1, 4. In April 2010, in response to the Supreme Court's ruling, the U.S. Court of Appeals for the 11th Circuit called the gifts "tasteless and disturbing" and ordered the case to be reviewed. Wellons v. Hall, 603 F.3d 1236 (11th Cir. 2010). In 2011, a federal trial-level judge concluded that the gifts did not influence the trial's fairness. See, Bill Rankin, "Death-Row Killer's Appeal Rejected," Atlanta Journal-Constitution, Aug. 6, 2011, B2; Bill Rankin, "Dignity of Death Ruling at Issue," Atlanta Journal-Constitution, Sept. 8, 2012, B3.

49. See, Derek Green, "Secret Courts: Is the 'Most Extraordinary Remedy' Becoming More Common?" News Media & the Law, Fall 2010, at 24.

50. Judicial Qualifications Commission Opinion 239, Georgia Courts Journal, Aug. 28, 2013, available at: http://w2.georgiacourts.gov/journal/index.php/this-issue/207-jqc-opinion-239- (last accessed Nov. 15, 2013). See, Arlinda Broady, "Commission: Closed Courtrooms Violate Law," Atlanta Journal-Constitution, Sept. 1, 2013, B4.

51. A copy of the settlement agreement in Fuqua v. Pridgen, No. 1:12-CV-93 (WLS), M.D. Ga., Nov. 4, 2013, is available at: http://www.gfaf.org/wp-content/uploads/2013/11/gfaf-open-courtrooms.pdf (last accessed Nov. 15, 2013). See, Robin McDonald, "Suit Accuses Cordele Judges of Closing Courtrooms, Daily Report, June 22, 2012, available at: http://arringtonlawfirm.com/blog/?p=1084 (last accessed Nov. 4, 2013); Robin McDonald, "At Issue: Closed Courts or Limited Seating," Daily Report, June 28, 2012, 1, 2; Robin McDonald, "Public Shut Out of Georgia Courts," Daily Report, July 3, 2012, 1, 2; Robin McDonald, "Public's Right

One fact, however, is clear: Nationwide fewer battles are being fought over public access to courtrooms than ever before.[52] What is unclear is whether this lack of public pressure will have any detrimental impact on public access to and perceived fairness of judicial proceedings in Georgia.

to Court Access Isn't Absolute, Judges Say," Daily Report, Aug. 3, 2012, 1, 2.

52. See, Adam Liptak, "In Shrinking Newsrooms, Fewer Battles for Public Access to Courtrooms," New York Times, Sept. 1, 2009, A10, A19.

The Problem of Cameras in the Courtroom

It was because of Georgia's commitment to openness that the state Supreme Court in 1982 approved plans to permit broadcasting of judicial proceedings in the state when consent of the court in which the case is to be heard is obtained.[53] Georgia, in fact, ranks among the states which allow the most electronic coverage, according to the Association of Electronic Journalists, and places "broad discretion in the presiding judge."[54]

Almost identical uniform rules regulating access to court documents and electronic and photographic recordings of proceedings are in place for Georgia Superior courts, State courts, Magistrate courts, and Probate courts.[55] Print and

---

53. See, generally, "How States Handle Cameras in the Courts," Broadcasting, June 3, 1991, 32; "Cameras in the Courtroom: Three Holdouts," The Quill (September 1998), 26-27; and RTNDA: The Association of Electronic Journalists, Freedom of Information – Cameras in the Court: A State-by-State Guide (2013), available at: http://www.rtnda.org/content/cameras_in_court (last accessed Nov. 15, 2013).

54. Id.

55. See, Rule 22, Electronic & Photographic Coverage of Judicial Proceedings, Uniform Rules of the Superior Court (undated), available at: http://www.georgiacourts.org/courts/superior/rules/rule_22.html (last accessed Nov. 15, 2013), also applicable to state courts; Rule 11, Electronic & Photographic Coverage of Magistrate Court Proceedings, Uniform Rules for the Magistrate Court (undated), available at: http://www.georgiacourts.gov/files/UNIFORM%20MAGISTRATE%20COURT%20RULES%20-%2001_25_13_.pdf (last accessed Nov. 15, 2013); and Rule 18, Electronic & Photographic Coverage of Judicial Proceedings, Uniform Rules of the Probate Court (undated), available at: http://georgiacourts.gov/files/UNIFORM%20PROBATE%20COURT%20RULES%20-%2007_01_12.pdf (last accessed Nov. 15, 2013). See, generally, Administrative Office of the Courts of Georgia, Rules of the Georgia Courts (undated), available at: http://www.georgiacourts.gov/index.php/georgia-courts/court-rules (last accessed Nov. 15, 2013).

electronic journalists, as well as technicians – "without partiality or preference to any person, news agency, or type of electronic or photographic coverage" – are allowed "full access to court proceedings for obtaining public information within the requirements of due process of law, so long as it is done without detracting from the dignity and decorum of the court."[56]

Access to juvenile courts, first approved by the Georgia Supreme Court in 1992,[57] was expanded by the state legislature in 1995 to include juvenile proceedings in most felony cases and "for all second offenses, except those involving sexual crimes other than rape."[58] These include delinquency and deprivation hearings.

"All court records are public and are to be available for

---

56. Id. See, for example, Morris Communications v. Griffin, 279 Ga. 735, 620 S.E.2d 800 (2005); and Savannah Morning News v. Jeffcoat, 280 Ga. App. 634, 634 S.E.2d 830 (2006) – where no basis was found that the presence of cameras would disrupt court proceedings. See also, Scott Simonson, "Judge Was Wrong to Ban Cameras in Murder Trial," Daily Report, Oct. 14, 2005, page number unknown.

57. Rule 26.1, Access to Juvenile Court Proceedings, & Rule 26.2, Electronic & Photographic News Coverage of Juvenile Court Proceedings, Uniform Rules for the Juvenile Courts of Georgia (undated), available at: http://www.georgiacourts.gov/files/UNIFORM%20JUVENILE%20COURT %20RULES%20-%2001 22 13.pdf (last accessed Nov. 15, 2013). See, O.C.G.A. 15-1-10.1. See also, O.C.G.A. 15-11-78(c).

58. Charles Walston, "New Law Opens Up Juvenile Court to Public," Atlanta Journal-Constitution, July 30, 1995, D4; Mark Silk, "Cases Involving Certain Offenses Open to Public," Atlanta Journal-Constitution, July 30, 1995, D4. These designated felony offenses include: kidnapping, arson, aggravated assault, aggravated battery, robbery, armed robbery without a firearm, attempted murder, attempted kidnapping, carrying or possessing a weapon, and hijacking a motor vehicle. O.C.G.A. 15-11-63. See, generally, "Access to Juvenile Courts," News Media & The Law (Spring 1999), supplement, 1-24.

public inspection,"[59] except in certain instances - when the harm resulting from an invasion of privacy "clearly outweighs" the public interest[60] or when "compelling circumstances" require limited access, and then for not more than thirty days.[61] In such cases, the court's order must indicate the record or file, or portion thereof, to which access is no longer granted, the nature and length of the limitation, and the reason for it.[62] All

---

59. Rule 21, Limitation of Access to Court Files, Uniform Rules for the Superior Courts (undated), available at: https://www.georgiacourts.gov/files/UNIFORM%20SUPERIOR%20COURT %20RULES Updated 05 23 13 .pdf (last accessed Nov. 15, 2013). The requirements of Rule 21, Limitation of Access to Court Files, are the same for both Superior Courts and State Courts. See, Uniform Rules of the State Courts (undated), p.1, available at: http://georgiacourts.gov/files/UNIFORM%20STATE%20COURT%20RULE S 8 11.pdf (last accessed Nov. 15, 2013). The term "records" includes civil pre-judgment records. See, for example, Atlanta Journal and Atlanta Constitution v. Long, 258 Ga. 410, 369 S.E.2d 755 (1988). However, the right of access is not absolute. See, for example, U.S. v. Eaves, 685 F. Supp. 1243 (N.D. Ga. 1988). See, Rule 4.6, Limitation of Access to Court Records, Uniform Probate Court Rules (undated), available at: http://georgiacourts.gov/files/UNIFORM%20PROBATE%20COURT%20RU LES%20-%2007 01 12.pdf (last accessed Nov. 15, 2013). See also, O.C.G.A. 15-11-79, Inspection of [Juvenile] Court Files and Records, which opens such records "only upon the order of the court." See also, O.C.G.A. 15-11-79.2, O.C.G.A. 15-11-82, O.C.G.A. 15-11-84.

60. For an instance in which privacy interest did not outweigh the public interest, see, Atlanta Journal and Atlanta Constitution v. Long, 258 Ga. 410, 369 S.E.2d 755 (1988); and 259 Ga. 23, 376 S.E.2d 865 (1988). See also, "High Court Orders Judge To Open Suit Against Priest," News Media & the Law (Summer 1989), 8-9.

61. See, generally, "Judicial Records: A Guide to Access in State and Federal Courts," News Media & the Law (Summer 1990), supplement, 1-16.

62. See, BankWest v. Oxendine, 266 Ga. App. 771, 598 S.E.2d 343 (2004); Wall v. Thurman, 283 Ga. 533 (2008) (where trial orders sealing certain records were reversed for not making such a finding of fact as required by Uniform Superior Court Rule 21).

such orders are automatically sent to the Georgia Supreme Court for review and possible amendment. However, evidence electronically produced by police during a criminal investigation is not considered a "court record" and, thus, is not subject to disclosure.[63]

Unless forbidden by the trial-level judge after an appropriate hearing, journalists may attend and "unobtrusively" take notes or make sketches at all judicial proceedings in any Georgia Superior, State, or Probate court. This unobtrusive note-taking also includes the use of laptop computers. Because of the potentially "distractive nature" of electronic and photographic equipment, the presiding judge must make his or her own determination, in the form of a specific finding, as to whether broadcast coverage will not detract from judicial decorum or deprive a defendant of due process of law.[64] Such "broadcast coverage" subject to court approval apparently also includes what one Georgia court called "twittering"[65] – the description and posting of courtroom proceedings directly from inside the courtroom to the twitter.com website,[66] where the

---

63. See, In re Pacific & Southern Co. Inc., d/b/a WXIA-TV, 257 Ga. 484, 361 S.E.2d 159 (1987).

64. See, for example, Georgia Television Co. d/b/a WSB-TV v. Georgia, 257 Ga. 764, 363 S.E.2d 528 (1988). Consent of the parties involved is not required.

65. See, U.S. v. John Mark Shelnutt, 37 Media Law Reporter 2594 (M.D. Ga. 2009).

66. Available at: http://twitter.com/ (last accessed Nov. 15, 2013). See, generally, Ahnalese Rushmann, "Courtroom Coverage in 140 Characters," News Media & the Law (Spring 2009), 28-30; Mark Tamburri, Thomas Pohl & Patrick Yingling, "A Little Bird Told Me about the Trial: Revising Court Rules to Allow Reporting from the Courtroom via Twitter," 15 Electronic Commerce & Law Report 1415 (2010); Adriana Cervantes, "Will Twitter Be Following You in the Courtroom? Why Reporters Should Be Allowed to Broadcast During Courtroom Proceedings," 33 Hastings Communication & Entertainment Law Journal 133 (2010).

short messages (called "tweets") are immediately disseminated to "subscribers" who are following the reporter's postings.

Other factors courts must also consider include the nature of the proceeding, the consent or objection of the parties, effects on the administration of justice, and the "truth-finding functions" of the courts. Where prejudicial news coverage is present, the state is required to protect the defendant's rights.[67] Yet journalists should remember that where the record shows no specific finding - no written order or judgment with respect to the removal of the media from a courtroom nor any request by the media that the judge enter such an order - there is nothing to appeal.[68]

However, disallowing coverage because it might "stifle, inhibit, frustrate or prevent the Socratic dialogue beneficial to the free exchange of ideas between court and counsel" was not deemed to be an appropriate "specific finding."[69] On the other hand, a Clayton County attorney's contention that the presence of cameras "would impair [his] ability to present his case, due to 'camera shyness' and the intimidation factor of the camera" was accepted by Judge John C. Carbo III as a justification to bar television coverage of a trial.[70]

---

67. See, for example, WALB-TV v. Gibson, 269 Ga. 564, 501 S.E.2d 821 (1998); Calley v. Callaway, 382 F.Supp. 650 (M.D. Ga. 1974), reversed on other grounds, 519 F.2d 184 (5th Cir. 1975), certiorari denied, Calley v. Hoffman, 425 U.S. 911 (1976). See also, "Georgia Court Opens Coverage of Second Trial," News Media & the Law (Summer 1998), 5-6.

68. See, for example, Georgia Television Co. d/b/a WSB-TV v. Castellani, 257 Ga. 549, 361 S.E.2d 381 (1987).

69. Georgia Television Co. d/b/a WSB-TV v. Napper, 258 Ga. 68, 365 S.E.2d 275 (1988) at 69.

70. Still photographers were not affected by the ruling. Trisha Renaud, "Camera-Shy Ruling Draws Double Take: Lawyer's Unease Proves an Easy Way to Get TV Banned from Trial," Daily Report, Nov. 11, 1991, 1, at 7.

While local rules may not conflict with the state's uniform rules,[71] the broadcasting of judicial proceedings may be evaluated according to court rules and generally restricted according to O.C.G.A. 15-1-10.1:[72]

- Broadcasters must file "a timely written request"[73] with the judge involved, specifying the case to be reported; the portion - trial, hearing or proceeding - to be reported; the equipment to be used; and the person

---

71. See, for example, Multimedia WMAZ, Inc. v. Georgia, 256 Ga. 698, 353 S.E.2d 173 (1987). See, generally, Administrative Office of the Courts of Georgia, Rules of the Georgia Courts (undated), available at: http://www.georgiacourts.gov/index.php/georgia-courts/court-rules (last accessed Nov. 15, 2013).

72. Statutory factors to be considered include: 1) the nature of the proceeding; 2) the consent or objection of the parties or witnesses whose testimony will be presented; 3) whether the proposed coverage will promote increased public access to the courts and openness of judicial proceedings; 4) the impact upon the integrity and dignity of the court; 5) the impact upon the administration of the court; 6) the impact upon due process and the truth finding function of the proceeding; 7) whether the proposed coverage would contribute to the enhancement of or detract from the ends of justice; 8) any special circumstances of the parties, victims, witnesses, or other participants – such as the need to protect children - and 9) any other factors which the court may determine to be important.

73. The request must follow the form of Rule 22, Exhibit A, Uniform Rules for the Superior Courts (undated), available at: https://www.georgiacourts.gov/files/UNIFORM%20SUPERIOR%20COURT %20RULES Updated 05 23 13 .pdf (last accessed Nov. 15, 2013), which also applies to state courts; Rule 11(O), Uniform Rules for the Magistrate Court (undated), available at: http://www.georgiacourts.gov/files/UNIFORM%20MAGISTRATE%20COU RT%20RULES%20-%2001 25 13 .pdf (last accessed Nov. 15, 2013); and Rule 10.10, Exhibit A, Uniform Rules of the Probate Court (undated), available at: http://georgiacourts.gov/files/UNIFORM%20PROBATE%20COURT%20RU LES%20-%2007 01 12.pdf (last accessed Nov. 15, 2013).

responsible for the equipment's installation and operation;

- Requests will be considered without partiality and approval subject to courtroom space limitations;

- If a "pool" arrangement is required by the court, journalists will arrange pooled coverage and present a schedule and description of the coverage to the judge;

- Cameras should be positioned and ready to operate before the court convenes and will not be allowed to disturb court proceedings;

- Overhead lights in the courtroom will be controlled only by court personnel and no camera lights or flashes will be allowed, unless approved in advance by the court;

- Additional microphones used to make audio recordings of court proceedings must be approved by the court in advance and unobtrusively attached to the court's public address system;

- Cameras will be assigned designated portions of the courtroom and may not be moved during court proceedings;

- Cameras which are not quiet when recording and are "distractive to the court proceedings" may be excluded from the courtroom;

- Pictures in which the jury is the central image are forbidden, "except where the jury happens to be in the background of other topics being photographed;"

- Journalists must be able to produce proper identifying credentials at all times;

- Disruption of court proceedings as a result of a technical or equipment problem is forbidden;

- Journalists "should do everything possible to avoid attracting attention to themselves" to protect the dignity

and decorum of the courts;
- All other photographing and broadcasting is prohibited; and
- No interviews may be conducted in the courtroom, without the permission of the judge.

Rules and forms approved by the Supreme Court in 1992 allowing broadcast coverage of certain juvenile court proceedings are almost exactly the same as the state's uniform rules discussed above.[74] Previously, there were no provisions opening Georgia juvenile courts to electronic media coverage.[75]

The Georgia Supreme Court allows photographic and

---

74. The primary difference is that in juvenile cases, there is no jury and all court actions are to be in the best interests of the child. For example, the rules prohibit any and all pictures of the child involved. See, Council of Juvenile Court Judges, Uniform Rules for the Juvenile Courts (undated), http://www.georgiacourts.gov/files/UNIFORM%20JUVENILE%20COURT %20RULES%20-%2001_22_13.pdf (last accessed Nov. 15, 2013). At times, however, courts appear have too much confidence that a juvenile's best interests are best promoted and protected by secrecy. See, Julie Bolen & Alice McQuade, "Juvenile Courts' Secrecy Harmful," Atlanta Journal-Constitution, Sept. 18, 2006, A15.

75. Before 1995, only juvenile felony murder, theft, and armed robbery proceedings were open. See, In re: Ross, 16 Media Law Reporter 2087 (Ga. Juvenile Court 1989). O.C.G.A. 15-11-58 provides that juvenile court records may be inspected pursuant to a court order. Records may be released if the release is required by the state constitution or is in the child's best interests. See, 1987 Opinions of the Attorney General, No. U87-18, 127. For a discussion of the problems facing juvenile courts, see, Joseph B. Sanborn Jr., "The Right to a Public Trial: A Need for Today's Juvenile Court," 76 Judicature 230 (February-March 1993); Beverly Shepard, "Increasingly Violent Kids Confound Juvenile Courts," Atlanta Constitution, April 13, 1993, D1, D3; Regina Akers, "Telling Youths' Crimes: Critics Seek Lifting of Juvenile Secrecy," Kansas City Star, Aug. 14, 1993, A1, A12-A13; Mark Silk, "Judges Push for More Openness in Juvenile Court," Atlanta Journal-Constitution, Oct. 24, 1993, F11.

broadcast coverage if the coverage does not "distract from the dignity of the Court proceedings"[76] and retains the exclusive right to limit or terminate coverage. The state Court of Appeals permits photograph or videotape coverage of oral argument in conjunction with the court's standing order regarding media in the courtroom.[77] Requests for installation of electronic equipment generally requires a week's notice[78] and journalists must agree to provide the court with video or audio tape copies of all proceedings covered.

Federal courts for the Northern and Southern districts of Georgia have specific rules prohibiting the photographing, recording, and broadcasting of judicial proceedings, although Middle District federal courts do not.[79] Local Rule 83.4 of the Northern District's rules states:

> The taking of photographs and operation of tape recorders in the courthouse and radio or television broadcasting from the courthouse during the progress of or in connection with

---

76. Rule 76, Rules of the Supreme Court of Georgia (undated). See, Media Rules, Rules 75-91, Rules of Supreme Court of Georgia (undated), available at: http://www.gasupreme.us/rules/#xiv (last accessed Nov. 15, 2013).

77. Rule 28(i), Court of Appeals of Georgia, Rules (2013), available at: http://www.gaappeals.us/rules2/rules.php?name=ARGUMENT (last accessed Nov. 15, 2013).

78. Request To Install Audio and Visual Recording and Transmittal Equipment for Electronic and Photographic News Coverage of Oral Argument, Court of Appeals of the State of Georgia (2013), available at: http://www.gaappeals.us/announce media-form.php (last accessed Nov. 15, 2013).

79. See, U.S. District Court for the Middle District of Georgia, Local Rules (Dec. 1, 2009), available at: http://www.gamd.uscourts.gov/local%20rules/local%20rules%20amended%2012-1-09.pdf (last accessed Nov. 15, 2013).

judicial proceedings, including proceedings before a United States Magistrate Judge, whether or not court is actually in session, is prohibited.... To facilitate the enforcement of this rule, no photographic, broadcasting, sound or recording equipment ... will be permitted to be operated on the floors of the courthouse occupied by the court, except as otherwise permitted by order of the judicial officer before whom the particular case or proceeding is pending. Portable computers, cellular telephones, pagers and personal communication devices without cameras ... shall not be operated in any courtroom or hearing room nor shall they be operated in any public area where their operation is disruptive of any court proceeding unless otherwise permitted by order of the court.[80]

The Southern District's rule appears to be more restrictive:

The taking of photographs and operating of tape recorders in the courtroom or its environs and radio or television broadcasting from the courtroom or its environs during the progress of or in connection with judicial proceedings, including proceedings before a United States

Magistrate Judge, Bankruptcy Judge, or Administrative Law Judge, whether or not court is actually in session, are prohibited.... The courtroom and its environs ... shall include any portion of any United States courthouse building and the exterior steps to such buildings, and parking areas adjacent to such buildings if such areas are owned by the United States Government. Where the interest of justice or public safety may so require, the Court may direct the Marshal to extend the environs of the courtroom ... to the curb or edge of the public streets or thoroughfares adjacent to any United States courthouse building.... At the request of the United States Marshal or the United States Attorney, the Court may direct other limitations on photography and broadcasting to maintain the secrecy of grand jury proceedings, to protect jurors and witnesses, and to further the interest of justice in unusual, hazardous, or inflammatory circumstances.... Nothing herein contained shall be construed unreasonably so as to restrict the constitutional rights of any individual....[81]

The Eleventh Circuit Court of Appeals' "Federal Rules of Appellate Procedure" do not provide for electronic coverage of

---

81. Local Rules 83.23-83.26, U.S. District Court for the Southern District of Georgia, Local Rules (undated), available at: http://www.gasd.uscourts.gov/lr/lr1.htm#lr83 (last accessed Nov. 15, 2013).

that court's oral arguments or its rulings.[82] Neither do the rules of the U.S. Supreme Court.[83]

82. See, U.S. Court of Appeals, Eleventh Circuit, Federal Rules of Appellate Procedure (Aug. 1, 2007), available at: http://www.ca11.uscourts.gov/documents/pdfs/BlueAUG07.pdf (last accessed Nov. 15, 2013). See also, U.S. Court of Appeals, Eleventh Circuit, Rules and Addenda (undated) available at: http://www.ca11.uscourts.gov/rules/index.php (last accessed Nov. 15, 2013). The Ninth Circuit Court of Appeals is experimenting with the limited use of video cameras in federal courtrooms. See, John Schwartz, "Judge Opens Federal Court to Video in Civil Cases," New York Times, Dec. 19, 2009, A12.

83. See, Rules of the Supreme Court of the United States (2010), available at: http://www.supremecourt.gov/ctrules/2010RulesoftheCourt.pdf (last accessed Nov. 15, 2013).

Unintended Consequences

In recent years there has been growing use of corporate documents, produced and filed with trial courts as part of pre-trial discovery in civil cases, to inform the public of threats to the public's safety or to its welfare. One such example has been the past litigation questioning the safety of Firestone tires.[84] Journalists have used these suits to obtain more information about comparative tire safety, which has led some to question the appropriateness of this method of news-gathering. Other questions have also been raised:

- While pre-trials records in civil cases are open to public inspection as a means of assuring the fairness of trials and public confidence in the judicial process, at what point does the use of pre-trial records in news-gathering and reporting become an abuse of the discovery process?[85]
- Should courts seal depositions or allegations contained in lawsuits to prevent public disclosure?[86]
- Should it make a difference if a party is a public person or that the issue is only one of public curiosity?[87]

---

84. See, Van Etten v. Bridgestone/Firestone & Ford Motor Co., 117 F.Supp.2d 1375 (S.D. Ga. 2000); reversed, Chicago Tribune v. Bridgestone/Firestone, 263 F.3d 1304 (11th Cir. 2001).

85. Discovery, according to the 11th Circuit federal appellate court, "is essentially a private process because the litigants and the courts assume that the sole purpose of discovery is to assist trial preparation...." U.S. v. Anderson, 799 F.2d 1438 (11th Cir. 1986) at 1441. See, for example, Robin McDonald, "Lockheed Withheld Discovery Docs," Daily Report, May 18, 2010, 1, 10.

86. See, for example, Robin McDonald, "Judge Rejects Jones' Effort to Seal Records," Daily Report, Sept. 28, 2007, 1, 5.

87. See, for example, Carrie Teegardin, "Secrecy Veils Suit Against Regents Head," Atlanta Journal-Constitution, March 15, 2009, B1, B9;

- Should settlement records in a civil case be open to the public?[88]
- In what circumstances should court records filed under seal be available to the public?[89]
- How should the public's interest be measured?[90]

It is important to recognize the growing concern that "third parties – who have no cause of action before the court – us[e] the discovery process as a means to unearth documents to which they otherwise would have no right to inspect and copy."[91] It is yet another challenge to the balance between one's right to a fair trial and the right of public access to the judicial

---

Carrie Teegardin, "Case, Seal by Court, Resolved – With No Details," Atlanta Journal-Constitution, April 12, 2009, B7. See also, Bill Rankin, "Speaker Blasts Effort to Make Divorce File Public," Atlanta Journal-Constitution, May 22, 2008, D12; Bill Rankin, "Speaker's Sealed Divorce Could Set Precedent," Atlanta Journal-Constitution, June 13, 2008, A1, A7; Jim Galloway, "Scott Divorce Records Stay Sealed for Now," Atlanta Journal-Constitution, Oct. 27, 2010, page number unknown; Grayson Daughters, "Gingrich Divorce Records Pose Questions for Carroll County Court," ATLaw, Dec. 28, 2011, available at: http://www.atlawblog.com/2011/12/gingrich-divorce-records-pose-question-for-carroll-county-court/ (last accessed Nov. 4, 2013).

88. See, Savannah College of Art & Design v. School of Visual Arts, 270 Ga. 791, 515 S.E.2d 370 (1999).

89. See, Estate of Martin Luther King, Jr., Inc. v. CBS, 184 F.Supp.2d 1353 (N.D. Ga. 2002). See also, Eric Stirgus, "Brian Nichols Case: Media Seek To Have Records Unsealed," Atlanta Journal-Constitution, Oct. 27, 2007, B4.

90. See, for example, Rhonda Cook, "Court: Records Can Stay Private – Defense Dispute: Lawyer Rebuffed in Fight to See Account of Public Defender Spending," Atlanta Journal-Constitution, Nov. 22, 2007, D17.

91. Chicago Tribune v. Bridgestone/Firestone, 263 F.3d 1304 (11th Cir. 2001) at 1316 (Black, J., concurring). See, for example, "Prosecutors Seek Lid on Coke Trial: Leaking of Trade Secrets Emerges as Big Concern," Atlanta Journal-Constitution, Jan. 5, 2007, G6.

process, complicated by growing Internet access to court records.[92]

---

92. See, NCSC: National Center for State Courts, Public Access to Court Records: Resource Guide (undated), available at: http://www.ncsc.org/Topics/Access-and-Fairness/Privacy-Public-Access-to-Court-Records/Resource-Guide.aspx (last accessed Nov. 15, 2013). See, for example, DeKalb County Online Judicial System (undated), available at: http://www.ojs.dekalbga.org (last accessed Nov. 15, 2013).

QUESTIONS

1. To what extent do Georgia judges have power to prevent disruptions of proceedings? How far does this power extend?

2. In Georgia, what is the test for determining when requests for venue changes will be approved?

3. What is the purpose of the four-part test established by the U.S. Supreme Court in *Waller v. Georgia* (1984)?

4. What responsibility does journalists' greater right of access to Georgia courtrooms bring, when compared with that of the general public?

5. Georgia rules allowing broadcast of certain juvenile proceedings still prohibit what?

6. When are court records not available for public inspection?

7. What is the rule regarding public access to criminal trials?

8. What is the Georgia test regarding whether prejudicial publicity has deprived someone of a fair trial?

9. How far from the courtroom can Middle District federal courts go to regulate electronic coverage of their proceedings?

Thought Question:

What factors should be considered when determining whether to allow broadcast coverage of criminal proceedings in Georgia? Why?

6. Reporter's Privilege in Georgia

O n March 13, 1990, then-Governor Joe Frank Harris signed into effect Georgia's first "shield" law (see, Figure 6, p. 145),[1] which provides journalists with a qualified privilege against the forced disclosure of confidential sources and information in many situations. Prior to this, journalists and their attorneys had fought regularly with trial attorneys seeking confidential information gathered by reporters to help in the preparation of both civil and criminal cases. Before 1990, journalists' attorneys could cite no substantive defense in countering claims that refusal by the media to divulge undisclosed information infringed on the constitutional rights of those accused to a fair and speedy trial.[2] Adopted by

---

1. See, O.C.G.A. 24-5-508. The Atlanta Constitution's entire one-paragraph story about the event ("Governor Signs 'Shield' Law for Reporter's Sources," March 14, 1990, D4) read as follows: "Reporters' confidential sources are promised anonymity in most circumstances under legislation Gov. Joe Frank Harris singed into law Tuesday, giving Georgia its first 'shield law.' The new law, passed during the 1990 General Assembly session that ended last week, says reporters must reveal sources only if the information is relevant to a court case and is necessary to properly prepare it, and only if the information cannot be reasonably obtained any other way. The law went into effect when Mr. Harris signed the bill."

2. The Sixth Amendment to the U.S. Constitution states: "In all criminal prosecutions, the accused shall enjoy the right to a speedy and public trial ... [and] to have compulsory process for obtaining witnesses in his favor, and to have the Assistance of Counsel for his defense." The part of Georgia's Constitution of 1983 which journalists contend is abused on occasion provides that "every person charged with an offense against the laws of this state ... shall have compulsory process to obtain the testimony of that person's own witnesses.... (Article I, §I, ¶XIV).

the Georgia General Assembly March 6, the law's passage also neutralized the legal effect of the state's 79-year-old precedent, *Plunkett v. Hamilton.*[3]

In that case, a unanimous Georgia Supreme Court denied Thomas Hamilton's request to be released from jail, following his contempt citation for refusing to testify before the Augusta police commission. Hamilton, a reporter for the *Augusta Herald*, had obtained information about a murder from an Augusta police officer and "regarded his obligation not to divulge the name of his informant as sacred as the obligation to tell the truth after being sworn by the commission."[4] He told the commission, just before being fined $50 or serving five days in jail, that "he believed he would forfeit the respect and confidence of the community at large if he divulged the name of his informant and that to do so would subject him to ridicule and contempt."[5] He contended that being forced to betray the confidence "would ruin me in my business. It would cause me to lose my position as a newspaper reporter ... and would prevent my ever engaging in the occupation ... again."[6]

Nonetheless, Justice Joseph H. Lumpkin of the Georgia Supreme Court - comparing journalists' promises of secrecy with those made by friends of a murderer or thief - concluded that every

> citizen or inhabitant owes to the state the duty of testifying, when lawfully called upon to do so, in order that the truth may be ascertained and impartial and complete justice done.... A promise not to testify when so required is

---

3. 136 Ga. 72, 70 S.E. 781 (1911).
4. Id. at 81.
5. Id.
6. Id.

substantially a promise not to obey the law. Such promises cannot be recognized, save in subordination to the requirements of the law. Neither can the wishes, or even the commands, of employers be allowed to outweigh the commands of the law. If the views sought to be maintained in this case were permitted to prevail, the power to ascertain the truth in judicial investigations, and to administer justice accordingly, would depend, not upon the law of the land, but upon the private promises of secrecy on the part of witnesses, or upon the wishes or orders of their employers. To sustain such a doctrine would render courts impotent and the effort to administer justice oftentimes a mockery.[7]

In 1972, the U.S. Supreme Court reached a similar conclusion in *Branzburg v. Hayes*.[8] Paul Branzburg was a reporter for the Louisville (Ky.) Courier-Journal who refused to tell a grand jury what he had discovered during an investigation into the local manufacture of hashish. Writing for a sharply divided 5-4 court, Justice Byron White agreed that "news gathering does ... qualify for First Amendment protection,"[9] but concluded that journalists have the same rights as other citizens, no less but also no more.[10] No privilege - qualified or not - protecting communication between a

---

7. Id. at 83-84.

8. 408 U.S. 665. The case involved the separate appeals of three different reporters - Paul Branzburg, Paul Pappas, and Earl Caldwell.

9. Id. at 681.

10. For a modern restatement of this argument, see, "Reporters' Duty Same as Public's," Atlanta Journal-Constitution, Dec. 10, 2004, A18.

journalist and his or her source exists in the U.S. Constitution. However, even though the Constitution does not provide the protection sought, "Congress has the freedom to determine whether a statutory newsman's privilege is necessary ... [and] state legislatures [are] free, within First Amendment limits, to fashion their own standards...."[11]

In a strongly worded dissent, Justice Potter Stewart (joined by Justices William Brennan and Thurgood Marshall) argued that before journalists can be required to testify before grand juries, the government must:

- Show that there is probable cause to believe that the newsman has information that is clearly relevant to a specific probable violation of law;
- Demonstrate that the information sought cannot be obtained by alternative means less destructive of First Amendment rights; and
- Demonstrate a compelling and overriding interest in the information.[12]

Stewart's dissent and White's invitation proved to be the catalyst for state legislatures. In the years since, about four-fifths of the states - including Georgia in 1990 - have adopted "shield" laws or recognized a reporter's privilege through court ruling.[13] Most clearly appear to have been patterned after Stewart's three-part test.

The underlying issues, however, have not been as easily resolved. From the journalists' perspective, for too long they

---

11. Id. at 706.

12. Id. at 743.

13. See, Reporters Committee for Freedom of the Press, "The Reporter's Privilege" (undated), available at: http://www.rcfp.org/privilege/ (last accessed Nov. 15, 2013).

have served as "free private investigators for litigants" and police.[14] Without some sort of protection, they contend, journalists' jobs will be more difficult, because all too often sources are unwilling to talk "on the record." Important issues and controversies, like Watergate, the Pentagon Papers, or the Abu-Ghraib prison scandal, might not otherwise be covered if sources cannot be promised confidentiality.[15] It is the information, they believe, which contributes to democracy's marketplace of ideas - not the identity of its source. On the other hand, opponents assert that journalists simply want to have it both ways. While they are fighting against governmental secrecy with such slogans as "the public's right to know," journalists are - in the same breath - demanding the right to keep secrets themselves, in the public's best interest.[16]

As a result, *Plunkett v. Hamilton*[17] was still the law in Georgia in 1988 when William Vaughn, a reporter for the

---

14. "State Justices Hear Debate on Reporter's 'Shield Law,'" Los Angeles Times, Feb. 7, 1990, A18. See also, Paul Kvinta, "Riot Squad Battles Reporter Shield," Daily Report, May 19, 1992, 1, 4-5; Kathleen Cullinan, "Ex-Reporter Can Guard Her Sources in Georgia Case," Reporters Committee for Freedom of the Press' News Media Update, 15:9 (May 11, 2009), page number unknown.

15. See, for example, Note, "Reporters and Their Sources: the Constitutional Right to a Confidential Relationship," 80 Yale Law Journal 317 (1970); Note, "Free Press, Privacy and Privilege: Protection of Researcher-Subject Communications," 17 Georgia Law Review 1009 (1983); Note, "A Press Privilege for the Worst of Times," 75 Georgetown Law Journal 361 (1986).

16. "'Shield' legislation poses serious difficulties - even dangers. First, if the people have a right to know, why would they not have a right to know the sources of a reporter's story?" (John C. Merrill, "The 'People's Right To Know' Myth," 45 New York State Bar Journal 461, November 1973, at 462). See, George Blake, "Rebuilding Credibility: Banning Anonymous Sources Is a Start," The Quill (April 1988), 21-23.

17. 136 Ga. 72, 70 S.E.781 (1911).

Clayton News/Daily, interviewed an alleged drug dealer, "Carlos," for an article, headlined, "Confessions of a Dope Dealer."[18] Subpoenaed to testify before a grand jury, Vaughn refused. A Clayton County Superior Court judge held Vaughn in contempt and ordered him to perform 100 hours of community service in a drug rehabilitation center in lieu of a 10-day jail term.[19] Vaughn appealed to the Georgia Supreme Court, arguing that both the federal and state constitutions gave him the right to protect the identity of his source and that before he could be forced to divulge that identity, prosecutors must meet the requirements of Justice Stewart's three-part test.[20] In *Vaughn v. Georgia*, the Georgia Supreme Court, however, disagreed 6-1,[21] citing *Branzburg*[22] to deny him any such right under the U.S. Constitution and "declin[ing] to interpret the Constitution of Georgia to afford any greater right...."[23]

A civil case decided soon afterward, *Howard v. Savannah College of Art & Design*,[24] set the stage for the Georgia Press Association's successful campaign for the state's new "shield" law.[25] In this case, Rosanne Howard, a reporter for the *Savannah News-Press*, contributed information that was used in a civil suit filed against the Savannah College of Art & Design by two women who had been raped in a dormitory there. When

---

18. Clayton News/Daily, June 29, 1988, 1.
19. See, Gary Headricks, "High Court Case May Mean Media Source Law," Atlanta Constitution, Feb. 25, 1989, F2; "High Court Finds Contempt for Silence in Grand Jury," The News Media & the Law (Fall 1990), 38-39.
20. 408 U.S. 665 (1972) at 743.
21. 259 Ga. 325, 381 S.E.2d 30 (1989).
22. 408 U.S. 665 (1972).
23. 259 Ga. 325, 381 S.E.2d 30 (1989) at 326.
24. 259 Ga. 795, 387 S.E.2d 332 (1990).
25. See, Susan Dewberry, "Witnesses: A Qualified Reporters' Privilege," 7 Georgia State Law Review 286 (Fall 1990).

the college sought additional information from her, Howard refused to answer, claiming a constitutional right to protect her sources. Justice Charles L. Weltner wrote the three-paragraph opinion, stating: "The trial court held: 'Georgia has no statutory qualified privilege.... [The journalist] has no qualified reporter's privilege under the law of this state.' This holding is correct."[26]

In essence, then, under Georgia law reporters could not keep secrets,[27] despite the existence of a qualified privilege already recognized in certain instances.[28]

Consequently, state Senators C. Donald Johnson, Jr., of Royston; Don M. Peevy of Lawrenceville; and Pierre Howard of Decatur[29] agreed to sponsor legislation drafted by Georgia Press Association counsel to provide for Georgia's first "shield" law[30] as part of the state code's section on rules of evidence concerning witnesses.[31] The bill contained three parts:

First, those qualified to assert the privilege included "any person, company, or other entity engaged in the gathering or

---

26. 259 Ga. 795, 387 S.E.2d 332 (1990) at 795-796. Any reporter's privilege, Weltner said, would have to come from the state legislature. See, "Weltner: No Shield for News Media," Daily Report, Jan. 23, 1990, 7.

27. See, David Hudson, "What To Do When the Newspaper Is Subpoenaed," Georgia Press Association Editor's Forum (Winter 1990), 13.

28. See, for example, Georgia Communications Corp. v. Horne, 164 Ga. App. 227, 294 S.E.2d 725 (1982) (where a radio show host's refusal to identify the source of allegedly defamatory statements might have been protected by privilege had the statements been related to any legitimate journalistic endeavor); Carver v. Georgia, 258 Ga. 385, 369 S.E.2d 471 (1988) (where unpublished information was protected by a balancing test which took into account the defendant's interest in obtaining the information from the reporter, the lack of alternative sources for the information, and the burden placed on the newspaper to produce the information sought).

29. Howard was elected lieutenant governor later that same year.

30. Senate Bill 636 (Georgia General Assembly 1990).

31. See, O.C.G.A. 24-5-508.

dissemination of news for the public through a newspaper, book, magazine, or radio or television broadcast"[32] and the privilege protects every confidential or non-confidential "information, document, or item obtained or prepared in the gathering or dissemination of news."[33] Before the state House of Representatives would agree to the definition of who the privilege was intended to protect, however, the House Judiciary Committee recommended that the word "or" in the phrase "... engaged in the gathering or dissemination ..." be changed to "and."[34] This change appears to guarantee that anyone seeking to assert the privilege will not be " a non-journalist,"[35] and may even limit the protection offered to free-lance journalists who, until their gathered information is written in news form and sold, cannot be properly be said to be engaged in the dissemination of news.[36]

Second, the privilege only applies "in any proceeding

---

32. Senate Bill 636 (Georgia General Assembly 1990).

33. Id.

34. In the House, the bill was handled by Rep. Charles Thomas of Temple, chair of the House Judiciary Committee.

35. Gregory C. Lisby, "Would New Shield Law Have Helped Billy Vaughn?" Georgia Press Association Editor's Forum (Spring 1990), 2.

36. Susan Dewberry. "Witnesses," 7 Georgia State Law Review 286 (Fall 1990) at 292. A precedent for this approach may be found in Jersawitz v. Hanberry, 610 F.Supp. 535 (N.D. Ga. 1985), affirmed, 783 F.2d 1532 (11th Cir. 1986), certiorari denied, 479 U.S. 883 (1986) (where an independent television producer was denied access to a maximum security prison based on a regulation stating that media representatives must be employed by the media). On the other hand, Georgia's shield law was held to protect a reporter (at the time a Georgia resident) who wrote a story in December 1988 (thirteen months before Georgia's shield law was enacted) while living in South Carolina and employed by a Columbia newspaper. See, David Hudson, "Reporter's Shield Law Applied in the Case of a Former South Carolina Reporter," The GPA Bulletin, April 10, 1992, 9.

where the one asserting the privilege is not a party."[37] Journalists involved as a party in a lawsuit are subject to the same laws of evidence as anyone else.

Third, unless the privilege is waived, those seeking the information must show that it:

- is highly material and relevant;
- cannot be reasonably obtained by alternative means; and
- is necessary to the proper preparation or presentation of the case of a party seeking the information, document, or item.[38]

Before the state House of Representatives would agree to this variation of Justice Stewart's three-part test,[39] however, the House Judiciary Committee recommended that the word

---

37. Senate Bill 636 (Georgia General Assembly 1990). This language would appear to include both civil and criminal cases.

38. Id. To compare the region's federal appellate court's approach to reporter's privilege with Georgia's, see, U.S. v. Caporale, 806 F.2d 1487 (11th Cir. 1986). Disclosure "may only be compelled from a reporter claiming privilege if the party requesting the information can show that it is highly relevant, necessary to the proper presentation of the case, and unavailable form other sources" (id. at 1504). In ruling on a motion in Izbicki v. Ridgeview Institute, No. 1:89-cv-306-RCF slip opinion (N.D. Ga. March 27, 1990), Judge Robert C. Freeman wrote that Georgia's "shield" law is broader than its federal counterpart in that it protects confidential and non-confidential information alike yet weaker in that it requires only that the information sought be "material and relevant" rather than "highly relevant" and "cannot be reasonably obtained by alternative means" rather than being "unavailable from other sources." See, Jane Okransinki, "Freeman reviews Reporter's Shield," Daily Report, March 30, 1990, 5; Jane Okransinki, 'District Judge Finds New State Law Broader Than Federal," Georgia Press Association Editor's Forum (Spring 1990), 1, 12.

39. See, Branzburg v. Hayes, 408 U.S. 665 (1972) at 743.

"highly" in the first part of the test be deleted.[40]

The final version of the bill (see, Figure 6, p. 145) passed the Senate by a vote of 41-0 and the House 107-4.

---

40. See Susan Dewberry, "Witnesses," 7 Georgia State Law Review 286 (Fall 1990) at note 48 for a comment by the bill's primary sponsor regarding the perceived redundancies involved in the terms "highly pregnant" and "highly relevant." Greg Lisby, however, disagrees: "What does "material and relevant" mean? How "material and relevant" is material and relevant? Is it "substantially" material and relevant? ... Or does the information need only be "marginally" material and relevant? ... While this may appear to be legal nit-picking to most, these are very important questions to journalists attempting to ascertain just how big and how thick a shield Georgia has fashioned here" ("Would a New Shield Law Have Helped?" GPA Editor's Forum, Spring 1990, at 2).

GEORGIA REPORTERS' SHIELD STATUTE
(Figure 6)

Any person, company, or other entity engaged in the gathering and dissemination of news for the public through any newspaper, book, magazine, radio or television broadcast, or electronic means shall have a qualified privilege against disclosure of any information, document, or item obtained or prepared in the gathering or dissemination of news in any proceeding where the one asserting the privilege is not a party, unless it is shown that this privilege has been waived or that what is sought:

(1) Is material and relevant;

(2) Cannot be reasonably obtained by alternative means; and

(3) Is necessary to the proper preparation or presentation of the case of a party seeking the information, document, or item.

- O.C.G.A. 24-5-508 (2013)

On March 28, 1990, when the law was a scant two weeks old, it survived its first test in a Douglas County court.[41] The case involved an effort to expose the involvement of Douglas County police in the interception of telephone conversations between attorneys and their clients in the county jail.[42] *Fulton County Daily Report* staff writer Trisha Renaud was required to

---

41. See, Stripling v. Georgia, 261 Ga. 1, 401 S.E.2d 500 (1991). See also, David E. Langford, "Reporter's Shield Passes First Test," Daily Report, March 30, 1990, 2; "Shield Law Upheld in First Court Test," Georgia Press Association Editor's Forum (Spring 1990), at 1.

42. Communication between attorneys and clients is privileged and is a type of informational relationships – including relationships between reporters and sources, husbands and wives, doctors and patients, ministers and parishioners, accountants and clients, and family violence or sexual assault victims and government agents providing services – protected by testimonial privilege from disclosure in court on the grounds of public policy. See, O.C.G.A. 24-5-501 through O.C.G.A. 24-5-509.

testify before Douglas County Superior Court Judge Robert Nolan about the identity of confidential sources who supplied her with information about the alleged wire-tapping. Declining to answer more than 50 questions, she cited the recently enacted reporter's privilege statute.

"If client-attorney conversations were taped in the jail," Judge Nolan said, "it's the most reprehensible thing this court has ever heard. If you can show that that happened in this case, then we're going to take the bars down and let the horses trot."[43] However, he denied motions to force the reporter to reveal her sources.

The new "shield" law was used a second time three weeks later to quash a subpoena and the reporter involved was not even required to appear in court.[44] In this case, attorneys for a man convicted of taking narcotics from the Hall County Sheriff Department's storeroom subpoenaed an editor at the Gainesville Times to testify about alleged prosecutorial misconduct. After two hours of arguments, Hall County Superior Court Judge J.D. Smith granted the newspaper's motion to quash the subpoena, because the information sought was available from alternative sources.

However, a subsequent attempt to invoke the new law failed. The case involved an unusual civil suit that accused a widower of murdering his wife. As part of the dispute, DeKalb County Superior Court Judge Hilton Fuller was asked to ascertain the dividing line between the professional and private life of a journalist, who was also a friend of the Krause

---

43. Mark Curriden, "State Law Protecting Journalists Survives 1st Test in Douglas Court," Atlanta Journal, March 29, 1990, B6.

44. See, David E. Langford, "Reporters Shield Survives Second Test," Daily Report, April 17, 1990, 2.

family.[45] At the time of Connie Vance Krause's disappearance
in 1989, WAGA-TV reporter Anthony D'Astoli spent hours
talking with police and Mrs. Krause's husband, Hans; helping
in the search and subsequent discovery of her body; and "acting
as the family's liaison with the news media."[46] When no one
was finally charged with the murder, Mrs. Krause's family
sued Mr. Krause, claiming that he killed his wife and should
not be allowed to collect any insurance money. D'Astoli,
however, refused to cooperate with the Vance family in its
lawsuit, maintaining that Georgia's new law shielded him from
having to do so.[47] Judge Fuller rejected that assertion as
"border[ing] on the absurd,"[48] while also requiring family
attorneys to show that they could not obtain the information
sought form D'Astoli elsewhere.

Georgia courts have also not required reporters to testify
about the source of an inaccurate story concerning jury
deliberations in a murder trial,[49] but have upheld a grand jury
subpoena for an audio-tape of a jailhouse interview with an
accused murderer because the reporter allowed a sheriff's

---

45. See, Trisha Renaud, "Shield Law Invoked in Krause Case: Is TV
Reporter Protecting Sources or Protecting Hans Krause?" Daily Report, Nov.
6, 1990, 4, 5.

46. Id. at 4.

47. D'Astoli said in an affidavit, "I have used my relationship with Hans
Krause to obtain valuable information in reporting on the story. Any personal
interest I may have had in assisting the family find Mrs. Krause was
completely consistent with my interest as a journalist in covering the story.
The more publicity there was about the story, the better the chances of finding
Mrs. Krause, and the better the news story" (id. at 5). His claim raises
interesting ethical questions regarding the use of personal relationships to gain
information, which are beyond the scope of this discussion.

48. Ken Foskett, "Judge: Friend of Krause Must Give Evidence in
Suit," Atlanta Journal-Constitution, Nov. 23, 1990, E14.

49. See, Nobles v. Georgia, 201 Ga. App. 483, 411 S.E.2d 294 (1991).

deputy to stay in the room during the meeting.[50] More recently, the Georgia Supreme Court ruled that the "shield" law protected a Savannah reporter from disclosing his unpublished information obtained during a jailhouse interview. The court explicitly held that the privilege applies both to confidential and non-confidential information and that a reporter ordered to disclose such information is entitled to an immediate, direct appeal to the Supreme Court.[51] Yet, published information cannot be grounds for a journalist's seeking the protection of the law.[52]

But in a decision that substantively re-interprets one requirement of the state's "shield" law, the Georgia Court of Appeals, in *Atlanta Journal-Constitution v. Jewell*, ruled in 2001 that journalists who are parties to lawsuits do not completely waive their claims to the law's protections when asserting a reporter's privilege.[53] Here, newspaper reporters refused to reveal their sources for accusations made that security guard Richard Jewell fit the profile of the bomber at the 1996 Atlanta Olympics, while at the same time asserting truth as a defense to Jewell's lawsuit for defamation. When a Fulton County State Court judge ruled that in order to use truth as a defense the reporters would have to identify their confidential sources, even though their sources had been promised anonymity, the reporters sought refuge in the "shield" law, even though it plainly states that its protections are only available to those "in any proceeding where the one

---

50. See, Katie Wood, "Did Reporter Waive Shield in Interview of Tokars Suspect?" Georgia Press Bulletin, July 22, 1993, 3.

51. In Re: Paul, 270 Ga. 680, 513 S.E.2d 219 (1999).

52. In Re: Morris Communications, 258 Ga. App. 154, 573 S.E.2d 420 (2002).

53. 251 Ga. App. 808, 555 S.E.2d 175 (2001).

asserting the privilege is not a party."[54]

The appellate court, however, concluded that general civil discovery procedures protected the anonymity of the reporters' sources, because "there is a strong public policy in favor of allowing journalists to shield the identity of their confidential sources unless disclosure is necessary in order to meet other important purposes of the law,"[55] such as the information being "relevant to the subject matter involved" and appearing "reasonably calculated to lead to the discovery of admissible evidence."[56] Thus, before such sources must be disclosed, "the trial court must require the plaintiff to specifically identify each and every purported statement he asserts was libelous, determine whether the plaintiff can prove the statements were untrue, taking into account all the other available evidentiary sources ... and determine whether the statements can be proven false through the use of other evidence, thus eliminating the plaintiff's necessity for the requested discovery."[57] In other words, "if the identity of the sources either is relevant and material in and of itself or is the only available avenue to other admissible evidence, then the trial court's balancing test should favor disclosure of the confidential sources."[58]

More broadly, the issue is simply one of balance: balance between constitutional guarantees of freedom of expression and

---

54. O.C.G.A. 24-5-508.

55. Atlanta Journal-Constitution v. Jewell, 251 Ga. App. 808, 555 S.E.2d 175 (2001) at 811.

56. Id. at 812. See, O.C.G.A. 9-11-26(b)(1). The court also noted that the "trial court has wide discretion ... to prevent the use of discovery directed to irrelevant or immaterial matter" (id.). See, Mead Corp. v. Masterack, 243 Ga. 213, 253 S.E.2d 164 (1979).

57. Id. at 813.

58. Id. As an example where alternative sources were not exhausted, see, Bill Rankin, "Shield Law Protects Ex-Reporter for AJC," Atlanta Journal-Constitution, May 5, 2009, B5.

those relating to justice achievable under the law. It is an ongoing debate for which there likely is no perfect resolution.[59]

---

59. See, for example, Janet Conley, "CNN Fights to Keep Footage Out of Suit," Daily Report, Jan. 16, 2008, 1, 9; Janet Conley, "CNN Loses Battle Over Release of Video," Daily Report, May 19, 2008, 1, 10.

QUESTIONS

1. On what grounds may we assume that free-lance writers are not entitled to the protection of Georgia's shield law?

2. Before 1990, on what legal precedent was the Georgia Supreme Court's response to the problem of reportorial privilege based?

3. Whom does the Georgia reporter's shield law protect? Whom does it not protect? Why?

4. What part of Georgia's proposed shield law was modified by the state House of Representatives before passage?

5. Immediately before the enactment of Georgia's shield law in 1990, what two court decisions reaffirmed the rule that there was no reporter's privilege in the state? To what two different types of cases did the two court decisions apply?

6. In *Plunkett v. Hamilton* (1911), the Georgia Supreme Court compared the confidentiality promises of a reporter with those of whom?

7. In what ways does Georgia's shield law not absolutely protect state journalists from being forced to testify?

Thought Question:
How do shield laws conflict with the public's "right to know"? How should journalists and others' opposing concerns be addressed? How does a reporter's privilege generally differ from other types of testimonial privilege?

7. Obscenity/Indecency in Georgia

The first law relating to obscenity or indecency in Georgia was enacted just after the end of the Civil War by the state legislature during the 1865-66 legislative session and was "almost by definition a by-product of class rivalry."[1] Aimed at protecting the so-called "fragile sensibilities of the fairer sex," it did not target printed material but forbade obscene and vulgar language in the presence of females: "Any person who shall, without provocation, use ... obscene and vulgar language in the presence of a female, shall be guilty of a misdemeanor."[2] A decade later, during the 1878-79 legislative term, the state's first statute against the possession and sale of obscene matter was passed: "If any person shall bring, or cause to be brought into this State for sale or exhibition, or shall sell or offer to sell, or shall give away or offer to give away, or having possession thereof, shall knowingly exhibit to another any indecent pictorial newspaper tending to debauch the morals, or any indecent or obscene book, ... such person ... shall be guilty of a misdemeanor."[3]

Interestingly, Georgia obscenity law was shaped almost exclusively over the next forty years by the decisions in four cases. And of these four, three concerned affronts to the morals of Southern women - not the sale or possession of obscene material with which obscenity law has become so concerned

---

1. D. Grier Stephenson, Jr., "State Appellate Courts and Written Obscenity: The Georgia Experience," 19 Mercer Law Review 287 (1968) at 289.
2. 1865-66 Georgia Laws 233.
3. 1878-79 Georgia Laws 163.

today. It was not until the 1957 U.S. Supreme Court decision in *Roth v. United States/Alberts v. California*[4] that Georgia obscenity law changed appreciably.

The first of the four cases was *Dillard v. Georgia.*[5] Here, James Dillard asked Mary Sanders, the wife of William Sanders, to "go to bed" with him. When she told her husband of the remark in Dillard's presence, he called her a "God-damned liar."[6] Responding to Dillard's argument that the words used were not "obscene and vulgar language," Justice H. K. McCay wrote, "Words get their point and meaning almost entirely from the time, place, circumstances, and intent with which they are used, and it seems to us a very unfair interpretation of this clause of the [law] to say, that it is directed simply against the use of certain words which are by common consent banished from decent society. If there are any such words in our language they are very few, and as we have said, even they are only obscene and vulgar accordingly as they convey obscene and vulgar ideas."[7] While voting with the unanimous court, Chief Justice Joseph E. Brown disagreed with the court's expansion of the law's scope to cover language - specifically Dillard's request that Mrs. Sanders "go to bed" with him - which "is in itself neither obscene nor vulgar, and has never before been so held in any Court…. I do not think it the proper province of the courts to extend this penal statute … so as to embrace offenses against morality, decency or good breeding…."[8]

Already, Georgia courts were beginning to confront the problem of definition. What exactly, what legally, is obscenity?

---

4. 354 U.S. 476.

5. 41 Ga. 278 (1870).

6. Id. at 279.

7. Id. at 280.

8. Id. at 282.

In *Dillard*, the majority of the Georgia Supreme Court seemed to think that the statute included not only so-called common four-letter words, but also words with what might be termed a four-letter meaning. Improper sexual advances were deemed obscene in Georgia as a result of this case.

Only one case in the state before 1900 involved a conviction for selling obscene literature, *Montross v. Georgia.*[9] In an attempt to determine whether copies of the *National Police Gazette* could be distributed in Atlanta without violating state obscenity laws, the would-be distributor gave a copy to Atlanta's police chief. Unimpressed, the chief charged him with distributing obscene literature. Montross claimed that the articles and pictures in the Gazette were no worse than items found every day in Atlanta's daily newspaper - the *Constitution.* The Georgia Supreme Court upheld the trial judge's refusal to allow Montross to demonstrate his contention and ruled that the Gazette was "indecent with an unmistakable tendency to vitiate the public taste and debauch the public morals,"[10] concluding that "no respectable magistrate could for a moment tolerate a spectacle so gross and outrageous."[11]

Had the court allowed Montross to compare his publication to one already accepted by the community, Georgia might have established the "community standards" test twenty-six years earlier than it did.[12] As it was, *Montross* reaffirmed that the courts had the authority to censor anything which "tend[ed] to debauch the public morals," while not defining exactly what that was.

---

9. 72 Ga. 261 (1884).
10. Id. at 266.
11. Id. at 268.
12. See, Redd v. Georgia, 7 Ga. App. 575, 67 S.E. 709 (1910).

Georgia's first definition of obscenity was developed in *Holcombe v. Georgia*,[13] where a Cartersville minister who was attempting to clear his church's auditorium of women to conduct a men's lecture reportedly told a woman who was slow in leaving, "You woman with the big fat rump pointed towards me, get out of the way."[14] Holcombe did not deny the incident took place, but explained that he had said: "Gentlemen, there is a big old woman weighing about 400 pounds with her rump turned this way. If she would turn around and let me speak to her head, I might explain to her the object of this meeting, and we might go on."[15] The minister was found guilty of addressing "obscene and vulgar language" to a woman. Expanding the scope of the Georgia law even further than was done in *Dillard*,[16] Judge Arthur G. Powell stated that the statute was not "aimed alone at language suggestive of sexual intercourse, or tending to excite lewdness, or to debauch the public morals [but at] any foul words which would reasonably offend the sense of modesty and decency of ... women."[17]

Borrowing from *Century Dictionary*, Judge Powell defined obscenity as something

> offensive to the senses, repulsive, disgusting, foul, filthy, offensive to modesty or decency, impure, unchaste, indecent, lewd.[18]

He also touched upon the concept of community standards, which would be brought into Georgia obscenity law in *Redd v.*

---

13. 5 Ga. App. 47, 62 S.E. 647 (1908).
14. Id. at 48.
15. Id. at 49.
16. 41 Ga. 278 (1870).
17. 5 Ga. App. 47, 62 S.E. 647 (1908) at 50.
18. Id.

Georgia,[19] when he suggested that anyone doubting that Holcombe's words were vulgar and obscene,

> as commonly and ordinarily understood, may
> easily solve that doubt by quoting the language
> to his different male acquaintances ... and
> asking them if they would consider it obscene
> and vulgar to use that language in the presence
> of ladies.[20]

Two years later, Judge Powell again found himself called upon to determine what was appropriate in the presence of women. In *Redd v. Georgia,*[21] two men were convicted of open lewdness and public indecency[22] when they allowed a bull and cow to copulate, "adjacent to a highway and in the presence of a lady and several children,[23] some of them little girls, when there was a thicket nearby which could have been used. Judge Powell concluded that "a fair test to determine whether an act is notoriously indecent within the purview of this law is to consider whether the general run of the citizenry of the State would readily recognize it as such (all the attendant facts and circumstances and the motives of the actor being considered), and also whether it tends to debauch the morals."[24] In this case, he decided, it was.

---

19. 7 Ga. App. 575, 67 S.E. 709 (1910).

20. 5 Ga. App. 47, 62 S.E. 647 (1908) at 51.

21. 7 Ga. App. 575, 67 S.E. 709 (1910).

22. 1865-66 Georgia Laws 233. This law provided that "any person who shall be guilty of open lewdness, or any notorious act of public indecency, tending to debauch the morals" would be guilty of a misdemeanor.

23. 7 Ga. App. 575, 67 S.E. 709 (1910) at 576.

24. Id. at 580.

Thus, most early Georgia case law dealt with public decency – or indecency – rather than obscenity. In the years following, the number of obscenity rulings reported in Georgia case law declined sharply. Censorship efforts, however, did not.

In 1913, the Atlanta Board of Aldermen passed an ordinance providing for the inspection of films by a board of censors[25] and vested this power in the board of trustees of the city's public library,[26] which in turn first hired John Peacock and later Zella Richardson to review all movies to be shown in Atlanta. Though not a state censor, Peacock and Richardson in essence dictated what movies would be shown elsewhere in Georgia for years as they controlled what was shown in Atlanta - the largest market in the state with about 400,000 persons. Film distributors who were denied a permit to show a particular movie could appeal the ruling to the library board and then to the courts. Peacock's decisions were appealed twice during his twelve-year term of office; his judgment was reversed only once. Richardson's decisions were challenged six times during her twenty-year tenure; only once was her opinion reversed.[27] After Richardson's retirement, Christine Smith was chosen out of 218 applicants for the post - a clear indication of the job's appeal and social acceptance.[28]

---

25. See, Code of the City of Atlanta 5-305 (1942). See also, 1915 Georgia Laws 480, at 493-494, for the portion of the city's charter authorizing it to adopt a film censorship ordinance.

26. See, Code of the City of Atlanta, 58-107, 58-108 (1942). See also, Code of the City of Atlanta, 66-504, 66-505, 66-506, 66-507 (1942).

27. Rebecca Franklin, "'The Standard Has Risen:' Films Show Improvement, Mrs. Richardson Declares," Atlanta Journal, Feb 4, 1945, C13. See also, "Mrs. Richardson, Church and Civic Leader, Dies," Atlanta Journal, April 29, 1946, 1, 4.

28. "Miss Smith New Movie Censor," Atlanta Journal, Feb 3, 1945, 5.

Through the 1950s, however, "Atlanta film censorship was often less concerned with morals than with sectional prejudice."[29] Charged with protecting the Atlanta film-going public from obscene films that would harm "the peace, health, morals, and good order" of Atlanta,[30] Smith later admitted that "the temper of the public can have a bearing on whether a movie is harmless entertainment or incitation to a breach of the peace.... This factor is the chief reason some Southern cities have refused permits to movies shown long ago in the South and now offered as reissues. The intervening years have so changed the emotions of the audience that the showing of the same movie would produce entirely different reactions from those of ten years ago."[31] For example, Smith refused to allow D. W. Griffith's "Birth of a Nation" (1915) to be shown again in the area because of her "instinctive fear of Negro men," a result of her "vivid memory" of a scene from the movie "in which an impressionable girl jumps from a cliff to avoid the caress of an ex-slave."[32] On similar racial grounds, "Imitation of Life" (1934) and "Lost Boundaries" (1949) were both banned because of their racial themes.[33]

By 1960, the censor had had her rulings appealed to the courts three times: in 1946 for her ban of "Scarlet Street" (1945), in 1950 for her ban of "Lost Boundaries" (1949), and

29. Frank Daniel, "Impossible Job: Atlanta Is Well Rid of Censors," Atlanta Journal, July 20, 1964, 19.

30. Code of the City of Atlanta, 5-306 (1942).

31. Christine Smith, "Life of a Movie Censor," Atlanta Journal Magazine, Nov. 25, 1945, 8.

32. Frank Daniel, "She Saw 4,490 Films: Not Prejudiced Nor Narrow, Movie Censor Here Says," Atlanta Journal, Oct. 26, 1961, 42.

33. "'Imitation of Life' Banned Here on Racial Angle," Atlanta Journal, Oct. 2, 1945, 1; "Suit Challenges Ban on Movie by City Censor," Atlanta Journal, Nov. 19, 1949, 2.

in 1955 for her ban of "Blackboard Jungle" (1955).[34] However, her ban of the British film, "Room at the Top" (1959) - which had been nominated for five Academy awards - and the Greek film "Never on Sunday" (1960), was the beginning of the end of her efforts.[35] The Georgia Supreme Court struck down the city's ordinance as a "prior rating or censorship of movies"[36] and then revoked her power to classify movies with a system rating their suitability for certain audiences[37] in back-to-back rulings, beginning with *K. Gordon Murray Productions v. Floyd*.[38] In the words of Chief Justice W. H. Duckworth, "The house may [not] be burned in order to get the rats out of it."[39] Because the censor's position had become "a frequent embarrassment,"[40] Christine Smith Gilliam resigned in 1964.

---

34. Phil Smith, "Movie Censor Hits Movie Bed Scenes," Atlanta Journal, Sept. 28, 1960, 4. In the first two cases, her rulings were upheld.

35. "Movie Censor Mrs. Gilliam Dies Here," Atlanta Journal, Aug. 11, 1971, C11. The former Miss Smith married Edwin A. Gilliam, an Atlanta city alderman, in 1954.

36. Bill Hedgepeth, "Film Censor Voices Dismay at Ruling," Atlanta Journal, Oct. 15, 1963, 19.

37. Under the system, a movie could "be rated 'Approved,' for showing to everyone, or 'Unsuitable for the Young,' or 'Objectionable,' to limit its showing" ("City's Movie Censor Rule Is Upheld," Atlanta Journal, Feb. 27, 1963, 23). See, Atlanta v. Columbia Pictures Corp., 218 Ga. 714, 130 S.E.2d 490 (1963) at 715 for the pertinent provisions of the city's ordinance on film rating, adopted June 1962 by the Atlanta Board of Aldermen.

38. 217 Ga. 784, 125 S.E.2d 207 (1962). See, Atlanta v. Columbia Pictures Corp., 218 Ga. 714, 130 S.E.2d 490 (1963); Atlanta v. Twentieth Century-Fox Film Corp., 219 Ga. 271, 133 S.E.2d 12 (1963). For a discussion of this last case, see, Richard L. Brannon, "Constitutional Law: Motion Picture classification," 26 Georgia Bar Journal 475 (1964); Richard M. Olnick, "Constitutional Law - Freedom of Speech and Press - Movie Censorship," 15 Mercer Law Review 514 (1964).

39. K. Gordon Murray Productions, Inc. v. Floyd, 217 Ga. 784, 125 S.E.2d 207 (1962) at 792.

40. Daniel, "Impossible Job," Journal at 19.

The position was subsequently abolished.

Meanwhile, Georgia began its first major campaign against obscene literature in 1953, with the onset of the paperback book revolution in the years after World War II.[41] The ability to produce paperbacks made books far more accessible than they had ever before been. Even teen-agers could now afford to buy and read novels previously available only to adults. Coupled with the rising popularity of so-called foreign "girlie" magazines and the 1953 introduction of *Playboy* magazine, the state legislature unanimously voted to establish the Georgia Literature Commission to combat immorality as represented by "the ever-present obscene literature available to persons of all ages."[42] Obscenity was defined in a manner reminiscent of the definition in *Holcombe*:[43]

> any literature offensive to the chastity or modesty, expressing or presenting to the mind or view something that purity and decency forbids to be exposed.[44]

---

41. See, Gregory C. Lisby, "'Trying To Define What May Be Indefinable': The Georgia Literature Commission, 1953-1973," The Georgia Historical Quarterly, 84:1 (Spring 2000), 70-97. See also, Gregory C. Lisby, "The Georgia Literature Commission," New Georgia Encyclopedia (Dec. 1, 2006), available at: http://www.georgiaencyclopedia.org/nge/Article.jsp?id=h-755&hl=y (last accessed Nov. 15, 2013); Gregory C. Lisby, "The Georgia Literature Commission," 154-155, in Hugh Ruppersburg (ed.), The New Georgia Encyclopedia Companion to Georgia Literature (2007).

42. Stephenson, "State Appellate Courts and Written Obscenity," Mercer Law Review at 300. See, Horace W. Fleming, Jr., "The Georgia Literature Commission, " 18 Mercer Law Review 325 (1967).

43. 5 Ga. App. 47, 62 S.E. 647 (1908).

44. Section 1(b), 1953 Georgia Laws 135. 1878-79 Georgia Laws 163 made it a crime to sell or distribute obscene material.

The commission - "a study agency [with] no powers of censorship nor authority to punish offenders"[45] - was to consist of three members, citizens of "the highest moral character,"[46] who would meet monthly to investigate "literature which they [had] reason to suspect [was] detrimental to the morals of the citizens" of Georgia.[47] If the commission determined something to be obscene, it had the power to inhibit distribution by, first, notifying the distributor and, then, thirty days later recommending prosecution by the proper solicitor general. Then-Governor Herman Talmadge appointed Atlanta minister James P. Wesberry, Royston newspaper publisher Hubert L. Dyar, and Greensboro theater owner William R. Boswell to serve four-year terms.[48]

---

45. Then-Gov. Herman Talmadge, quoted in James P. Wesberry, Every Citizen Has a Right to Know; A Report of the Georgia Literature Commission (1954), v. In 1953, at the time the commissioners were sworn in, Talmadge was quoted as saying, "Censorship in a free country is repugnant to me and had the commission ... any authority of censorship, I would have unhesitatingly vetoed it because such would be in contravention of our Constitution and our conception of free minds and free men" (James P. Wesberry, The Georgia Literature Commission, 1957 Report (1957), 3).

46. Section 2, 153 Georgia Laws 135.

47. Section 4, 1953 Georgia Laws 136. Literature was defined as "any book, pamphlet, paper, drawing, lithograph, engraving, photograph, or picture" (Section 1(a), 1953 Georgia Laws 135), but specifically did "not include pictures used in projection of motion pictures or television" (1953 Georgia Laws 474). "Weekly and daily newspapers, all Federal and State matters, and all reading matter used in the recognized religions and in scientific or educational institutions of the United States" were exempt (Wesberry, Every Citizen Has a Right to Know, at 6-7).

48. Boswell resigned from the commission in 1961 and R. Clayton Bowers, principal of Troup County High School in LaGrange, was appointed to succeed him. Bowers served until his death in 1964. He was succeeded by Marcus B. Calhoun, a Thomasville attorney, who was succeeded in 1967 by Moultrie chiropractor William R. Dyer. He was succeeded by William Pirkle,

The commission quickly discovered that Georgia's statutory definition of obscenity was inadequate and, with the assistance of the state attorney general's office, developed an eight-part test to aid in its deliberations:[49]

- What is the general and dominant theme?
- What degree of sincerity of purpose is evident?
- What is the literary or scientific worth?
- What channels of distribution are employed?
- What are contemporary attitudes of reasonable men towards such matters?
- What types of readers may reasonably be expected to peruse the publication?
- Is there evidence of pornographic intent?
- What impression will be created in the mind of the reader, upon reading the work as a whole?

Most of the commission's early work was through a program of mutual cooperation with publishers, distributors, and retailers, although the commission became increasingly ineffective in its dealing with magazines, as it could prohibit distribution of a particular issue found to be obscene, but not any future issue. In late 1956, the commission was sued in

who died in 1973, as did Hubert Dyar. Neither was replaced. Only Wesberry served throughout the commission's 20-year existence.

49. Wesberry, Every Citizen Has a Right to Know at 7. Interestingly, parts of the test appear in later U.S. Supreme Court rulings on obscenity. Parts 6, 5, 1 and 8, and 7 seem to constitute the entire 1957 Roth test: "whether to the average person, applying contemporary community standards, the dominant theme of the material taken as a whole appeals to prurient interest" (354 U.S. 476 (1957) at 489). Part 3 appears analogous to the third part of the 1973 Miller test, also known as the LAPS test: "whether the work, taken as a whole, lacks serious literary, artistic, political, or scientific value" (Miller v. California, 413 U.S. 15, at 24).

federal district court by four out-of-state publishing companies, who charged that the statute establishing the commission was unconstitutional. On January 4, 1957, a special three-judge appellate panel ruled that the statute as "correctly construed" did not raise a constitutional question.[50] Because the court concluded that the commission did not have any powers of censorship - it could only recommend to distributors that a publication not be sold or to solicitors general that a distributor be prosecuted - the suit was subsequently dismissed.[51]

The statute was, however, amended by the legislature the following year to reflect the U.S. Supreme Court's definition of obscenity in *Roth v. United States/Alberts v. California* and to strengthen the commission's procedures of operation.[52] First, the definition of literature was expanded to include the word "periodical."[53] But, more importantly, obscenity was re-defined as

> any literature which if, considered as a whole, its predominant appeal is [to] prurient interests, i.e., a shameful or morbid interest in nudity,

50. News Publishing Corp., Dee Publishing Co., Nugget Magazine, Inc., Mystery Publishing Co. v. Wesberry, unpublished decision (Jan. 21, 1957). See, "Literature Panel Act Upheld by U.S. Court," Atlanta Constitution, Jan. 5, 1957, 1.

51. "Suit Against Literary Board Dismissed by Judge Sloan," Atlanta Journal, Jan. 22, 1957, 9. As a result, the commission redoubled its efforts against obscenity, using stream-lined procedures adopted Jan. 25, 1957 (Wesberry, The Georgia Literature Commission at 15-17). See, Dorothy Cremin, "Censors Aim Harder Blow at Obscenity," Atlanta Journal-Constitution, Jan. 27, 1957, C1.

52. See also, 1964 Georgia Laws 161-165, which provided for the appointment of a full-time executive secretary and allowed the commission the power to seek declaratory judgements to stop distribution of obscene literature and to issue subpoenas to require testimony at its hearings.

53. Section 1(a), 1958 Georgia Laws 391.

sex or excretion, and if it goes substantially beyond customary limits of candor in description or representation of such matters.[54]

Through 1967, the commission was required to take legal action in only six instances.[55] However, it was the legal battle in one of these cases that (as was true with the Atlanta movie censor) signaled the beginning of the end of the commission's efforts.[56]

On August 19, 1966, the commission sought and received a declaratory judgment in Muscogee County Superior Court that Alan Marshall's *Sin Whisper* was obscene. A unanimous Georgia Supreme Court also sided with the commission, concluding that "in our view, the book is filthy and disgusting. Further description is not necessary, and we do not wish to sully the pages of the reported opinions of this court with it."[57] The U.S. Supreme Court, however, reversed the judgment in *Corinth Publications v. Wesberry*, without comment in a memorandum decision - without any explanation as to why the book was not obscene, without any comment about the standards applied by Georgia courts determining it to be obscene, and without any ruling on the constitutionality of the

54. Section 1(b), 1958 Georgia Laws 391. See also, Roth v. U.S./Alberts v. California, 354 U.S. 476 (1957) at 487.

55. The books involved were Turbulent Daughters (1958), Rambling Maids (1958), Strip Artist (1964), Campus Lust (1965), Lust Avenger (1965), and Sin Whisper (1965).

56. The book was distributed by Peachtree News Agency of Chamblee and sold by Mike's News Stand in Columbus.

57. Corinth Publications, Inc. v. Wesberry, 221 Ga. 704, 146 S.E.2d 764 (1966) at 710.

commission itself.[58] The commission ceased operations sometime after 1973, a victim of then-Governor Jimmy Carter's zero-based budgeting system, which required state agencies to justify their existence each fiscal year. Coupled with his and successive governors' failure to appoint replacements for the two commission members who died that year,[59] the agency was thereafter unable to conduct business as it never was able to have a quorum of its members present.

Throughout the 1960s, obscenity more and more became a federal question, rather than a state one. With increasing frequency, the U.S. Supreme Court - sometimes called the "High Court of Obscenity" during that period - accepted the task of deciding several cases involving challenges to Georgia's obscenity laws.

In 1968, for example, Robert E. Stanley was convicted of possessing obscene materials in violation of state law,[60] when several reels of film were discovered in a desk drawer by federal and state agents searching for evidence of alleged gambling activities. The Georgia Supreme Court upheld his conviction,[61] only to be overturned by the U.S. Supreme Court on the grounds that "the mere private possession of obscene matter cannot constitutionally be made a crime."[62] Writing for a

---

58. 388 U.S. 448 (1967), previous judgment vacated, 223 Ga. 497, 156 S.E.2d 346 (1967). See, "State Court Reversed on 'Sin Whisper,'" Atlanta Constitution, June 13, 1967, 8.

59. Because the commission was not mentioned in the Executive Reorganization Act of 1972, it continued unchanged as an independent agency. Although the 1953 statute creating the commission has never been rescinded by the General Assembly, the Georgia Constitution of 1983, Article IV, lists six constitutional boards and commissions, and the Georgia Literature Commission is not among them.

60. 1956 Georgia Laws 801; amended, 1963 Georgia Laws 78.

61. Stanley v. Georgia, 224 Ga. 259, 161 S.E.2d 309 (1968).

62. Stanley v. Georgia, 394 U.S. 558 (1969) at 559.

unanimous court, Justice Thurgood Marshall stated in *Stanley v. Georgia* that the

> mere categorization of these films as "obscene" is insufficient justification for such a drastic invasion of personal liberties.... Whatever may be the justifications for other statutes regulating obscenity, we do not think they reach into the privacy of one's own home. If the First Amendment means anything, it means that a State has no business telling a man, sitting alone in his own house, what books he may read or what films he may watch. Our whole constitutional heritage rebels at the thought of giving government the power to control men's minds.[63]

If nudity may then be viewed in the privacy of one's home, is there a constitutional right to view it in public? This was the question that arose in 1971 when Southeastern Promotions sought to book the Atlanta Civic Center for a presentation of the musical play, "Hair." Informed that "Hair" was not the type of family entertainment suitable for a public auditorium since it contained nudity, the company filed suit in federal district court.[64] Ruling that "the entire musical play 'Hair' [including the 35 seconds of nudity under subdued lighting] is ... entitled to First Amendment protection,"[65] the district court concluded that the auditorium, as a public forum, had to be made available to all and that mere "foul words and nudity ...

---

63. Id. at 565.

64. Southeastern Promotions, Ltd. v. Atlanta, 334 F.Supp. 634 (N.D. Ga. 1971).

65. Id. at 639.

are in and of themselves constitutionally protected forms of expression which may not be censored...."[66]

That same year, District Attorney Lewis Slaton and Solicitor General Hinson McAuliffe began a drive to force hard core pornographic films and publications out of Georgia. In what is probably the best known of these cases, Judge Jack Etheridge of the Fulton County Superior Court held that the films, "It All Comes Out in the End" (1970) and "Magic Mirror" (1970), being shown at Paris Adult Theaters, were not obscene, because "the portrayal of the sex act is undertaken, but the act itself is consistently only a simulated one if, indeed, the viewer can assume an act of intercourse or of fellatio is occurring from the machinations which are portrayed on the screen."[67]

The Georgia Supreme Court reversed the trial-level court, holding that the films were hard core pornography and concluding that "it is plain what they purport to depict, that is, conduct of the most salacious character."[68] The U.S. Supreme Court overturned that ruling and ordered the Georgia Supreme Court to re-evaluate state obscenity laws in view of recent standards set forth in *Miller v. California*.[69] This the Georgia

---

66. Id. at 642.

67. Judge Etheridge quoted in Slaton v. Paris Adult Theater I, 228 Ga. 343, 185 S.E.2d 768 (1971) at 343. Other films targeted included "I Am Curious (Yellow)" - see, Evans Theatre Corp. v. Slaton, 227 Ga. 676, 182 S.E.2d 464 (1971) - and "Deep Throat" - see, S.S.W. Corp. v. Slaton, 231 Ga. 734, 204 S.E.2d 155 (1974).

68. Id. at 347.

69. Paris Adult Theater I v. Slaton, 413 U.S. 49 (1973). See also, Miller v. California, 413 U.S. 15 (1973), in which the U.S. Supreme Court ruled that "the basic guidelines [for obscenity] must be: a) whether the average person, applying contemporary community standards, would find that the work, taken as a whole, appeals to the prurient interest; b) whether the work depicts or describes, in a patently offensive way, sexual conduct specifically

Supreme Court did, concluding that the Georgia statute[70] was consistent with the new *Miller* standards and that the films could still not be shown in Georgia.[71]

The Georgia Supreme Court, applying the new *Miller* standards to "Carnal Knowledge" (1971), then being shown in an Albany movie theater, decided that this film was also obscene.[72] A unanimous U.S. Supreme Court, with Justice William Rehnquist writing for the majority, disagreed in *Jenkins v. Georgia*, determining that the film "could not be found under the *Miller* standards to depict sexual conduct in a patently offensive way."[73] In other words, it had at least some serious artistic value. Clearly, the new *Miller* standards had not had the effect many had hoped; defining obscenity was almost as difficult as it ever was, which led one Georgia federal judge to lament, "It is a strange sort of Bill of Rights that guarantees the inalienable right to sell unspeakable filth."[74]

In 1975, Georgia enacted a new obscenity statute, more fully incorporating the *Miller* standards and, as demanded in *Miller*, defining sexual conduct according to applicable state law. Under Georgia law (see, Figure 7, p. 171), material was "obscene" if:

---

defined by the applicable state law; and c) whether the work, taken as a whole, lacks serious literary, artistic, political, or scientific value" (id. at 24). For an earlier, contrary view of the "state" community standard, see, for example, Feldschneider v. Georgia, 127 Ga. App. 745, 195 S.E.2d 184 (1972).

70. 1968 Georgia Laws 1249, 1302.

71. Slaton v. Paris Adult Theater I, 231 Ga. 312, 201 S.E.2d 456 (1973).

72. Jenkins v. Georgia, 230 Ga. 726, 199 S.E.2d 183 (1973).

73. 418 U.S. 153 (1974) at 161.

74. Chief Judge Alexander Lawrence in Gornto v. McDougall, 336 F.Supp. 1372 (S.D. Ga 1972) at 1377.

1) To the average person, applying contemporary community standards, taken as a whole, it predominantly appeals to the prurient interest, that is, a shameful or morbid interest in nudity, sex, or excretion;

2) The material taken as a whole lacks serious literary, artistic, political, or scientific value; and

3) The material depicts or describes, in a patently offensive way, sexual conduct specifically defined [as follows]:

   A) Acts of sexual intercourse, heterosexual or homosexual, normal or perverted, actual or simulated;

   B) Acts of masturbation;

   C) Acts involving excretory functions or lewd exhibition of the genitals;

   D) Acts of bestiality or the fondling of sex organs of animals; or

   E) Sexual acts of flagellation, torture, or other violence indicating a sadomasochistic sexual relationship.[75]

"Any device designed or marketed as useful primarily for the stimulation of human genital organs' was also by definition obscene,[76] as was the commercial marketing or "exploitation" of any non-obscene material in a prurient fashion.[77] However, the law did not apply if distribution of obscene material was restricted to college-level students and teachers studying it or to

---

75. O.C.G.A. 16-12-80(b) (2006).

76. O.C.G.A. 16-12-80(c) (2006).

77. O.C.G.A. 16-12-80(d) (2006). See, Morrison v. Georgia, 272 Ga. 129, 526 S.E.2d 336 (2000); Inserection, A Fantasy Store v. City of Marietta, 278 Ga. 170; 598 S.E.2d 452 (2004).

patients of doctors or psychiatrists who prescribed it. That was considered to be an "affirmative defense."[78]

GEORGIA'S 1975 OBSCENITY LAW: A SUMMARY
(Figure 7)

(a) Prohibited the "knowing" dissemination of "obscene" material – including the advertising of such material;

(b) Defines "obscene" material, according to the standards set forth in the U.S. Supreme Court's 1973 *Miller* test;

(c) Designated as "obscene" "any device designed or marketed as useful primarily for the stimulation of human genital organs;"

(d) Noted that non-obscene material may be legally "obscene" if its distribution is "commercial exploitation" "solely for the sake of [its] prurient appeal;"

(e) Allowed two groups to receive "obscene" material legally:

- a person studying such material in an institution of higher education; and
- a person who is prescribed such material by a "licensed medical practitioner or psychiatrist;"

(f) Determined the distribution of "obscene" material to be a "high and aggravated" misdemeanor.

- **O.C.G.A. 16-12-80 (2006)**

The courts have recognized that the distinction between what is and what is not obscene is a "dim and uncertain" line requiring "sensitive [definitional] tools."[79] As a result, the state bears the burden of proof in all obscenity cases.[80] However, it

---

78. O.C.G.A. 16-12-80(e) (2006).

79. See, Carter v. Gautier, 305 F.Supp. 1098 (M.D. Ga 1969). See also, Central Agency, Inc. v. Brown, 306 F.Supp. 502 (N.D. Ga. 1969).

80. See, for example, Sanders v. Georgia, 231 Ga. 608, 203 S.E.2d 153 (1974).

is possible for films containing nothing more than a public portrayal of hard core sexual conduct, shown only for the resulting commercial gain, to be "statutorily obscene."[81]

Beginning in 1977, McAuliffe initiated a series of lawsuits against various "men's magazines," which, to that point, had been sold legally in Atlanta. The following year, the publishers of *Oui*, *Playboy*, and *Penthouse* sued McAuliffe, who had been making high-profile arrests of magazine retailers, arguing that his tactics were a prior restraint in violation of the First and Fourteenth amendments and that their magazines were not obscene. The district court judge, Richard Freeman, agreed, finding that the January 1978 issues of the magazines had "significant literary, artistic, political, and scientific value which, independent of any other determinations which we have made, preclude finding them obscene."[82]

But because the court did not rule on the question of whether McAuliffe's tactics were a form of prior restraint, *Penthouse* - joined by *Playboy*, *Hustler*, *High Society*, *Eros*, and *Gallery* - appealed to the Fifth Circuit U.S. Court of Appeals. McAuliffe's tactics were found to be illegal, but at the same time the court found that the January 1978 issues of *Penthouse* and *Oui* were obscene, according to the *Miller* guidelines.[83] "The issue with respect to *Penthouse* and *Oui*," the court ruled, "is close but the numerous pictorials and

---

81. See, for example, Clayton v. Georgia, 149 Ga. App. 374, 254 S.E.2d 495 (1979).

82. Penthouse International, Ltd. v. McAuliffe, 454 F.Supp. 289 (N.D. Ga. 1978) at 304.

83. 413 U.S. 15 (1973) at 24.

obscene letters were not saved by the articles possessing some literary merit."[84]

The fight, however, may never be over, because while the courts have been willing to rule that individual issues of specific magazines violate Georgia's obscenity laws,[85] they are only willing to do so on a case-by-case or issue-by-issue basis.

In more recent years, the Georgia Supreme Court struck down a state indecency statute in *Cunningham v. Georgia*, because it prohibited "profane and lewd" language, in addition to obscenities,[86] signaling what may be the end of indecency regulation involving adults, when the words are not aimed at offending or provoking a particular audience to violence.

The protection of minors, however, is a proper object of regulation and appears to be the focus of future regulator efforts, though and a Riverdale shoe salesman who uttered a "barnyard epithet" in front of a child was not charged with violating the Georgia statute prohibiting the using of profane language in the presence of a child because the child was only 15 months old and unable to understand what was said.[87] The U.S. Supreme Court did refuse to hear and, thus, upheld a Georgia obscenity statute in 1991 aimed at keeping sexually explicit material deemed "harmful to minors" out of their possession while at the same time hampering adult access to

---

84. Penthouse International, Ltd v. McAuliffe, 610 F2d 1353 (1980) at 1372. For an item-by-item discussion of the judges' concerns, see, 1372-1373.

85. In this case, the September 1984 issue of Penthouse magazine. See, Penthouse International, Ltd. v. Webb, 594 F.Supp. 1186 (N.D. Ga. 1984).

86. 260 Ga. 827, 400 S.E.2d 916 (1991), interpreting O.C.G.A. 40-1-4. See, Mark Curriden, "The 'S' Word OK on Cars, High Court Decides, 4-3," Atlanta Journal-Constitution, Feb. 23, 1991, A1.

87. Scott Bowles, "Charges Dropped in Profanity Case," Atlanta Journal-Constitution, June 4, 1991, D3. See, O.C.G.A. 16-11-39.

otherwise protected expression.[88] And, in 1993, Georgia became the second state to outlaw the electronic transmission of computer-generated pornography to minors.[89]

On Feb. 15, 2006, the federal appellate court in Atlanta ruled that Georgia's obscenity statute was unconstitutional in that it improperly regulated commercial expression that was protected by the First Amendment.[90] In its ruling in *This That & the Other Gifts v. Cobb County*,[91] the court concluded that, because the state statute allowed "obscene" materials to be legally sold to certain groups, a complete ban on the advertising of personal sexual devices was more extensive than necessary.[92] This made Georgia "the only state in the nation without an

---

88. O.C.G.A. 16-12-102 through O.C.G.A. 16-12-104. See, American Booksellers Association, Inc. v. Webb, 643 F.Supp. 1546 (N.D. Ga. 1986), reversed, 919 F.2d 1493 (11th Cir. 1990), rehearing denied, 930 F.2d 925 (11th Cir. 1991), certiorari denied, 500 U.S. 942, (1991). See, Michelle Hiskey, "Court: Ga. Obscenity Law Stays on Books," Atlanta Journal-Constitution, May 29, 1991, D2; "New Obscenity Law Is a Dangerous Tool," Atlanta Constitution, June 1, 1991, A16.

89. Florida was the first. See, O.C.G.A. 16-12-100.1. See also, Lucy Soto, "Wall a Pioneer in Fight Against On-Line Porn," Atlanta Journal-Constitution, June 17, 1995, J1.

90. See, Meredith Hobbs, "Adult Entertainment Lawyer Prevails at 11th Circuit in Battle Over Obscenity Law," Daily Report, March 24, 2006, Law.com, available at: http://www.law.com/jsp/article.jsp?id=900005548322&Adult Entertainment Lawyer Prevails at 11th Circuit in Battle Over Obscenity Law (last accessed Nov. 15, 2013).

91. 439 F.3d 1275 (11th Cir. 2006). See also, This That & the Other v. Cobb County, 285 F.3d 1319 (11th Cir. 2002).

92. In reaching this conclusion, the court applied the Central Hudson test to the advertising prohibition in Georgia's obscenity law. See, Central Hudson Gas & Electric Corp. v. Public Service Commission, 447 U.S. 551 (1980) at 566.

obscenity statute,"[93] though obscenity can be and is still regulated under the U.S. Supreme Court's *Miller* test.[94]

In the five years since the court's ruling, the Georgia General Assembly has failed twice to enact a new statute, which would have allowed the advertising – not just dissemination – of "obscene" material to any individual legally able to receive it. The legislature's first attempt – Senate Bill 631 – in the 2005-2006 legislative session was hampered by the fact that the court's ruling was handed down about half-way through the legislature's 40-day annual session. The bill was given a favorable report by the Senate Judiciary Committee, but was not introduced in the state House of Representatives and, as a result, not enacted into law prior to adjournment.[95] Its second attempt – House Bill 226 – in the 2007-2008 legislative session was passed by the House and revised by the Senate Judiciary Committee but not voted on by the Senate or enacted into law prior to adjournment.[96] Nothing has happened legislatively since, and the old statute remains improperly listed as part of the current Official Code of Georgia Annotated.

However, as of late 2013, Georgia remains without a state obscenity statute defining and regulating the dissemination of "obscene" materials,[97] depending upon how the federal court's

---

93. "Federal Court Declares Georgia's Obscenity Statute Unconstitutional," Cook, Youngelson & Wiggins, Attorneys (undated), previously available at: http://www.cywlaw.com/lawyer-attorney-1122615.html (copy on file with author).

94. Miller v. California, 413 U.S. 15 (1973) at 24.

95. See, Georgia General Assembly, Senate Bill 631 (2006), available at: http://www.legis.ga.gov/Legislation/en-US/display/20052006/SB/631 (last accessed Nov. 15, 2013).

96. See, Georgia General Assembly, House Bill 226 (2007), available at: http://www.legis.ga.gov/Legislation/en-US/display/20072008/HB/226 (last accessed Nov. 15, 2013).

97. The research in this work is current through Nov. 15, 2013.

ruling is interpreted. Some have argued that the impact of the federal court's ruling is, at best, uncertain and that the court struck down "at least a portion" of the law, but not the entire statute.[98] Others believe the entire statute "was struck down in 2006."[99] The federal appellate court's response on April 14, 2006, to Cobb County's "Petition for Rehearing and Petition for Rehearing En Banc" "clearly holds" that the "entire" Georgia obscenity statute was unconstitutional (see Figure 8, pp. 177-178.)

---

98. Doug Nurse, "Obscenity Ruling's Impact Uncertain," Atlanta Journal-Constitution, Feb. 23, 2006, page number unknown, available at: http://www.highbeam.com/doc/1G1-142447870.html (last accessed Nov. 15, 2013); previously available at: http://www.ajc.com/metro/content/metro/stories/0223adultstores.html (copy on file with author). See also, "Court Nixes Part of Ga. Obscenity Law," Southern Voice, undated, previously available at: http://www.legalview.info/msn/court-nixes-part-of-ga-obscenity-law/6828/ (copy on file with author); Coley Ward, "It's Obscene! And Now It Could Be Legal," Creative Loafing, Feb. 22, 2006, available at: http://clatl.com/atlanta/its-obscene-and-now-it-could-be-legal/Content?oid=1256044 (last accessed Nov. 15, 2013).

99. Sarah Campbell, "Tennessee Attorney Will Represent Coweta in Starship Case," Newnan Times-Herald, Feb. 12, 2010, available at: http://www.times-herald.com/Local/Tennessee-attorney-will-represent-Coweta-in-Starship-case--992273 (last accessed Nov. 15, 2013). See, "Georgia Obscenity Law Struck Down by 11th Circuit," Associated Press News Service, Feb. 23, 2006, available at: http://www.firstamendmentcenter.org/ga-obscenity-law-struck-down-by-11th-circuit (last accessed Nov. 15, 2013); and "Court Strikes Down Georgia Obscenity Law," First Coast News, Feb. 23, 2006, available at: http://www.firstcoastnews.com/news/local/storye.aspx?storyid=52469 (last accessed Nov. 15, 2013).

GEORGIA'S OBSCENITY STATUTE UNCONSTITUTIONAL
(Figure 8)

IN THE UNITED STATES COURT OF APPEALS

FOR THE ELEVENTH CIRCUIT

No. 04-16419

FILED
U.S. COURT OF APPEALS
ELEVENTH CIRCUIT

APR 1 4 2006

THOMAS K. KAHN
CLERK

THIS THAT AND THE OTHER GIFT AND TOBACCO, INC.,
d.b.a. This That & The Other,
CHRISTOPHER PREWETT,

Plaintiffs-Appellants,

versus

COBB COUNTY, GEORGIA,
PAUL FOSTER,
in his official capacity as
Business License Division Manager
for Cobb County, Georgia,
THURBERT E. BAKER, in his official capacty
as Attorney General for the State of Georgia,

Defendants-Appellees.

On Appeal from the United States District Court
for the Northern District of Georgia

ON PETITION FOR REHEARING AND PETITION FOR REHEARING EN BANC

BEFORE BLACK, HULL and FARRIS*, Circuit Judges.

*Honorable Jerome Farris, United States Circuit Judge for the Ninth Circuit, sitting by designation.

GEORGIA'S OBSCENITY STATUTE
UNCONSTITUTIONAL
(Figure 8, continued)

PER CURIAM:

The Petition for Rehearing is DENIED as our panel opinion clearly holds that, based on the law of the case, the entire O.C.G.A. § 16-12-80 is unconstitutional and directs the district court to enter summary judgment for the plaintiffs. *This That and The Other Gift and Tobacco, Inc. v. Cobb County, Ga.*, 439 F.3d 1275, 1283-85 (11th Circ. 2006). No Judge in regular active service on the Court having requested that the Court be polled on rehearing en banc (Rule 35, Federal Rules of Appellate Procedure), the Petition for Rehearing En Banc is DENIED.

ENTERED FOR THE COURT:

_____
UNITED STATES CIRCUIT JUDGE

2

QUESTIONS

1. What two groups could legally view obscene material in Georgia, according to the state obscenity statute, before the 2006 ruling in *This That & the Other Gifts v. Cobb County*?

2. Georgia's 1975 obscenity statute essentially codified what U.S. Supreme Court decision?

3. In what Georgia case was the national right to possess pornography in the privacy of one's home established?

4. On what legal grounds did the U.S. Supreme Court, in *Jenkins v. Georgia* (1973), determine the film "Carnal Knowledge" (1971) not to be obscene?

5. What legal significance did the U.S. Supreme Court's decision in *Corinth Publications v. Wesberry* (1967) have for Georgia obscenity law?

6. As the result of what case did the Georgia Supreme Court classify Atlanta's film censorship ordinance as a "prior restraint"?

7. In what circumstances is indecent language not allowed in Georgia?

Thought Question:

How may Georgia obscenity/indecency law be viewed as an affirmation of the state's social and cultural status quo? How can anything be viewed as obscene in a society that values cultural pluralism and diversity?

8. Open Meetings/Records in Georgia

D emocracy, at its very core, requires openness,[1] because history teaches that "secrecy aids tyranny, abets corruption and hides incompetence."[2] Yet, the development of administrative law and the so-called "alphabet" agencies, social problems and solutions which have become increasingly complex, and the degree to which secrecy facilitates general efficiency of operation all have had the effect of keeping voters less and less in touch with the government they elected. Those who take their obligations of citizenship seriously "study their governors, challenge the decisions they make and petition or vote for change when change is needed. But no citizen can carry out these responsibilities when government is secret."[3] In Georgia, these obligations are

> enforceable in a court of law. Public men and women, above all others must act in good faith. Neither facile excuse nor clever dissimulation can serve in the stead of duty - faithfully performed. Because public men and women are amenable "at all times" to the people, they

---

1. For a discussion of the ramifications of this premise, see, for example, Perry Sentell Jr., "The Omen of 'Openness' in Local Government Law," 13 Georgia Law Review 97 (1978).

2. "The Public's Right to Know," Atlanta Constitution, Feb. 15, 1992, A22. "Publicity" – or government openness – "is justly commended as a remedy for social and industrial diseases. Sunlight is said to be the best of disinfectants." Louis Brandeis, Other People's Money (1933 ed.) at 62.

3. Reporters Committee for Freedom of the Press, Tapping Officials' Secrets: The Door to Open Government in Georgia (1989), i.

must conduct the public's business out in the open.[4]

Georgia's commitment to openness can be traced back to an 1831 statute which required "books of account" be available and open for public inspection.[5] Today, its "Open Georgia" website[6] – which went online in 2009, devoted to "transparency in government" and maintained by the state Department of Audits & Accounts – makes available state financial reports, employee salary and travel reimbursement information, state program reviews, grant and contract payments to vendors by state agencies, sales taxes being used for educational purposes, and other financial expenditure information in one, easy-to-find location.[7] And, since 2011, counties, municipalities, school districts, law enforcement agencies, and other governmental entities have been required to submit their annual reports and budgets to the Carl Vinson Institute for Government at the University of Georgia for posting on the institute's website, though only about half now comply.[8]

But though "the strong public policy of [Georgia] is in favor of open government [which] is essential to a free, open,

---

4. Chief Justice Charles Weltner concurring, in Davis v. Macon, 262 Ga. 407, 421 S.E.2d 278 (1992) at 407-408.

5. 1831 Georgia Laws 195.

6. Available at: http://www.open.georgia.gov/ (last accessed Nov. 15, 2013). See, O.C.G.A. 50-6-27, O.C.G.A. 50-6-32.

7. O.C.G.A. 50-6-32, O.C.G.A. 48-8-141.

8. O.C.G.A. 36-80-21. See, 2010 Georgia Laws 519. The statute applies to counties and municipalities with an annual budget in excess of $1 million. The institute's website is available at: http://www.cviog.uga.edu/ (last accessed Nov. 15, 2013). See also, Walter Jones, "Transparency Law Slow to Be Implemented," Athens Banner-Herald, June 3, 2012, available at: http://onlineathens.com/local-news/2012-06-03/transparency-law-slow-be-implemented (last accessed June 4, 2012).

and democratic society,"[9] state and local government entities have also always been slow to conform to Georgia's commitments to and demands for transparency, and the state itself has not consistently enforced its own sunshine laws,[10] because they were *"fuzzy"* and *"more confusing than constructive."*[11] As a result, a significant revision of the open meetings and open records statutes was enacted by the General Assembly in 2012,[12] including clearer language, making

---

9. O.C.G.A. 50-18-70.

10. See, Greg Bluestein, "Georgia Is Not Prosecuting Sunshine Cases," Daily Report, March 14, 2011, page number unknown.

11. Sam Olens & Jay Powell, "New Bill Aims to Bring Clarity to State's Fuzzy Sunshine Law," Atlanta Journal-Constitution, March 11, 2012, A21; Attorney General Sam Olens quoted in, "Attorney General Sam Olens Seeks to Strengthen & Clarify State Sunshine Laws," Georgia Dept. of Law, Feb. 28, 2011, available at: http://law.ga.gov/press-releases/2011-02-28/attorney-general-sam-olens-seeks-strengthen-and-clarify-state-sunshine (last accessed Nov. 15, 2013).

12. Georgia General Assembly, House Bill 397 (2012), available at: http://www.legis.ga.gov/Legislation/20112012/127646.pdf (last accessed Nov. 15, 2013). 2012 Georgia Laws 218. See, Kathleen Joyner, "Olens Looks to Revise Open Records Act," Daily Report, Feb. 16, 2011, 1, 4; Kathleen Joyner, "Olens Details Proposed Open Records Changes," Daily Report, Feb. 25, 2011, page number unknown; Kathleen Joyner, "Open Records Overhaul Filed, Daily Report, March 2, 2011, page number unknown; Kristina Torres, "Fines Likely to Rise for 'Sunshine Law' Violations, Atlanta Journal-Constitution, Aug. 31, 2011, B2; Bill Rankin, "Sunshine Laws May Get Improvements," Atlanta Journal-Constitution, Feb. 16, 2012, B1, B7; Kathleen Joyner, "Open Gov't Bill Moving Forward," Daily Report, Feb. 17, 2012, 1, 4; Kathleen Joyner, "Open Records Requests Carry New Price Tag Under Legislation," Daily Report, Feb. 24, 2012, 1, 4; Bill Rankin, "Sunshine Law Rewrite Makes It Through," Atlanta Journal-Constitution, March 30, 2012, A15; Aaron Sheinin & Bill Rankin, "Governor Signs Rewrite into Law," Atlanta Journal-Constitution, April 18, 2012, B1, B7. See also, Anna Adams & Lisa Scatamacchia, "State Government – HB 397," 29 Georgia State University Law Review 139 (2012), available at: http://digitalarchive.gsu.edu/gsulr/vol29/iss1/6 (last accessed Nov. 15, 2013).

enforcement easier, eliminating "some reasons governments have used to withhold electronic records, [reducing] the cost of copying paper documents, [while] also [making] more things private [and making] it easier to 'put the fear of God in people so they'll behave'."[13]

---

13. Ty Tagami, "New Law Lets More Light In," Atlanta Journal-Constitution, April 22, 2012, at B1. Tricia Knor of Cobb County, quoted in Ty Tagami, id., at B7. See, David Hudson, "Georgia Press Association General Counsel: Most Open Meetings Act Revisions 'Positive'," Daily Report, March 4, 2011, 5, 10; Shawn McIntosh, "Clearing Up Sunshine Laws," Atlanta Journal-Constitution, April 8, 2012, A19. A very good summary of the 2012 revisions, by the Georgia First Amendment Foundation, may be found at: http://www.gfaf.org/wp-content/uploads/2012/05/Georgias-Open-Meeting-and-Records-Laws-Effective-04-17-12-FINAL1.pdf (last accessed Nov. 15, 2013). The first test of the new law was scheduled to be Tisdale v. Cumming, No. A13A2226, Georgia Court of Appeals (July 19, 2013). See, Patrick Fox, "Cumming Faces Open Meetings Complaint," Atlanta Journal-Constitution, April 23, 2012, page number unknown. See also, Olens v. Gravitt, No. 12-CV-1205, Superior Court of Forsyth County (June 5, 2012); Jeffry Scott, "Attorney General Files Court Complaint Against Cumming Mayor Henry Gravitt," Atlanta Journal-Constitution, June 6, 2012, available at: http://www.ajc.com/news/forsyth/attorney-general-files-court-1453231.html (last accessed June 7, 2012); Kathleen Joyner, "AG Targets Cumming with First Sunshine Suit," Daily Report, June 7, 2012, page number unknown; Pat Fox, "Cumming Maintains in Court That It Did Not Violate Open Meetings Law," Atlanta Journal-Constitution, July 25, 2013, available at: http://www.ajc.com/news/news/cumming-maintains-in-court-that-it-did-not-violate-/nY4Ps/ (last accessed Nov. 6, 2013).There has been no resolution of either lawsuit as of Nov. 15, 2013.

DEFINITION OF "PUBLIC AGENCY"
(Figure 9)

(A) Every state department, agency, board, bureau, office, commission, public corporation, and authority;

(B) Every county, municipal corporation, school district, or other political subdivision of this state;

(C) Every department, agency, board, bureau, commission, authority, or similar body of each such county, municipal corporation, or other political subdivision of the state;

(D) Every city, county, regional, or other authority established pursuant to the laws of this state; and

(E) Any nonprofit organization to which there is a direct allocation of tax funds made by the governing authority of any agency ... and which constitutes more than 33 1/3 percent of the funds from all sources of such organization; provided, however, that this ... shall not include hospitals, nursing homes, dispensers of pharmaceutical products, or any other type organization, person, or firm furnishing medical or health services to a citizen for which they receive reimbursement from the state...; nor shall this term include a sub-agency or affiliate of such a nonprofit organization from or through which the allocation of tax funds is made.

- O.C.G.A. 50-14-1(a)(1) (2013)

Open Meetings

With the passage of the Georgia Open Meetings Act of 1965,[14] the Georgia General Assembly guaranteed access to meetings of "every" state, county, regional authority,

---

14. The act was approved March 5, 1965. See, 1965 Georgia Laws 118. Section 1 was codified as O.C.G.A. 50-14-1(a)(A-D); section 2 was codified as O.C.G.A. 50-14-6.

municipality, school district, or "other political subdivision"[15] - whether the body be appointed or elected - and to meetings of non-profit organizations which receive one-third or more of their funds from tax revenues (see, Figure 9, p. 185).[16]

Advisory groups and quasi-governmental bodies, however, are not subject to the law, because they "are organized and meet for the purpose of collecting information, making recommendations, and rendering advice, but ... have no authority to make governmental decisions and act for the State."[17] Additionally, neither the Office of the Governor,[18] nor state legislative bodies - such as the General Assembly and its committees, as determined by the Georgia Supreme Court in *Coggin v. Davey*[19] - nor the courts themselves are subject to the

---

15. O.C.G.A. 50-14-1-(a)(1)(A-D). Multi-state organizations would not fall in this category.

16. O.C.G.A. 50-14-1(a)(1)(E). This section was added in 1988, and includes university student government meetings. See, Chris Shattuck, "Student Government in Violation of State Law," GSU Signal, Oct. 25, 2011, 1, 2; Jocelyn Crawley, "University Condemns SGA Closed Meetings," GSU Signal, Nov. 1, 2011, 2. A recent question was whether this included local chambers of commerce. See, Mark Niesse, "Suit: Chamber Records Are Public," Daily Report, Nov. 28, 2012, 1, 7; David Wickert & Nancy Badertscher, "Gwinnett Chamber, Commission Sued," Atlanta Journal-Constitution, Nov. 29, 2012, B2.

17. McLarty v. Board of Regents, 231 Ga. 22, 200 S.E.2d 117 (1973) at 22-23 (where a student-faculty advisory committee making recommendations for the allocation of student activity funds was not subject to the law). See also, The Atlanta Journal v. Hill, 257 Ga. 398, 359 S.E.2d 913 (1987) (where a mayoral administrative review panel with no official power was not subject to the law).

18. See, Willoughby Mariano, "Olens Spot-On: Governor Exempt from Open Meetings Act, Atlanta Journal-Constitution, Aug. 16, 2011, B1, B3.

19. 233 Ga. 407, 211 S.E.2d 708 (1975). See, South Georgia Power Co. v. Baumann, 169 Ga. 649, 151 S.E.2d 513 (1929). The Georgia Constitution requires "sessions of the General Assembly and all standing committee meetings" to be open, but allows either house to make exceptions to this rule

provisions of the act.[20] The extent to which groups like the Atlanta Committee for the Olympic Games[21] - private, non-

(Georgia Constitution of 1983, Article III, § IV, ¶ IX). For example, the Senate confines reporters to the rear of the chamber (Senate Rule 17). The House allows reporters on the floor, only if they display their credentials at all times (House Rule 12). Reporters cannot move about on the floor of either house during proceedings. Photographers are allowed on the Senate floor under certain conditions, in the House photographers must take pictures from a designated area. The House allows committee meetings concerning acquisitions of real estate to be closed by majority vote (House Rule 8). It also has the authority to close conference committee meetings with the Senate (House Rule 146). In Murphy v. American Civil Liberties Union of Georgia, Inc., 258 Ga. 637, 373 S.E.2d 364 (1988), Justice Charles L. Weltner, concluding that the internal operating procedures of legislative conference and interim committees were not subject to judicial review, said a constitutional amendment was the only solution. See, "High Court Cannot Force Legislature to Follow Law," News Media & the Law (Winter 1989), 14-15.

20. See, Fathers Are Parents Too v. Hunstein, 202 Ga. App. 716, 415 S.E.2d 322 (1992).

21. See, David Hudson, "Covering the 1996 Olympics - From a Legal Standpoint," Georgia Press Association Editor's Forum (Winter 1991), 4; Bert Roughton Jr., "Secrecy by ACOG Elicits Anger, Bewilderment," Atlanta Journal-Constitution, May 24, 1993, B1, B5. See also, Kathey Pruitt & Melissa Turner, "Barnes Seeks Ruling, Says He Would Open Games Records," March 13, 1999, Atlanta Journal-Constitution, A1; Kathey Pruitt & Melissa Turner, "State May Seek Release of Records," Atlanta Journal-Constitution, March 16, 1999, F8; Colin Campbell, "Here's Some Radical Advice - Open Records," Atlanta Journal-Constitution, March 23, 1999, B2; Melissa Turner, "Personal Olympic Documents Put Off Limits," Atlanta Journal-Constitution, April 7, 1999, B1; Colin Campbell, "Files Finally Going Public, But at Such a Costly Price," Atlanta Journal-Constitution, April 29, 1999, B2; Melissa Turner, "Documents Give Clues, Not Whole Picture," Atlanta Journal-Constitution, May 1, 1999, A1, A4; Jere Longman, "Salt Lake City's Olympic Spirit Found in Atlanta," New York Times, May 1, 1999, B6; Colin Campbell, "More Secrecy Only Raises More Questions," Atlanta Journal-Constitution, May 1, 1999, A4; Melissa Turner, "State Rules Records Should Be Open," Atlanta Journal-Constitution, May 6, 1999, A1, A10; Colin Campbell, "Barnes: Open Bid Records So Public Has Confidence in Process," Atlanta Journal-Constitution, May 9, 1999, A13; Melissa

profit corporations which act on behalf of state and local governments doing such things as organizing the 1996 Summer Olympics - are public agencies appears to have been finally resolved in *Central Atlanta Progress v. Baker*, where private entities "working on behalf of public offices or agencies" are subject to open government requirements.[22]

A particular meeting is covered by the open meetings statute if it passes a two-part test:

- The meeting must be a quorum "of the governing body of an agency" or any committee thereof; and

---

Turner, "Media Sue To See Files on Games," Atlanta Journal-Constitution, May 20, 1999, D2; Colin Campbell, "With Records Kept Hidden, Payne Free To Cleanse Past," Atlanta Journal-Constitution, June 6, 1999, C3; Melissa Turner, "Access to Olympic Files Limited," Atlanta Journal-Constitution, June 18, 1999, A1, A20; Melissa Turner, "Payne Agrees To Open All But 8 Boxes," Atlanta Journal-Constitution, July 2, 1999, A9; Jay Croft, "Olympic Records Access Fight Goes to Fulton Judge," Atlanta Journal-Constitution, July 9, 1999, B2; Colin Campbell, "Public vs. Private: Olympics Case About More Than Papers," Atlanta Journal-Constitution, July 11, 1999, C3; Melissa Turner, "Treasure Trove of Records Will Open," Atlanta Journal-Constitution, July 18, 1999, F1, F3; Melissa Turner, "Viewing Records Is Not Easy," Atlanta Journal-Constitution, July 18, 1999, F1; "Media Seek Look at Boxes of Records," Atlanta Journal-Constitution, July 20, 1999, B1; Colin Campbell, "Result of Unanswered Olympic Questions Is ... More Questions," Atlanta Journal-Constitution, Aug. 15, 1999, F3; Christopher Quinn, "The Lawsuit: Paper, Baker Get Their Wish," Atlanta Journal-Constitution, Sept. 17, 1999, page number unknown; Colin Campbell, "Feds Funds for Games Justify Open Records," Atlanta Journal-Constitution, Jan. 6, 2000, B2; Colin Campbell, "Olympic Files Should Be Preserved," Atlanta Journal-Constitution, Feb. 15, 2000, B2; Melissa Turner, "Atlanta Olympic Records Going to Colorado," Atlanta Journal-Constitution, Feb. 29, 2000, D3; Colin Campbell, "Barnes: State Could Take Games Records," Atlanta Journal-Constitution, May 24, 2000, F1, F5; and Melissa Turner, "Treating History as Private Property," Atlanta Journal-Constitution, Aug. 6, 2000, B5.

22. 278 Ga. App. 733, 629 S.E.2d 840 (2006) at 737.

- The meeting is one "at which any official business, policy, or public matter" is to be "discussed or voted upon" or at which official action is to be taken.[23]

Meetings take place, according to the statute, whenever a quorum of any agency or any committee of the agency convenes, by prior arrangement to discuss or take action on official business or policy.[24] Both visual and sound recording is

---

23. Red & Black Publishing Co. v. Board of Regents, 262 Ga. 848, 427 S.E.2d 257 (1993) at 853. See also, O.C.G.A. 50-14-1(a)(3).

24. See, O.C.G.A. 50-14-1(a)(3). However, "the gathering of a quorum ... for the purpose of making inspections of physical facilities or property ... for the purposes of attending [meetings] ... for the purpose of meeting with [government] officials ... for the purpose of traveling to a meeting ... or gathering ... at social, ceremonial, civic, or religious events so long as no official business ... is ... discussed or voted upon" (id.). For an example of this, see, Maria Elena Fernandez, "Snellville Officials' Dec. 29 Confab Didn't Violate State Law, Solicitor Finds," Atlanta Journal-Constitution, Jan. 21, 1995, J12. See also, Gumz v. Irvin, 300 Ga. App. 426, 685 S.E.2d 392 (2009) (where an unscheduled "gathering" was not a meeting). The Georgia Press Association advises journalists attempting to cover closed meetings to carry a copy of the law with them and to insist politely but firmly on the importance of public participation:

> The Georgia Open Meetings law, Section 50-14-1 of the Official Code of Georgia Annotated, requires that all meetings of state and local boards or commissions and there committees be open to the public unless there is a specific statutory exemption. If I am ordered to leave (or forbidden to enter) this meeting, I ask that you advise me of the statutory authority for your action. Otherwise, my editors have instructed me to insist on my right to stay.

Georgia Press Association, Legal Survival Kit [1989] at 7. See also, David Hudson, "GPA Counsel Tells How to Cover a Closed Meeting," Georgia Press Association Editor's Forum (Summer 1989), 4. If all else fails, Hudson advises that all possible sources of information be interviewed about the

permitted, although the statute does not explicitly address the broadcasting of meetings.[25] The times and places of regular meetings must be posted in a "conspicuous place" at the meeting's location[26] and minutes generally made available within two business days.[27] Special or emergency meetings, or meetings being held at a different place or time, require twenty-four hours advance notice in the legal publication of the county.[28] Statutory requirements regarding minutes are the

---

meeting.

25. O.C.G.A. 50-14-1(c).

26. O.C.G.A. 50-14-1(d). Notice of regular meetings must be made a-vailable at lease one week in advance. See, for example, Duane D. Stanford, "Parole Board Didn't Give Notice of Meeting," Atlanta Journal-Constitution, Nov. 27, 2002, B3.

27. O.C.G.A. 50-14-1(e). Minimally, the minutes must contain "the names of the members present at the meeting, a description of each motion or other proposal made, the identity of the persons making and seconding the motion or other proposal, and a record of all votes. The name of each person voting for or against a proposal shall be recorded. It shall be presumed that the action taken was approved by each person in attendance unless the minutes reflect the name of the persons voting against a proposal or abstaining" (id.). This also holds true for non-roll-call votes. See, Cardinale v. Atlanta, 290 Ga. 521, 722 S.E.2d 732 (2012) at 524. Superior courts of Georgia have jurisdiction over violations of the law. See, O.C.G.A. 50-14-5. Suits must be filed within 90 days from the date of the agency's action. See, O.C.G.A. 50-14-1(b). Appeals filed beyond that time will fail. See, Anti-Landfill Corp. v. North American Metal, 299 Ga. App. 509, 683 S.E.2d 88 (2009).

28. O.C.G.A. 50-14-1(d). If circumstances require the meeting to be held with less than 24 hours notice, the agency must orally notify the county's legal publication or newspaper as quickly as possible. As with regularly scheduled meetings, a public agenda is not required. The additional requirement that a written notice of special meetings be posted 24 hours in advance is required in towns where the legal paper is published less than four times weekly. See, "New Changes In Open Meetings Law to Require More Notice of Special Meetings," Georgia Press Bulletin, July 22, 1993, 3. If circumstances require that a meeting be moved, the agency is not required to

same for those of regular meetings. Actions taken in improperly called or improperly closed meetings are not valid if action is taken within ninety days to challenge the agency's decision.[29] In addition, the attorney general may bring a civil or criminal action to force compliance with the law.[30]

The bottom line is simple: Whatever types of discussion may take place behind closed doors, all votes must be taken in public.[31]

Before any meeting can be properly closed to the public, the agency must vote on a formal motion to close the meeting and the specific reasons - along with the names of those voting for closure - entered in the minutes.[32] Once the discussion in the closed session, such as an agency's consultation with its attorney regarding pending legal action, turns to topics not

---

provide adequate seating for all who wish to attend. See, Maxwell v. Carney, 273 Ga. 864, 548 S.E.2d 293 (2001); Slaughter v. Brown, 269 Ga. App. 211, 603 S.E.2d 706 (2004).

29. O.C.G.A. 50-14-1(b). "Any person knowingly and willingly conducting or participating" in an illegal meeting is guilty of a misdemeanor and subject to a fine of $1,000. See, O.C.G.A. 50-14-6. "In most instances, the burden of forcing elected officials to abide by these statutes falls on the shoulders of journalists" (Walter Geiger, "Is Your City Council Violating the Open Meetings Law?" Georgia Press Bulletin, February 1994, 1). See also, H.G. Brown Family v. Villa Rica, 278 Ga. 819, 607 S.E.2d 883 (2005).

30. O.C.G.A. 50-14-5. See also, "State Government - Open and Public Meetings: Authorize Attorney General To Bring Civil or Criminal Actions To Enforce Georgia Open and Public Meetings Laws," 15 Georgia State University Law Review 242 (Fall 1998). Attorneys fees may also be awarded. See, Evans County Board of Commissioners v. Claxton Enterprise, 255 Ga. App. 656, 566 S.E.2d 399 (2002).

31. But, see, for example, Jeremy Redmon, "Secret Votes Common in Cobb – School Board Says It Will Change That Habit," Atlanta Journal-Constitution, July 11, 2009, A1, A12.

32. O.C.G.A. 50-14-4. See also, Georgia Press Association, "How a Government Agency Can Properly Close a Meeting," Legal Survival Kit [1989] at 6.

exempted from the Open Meetings Act, the meeting must then be re-opened to the public.[33]

The statute lists eight exemptions to openness and four justifications for closed executive sessions,[34] and does not diminish the scope of attorney-client privilege[35] or affect "those tax matters which are otherwise made confidential by state law."[36] The eight exemptions are:

1. Staff meetings held for investigative purposes;[37]
2. Deliberations of the state Board of Pardons and Parole;[38]
3. Meetings of the Georgia Bureau of Investigation or any other state law enforcement agency meetings, including grand jury deliberations;[39]
4. Adoption proceedings;[40]
5. Gatherings involving neutral third parties to help mediate disputes;[41]

---

33. See "Closing Off Constituents: Secretive DeKalb County Leaders Broke the Law," Atlanta Constitution, May 18, 1998, editorial page; and "DeKalb Leaders Broke the Law," Atlanta Constitution, June 2, 1998, editorial page.

34. O.C.G.A. 50-14-3(a)(1-8), O.C.G.A. 50-14-3(b)(1-4).

35. O.C.G.A. 50-14-2(1). See, Local Division 732, Amalgamated Transit Union v. Metropolitan Atlanta Rapid Transit Authority, 251 Ga. 15, 303 S.E.2d 1 (1983), certiorari granted and vacated on other grounds, 465 U.S. 1016 (1984); Schoen v. Cherokee County, 242 Ga. App. 501, 530 S.E.2d 226 (2000); Claxton Enterprise v. Evans County Board of Commissioners, 249 Ga. App. 870, 549 S.E.2d 830 (2001).

36. O.C.G.A. 50-14-2(2).

37. O.C.G.A. 50-14-3(a)(1).

38. O.C.G.A. 50-14-3(a)(2). Yet, see, O.C.G.A. 42-9-53, which requires hearings of the board to be open to the public.

39. O.C.G.A. 50-14-3(a)(3).

40. O.C.G.A. 50-14-3(a)(4).

41. O.C.G.A. 50-14-3(a)(5).

6. Meetings of public hospital authorities, health care facilities, public regulatory agencies, or similar bodies, when conducting staff evaluations[42] or discussing the granting of abortions;[43]

7. "Incidental conversation unrelated to the business of the agency;"[44]

8. E-mail communication not subject to open records requirements;[45]

The additional four justifications for closed executive sessions include:

9. Times during meetings when the agency is discussing – but not voting on - the future acquisition or disposal of real estate;[46]

---

42. O.C.G.A. 31-7-133.

43. O.C.G.A. 50-14-3(a)(6).

44. O.C.G.A. 50-14-3(a)(7).

45. O.C.G.A. 50-14-3(a)(8). "Doing business" by e-mail is, however, subject to open meetings/records requirements. See, Ty Tagami, "Cobb School Board Faces Complaints about Doing Business by Private E-Mail," Atlanta Journal-Constitution, July 29, 2011, available at: http://www.ajc.com/news/cobb/cobb-school-board-faces-1058604.html (last accessed Aug. 1, 2011).

46. O.C.G.A. 50-14-3(b)(1). The statute's 2012 requirement that "all votes at any meeting shall be taken in public" appears to eviscerate the ruling in Johnson v. Bibb County, 302 Ga. App. 266, 690 S.E.2d 912 (2010). Gwinnett County commissioners in the past have voted to purchase property in closed session, in violation of the Open Meetings Act. See, Duane Stanford, "Private Vote Called Illegal," Atlanta Journal-Constitution, May 18, 2005, page number unknown; Duane Stanford, "Gwinnett's Secret Vote Faulted," Atlanta Journal-Constitution, May 19, 2005, page number unknown; Duane Stanford, "Gwinnett Stands by Secret Vote," Atlanta Journal-Constitution, May 21, 2005, E1, E2; Duane Stanford, "Gwinnett Discloses Secret Vote for Parkland," Atlanta Journal-Constitution, Aug. 12, 2005, D1, D4; D. Aileen Dodd & Laura Diamond, "In Gwinnett, Critics

10. Times during meetings when the agency is discussing employment, compensation, including the "interviewing of applicants for the position of the executive head of an agency," except that all votes must be taken in public.[47]

11. Meetings of trustees of Georgia's public retirement

Decry Secrecy in Land Purchases," Atlanta Journal-Constitution, Aug. 13, 2005, E1, E3; Duane Stanford, "Parkland a Costly Purchase," Atlanta Journal-Constitution, Aug. 23, 2005, B1, B5; Duane Stanford, "Gwinnett Defends Secrecy," Atlanta Journal-Constitution, Aug. 28, 2005, C3; Duane Stanford, "Gwinnett Rethinks Land Secrecy," Atlanta Journal-Constitution, Sept. 1, 2005, C1, C6; Duane Stanford, "Gwinnett Halts Land Deals To Study Secret Vote Policy," Atlanta Journal-Constitution, Sept. 7, 2005, B1, B5; Duane Stanford & Aileen Dodd, "Board Insists on Land Secrecy," Atlanta Journal-Constitution, Sept. 18, 2005, C1, C4; Duane Stanford, "Lawyer: Gwinnett's Secrecy OK," Atlanta Journal-Constitution, Oct. 11, 2005, B1, B8; Duane Stanford, "Gwinnett May End Land Deal Secrecy," Atlanta Journal-Constitution, Oct. 12, 2005, D1, D5; Duane Stanford, "Gwinnett Schools in Secret Deals," Atlanta Journal-Constitution, April 14, 2006, A1, A10; "Gwinnett County To Vote in Public," Georgia FOI Access (Fall 2005), 3. Forsyth County has made claims similar to Gwinnett. See, Doug Nurse, "Secret Land Purchase Questioned," Atlanta Journal-Constitution, Aug. 24, 2005, B1, B5. Officials in Cobb, Fulton, DeKalb, Clayton, Paulding, Cherokee, and Douglas counties, however, disagree with Gwinnett and Forsyth's position. See, Richard Whitt & Doug Nurse, "Secrecy in Land Deals Loses Favor," Atlanta Journal-Constitution, Aug. 28, 2005, C1, C3. The city of Marietta has also done so. See, "Marietta's Secret Deals" (editorial) Atlanta Journal-Constitution, Aug. 31, 2007, A14.

47. O.C.G.A. 50-14-3(b)(2). See, Moon v. Terrell County, 249 Ga. App. 567, 548 S.E.2d 680 (2001). "Such proceedings are analogous to trials [and trials are] open to the public [while] the jury deliberation is not." Georgia Press Association, "How a Government Agency Can Properly Close a Meeting," Legal Survival Kit [1989] at 6. For recent applications of this exception, see, Camden County v. Haddock, 271 Ga. 664, 523 S.E.2d 291 (1999); Moon v. Terrell County, 249 Ga. App. 567, 548 S.E.2d 680 (2001). For a discussion of past concerns, see, Kelly Simmons, "UGA Approved Pay Raise in Secret," Atlanta Journal-Constitution, Feb. 21, 2005, A1, A10.

systems when trustees are discussing investments;[48]

12. Portions of meetings to discuss any record exempt from public disclosure which cannot be discussed without disclosing the confidential portions of the record.[49]

An agency may also close a meeting "to conduct an inspection of physical facilities under the agency's jurisdiction" or "to conduct a meeting at which no final official action is to be taken, with another agency or with officials of another agency at a location outside the agency's geographical jurisdiction."[50] Public officials must attest formally that public meetings have been legally closed.[51]

Other statutory exemptions include public school disciplinary proceedings and review,[52] executive sessions,[53] and professional license deliberations.[54]

---

48. O.C.G.A. 50-14-3(b)(3).

49. O.C.G.A. 50-14-3(b)(4). See also, O.C.G.A. 15-16-10(a)(10) (involving the development and implementation of courthouse security plans).

50. Georgia Press Association, "How a Government Agency Can Properly Close a Meeting," Legal Survival Kit [1989] at 6.

51. O.C.G.A. 50-14-4(b). See, "Baker: Clarke School Board Didn't Break Law," Atlanta Journal-Constitution, July 7, 2000, D9. See also, Alan Judd, "New Sunshine Laws Have Officials Feeling Exposed," Atlanta Journal-Constitution, July 9, 1999, B2; "State Government - Open and Public Meetings: Require that an Agency Holding a Meeting Make Available an Agenda of All Matters Expected To Be Discussed; Require the Agency to Post and Distribute Its Agenda; Require the Chairperson of a Closed Meeting To Execute and File with the Minutes a Notarized Affidavit Stating Why the Meeting Was Closed," 16 Georgia State University Law Review 256 (Fall 1999). However, see also, "Sunshine Law Violations Not Prosecuted," Atlanta Journal-Constitution, March 11, 2007, F10.

52. O.C.G.A. 20-2-757.

53. O.C.G.A. 36-80-1. See also, Deriso v. Cooper, 245 Ga. 786, 267 S.E.2d 217 (1980) (where executive sessions of a county board of education may only be held to discuss matters within the seven exemptions to the open meetings law). The agency does not have free rein to determine individuals

The biggest issues today seem to be what is a meeting,[55] and when or whether a group – such as, the University of Georgia Foundation[56] – must hold public meetings,[57] though

> if there is the slightest doubt, or any question whatsoever, as to whether a matter can be the subject of a closed meeting, DO NOT CLOSE.

---

invited to attend such meetings. See, 1998 Opinions of the Attorney General, No. U98-3, page number unknown.

54. O.C.G.A. 43-1-2(k).

55. See, "As Curtains Close in DeKalb," Atlanta Journal-Constitution, Jan. 15, 2003, A12; J. Stanley Hawkins, "Draw the Line on Journalists' Attempts to Gain Access," Atlanta Journal-Constitution, Jan. 15, 2003, A13.

56. The foundation is a private fund-raising entity which supplements the salary of the university's president and argued that it was not subject to open meetings laws. See, Dana Tofig, "Foundation Business Must Be Public," Atlanta Journal-Constitution, Nov. 15, 2003, F6; Dana Tofig, "Meeting 'in Contradiction' of Opinion on Openness," Atlanta Journal-Constitution, Jan. 7, 2004, A7; Patti Ghezzi & Alan Judd, "Meeting Closed in Defiance of Opinion by State's Attorney," Atlanta Journal-Constitution, Feb. 14, 2004, A1, A12; Alan Judd, "Closed Meetings at UGA Investigated," Atlanta Journal-Constitution, Feb. 17, 2004, page number unknown; Kelly Simmons, "Baker to UGA Foundation: Open Meetings," Atlanta Journal-Constitution, Feb. 27, 2004, D1; Kelly Simmons, "UGA Group Agrees to Open Meetings," Atlanta Journal-Constitution, March 10, 2004, D4.

57. See, for example, Jen Sansbury, "Closed Gatherings Skirt Ethics Laws," Atlanta Journal-Constitution, Jan. 13, 2003, B1. See also, Henry Farber, "Sandy Springs Takes Shape in the Dark," Atlanta Journal-Constitution, July 21, 2005, A1, A11; Henry Farber & Michael Pearson, "Sandy Springs' Closed Meetings Stir Concerns," Atlanta Journal-Constitution, July 22, 2005, D1; Henry Farber & Doug Nurse, "Open Meetings of Task Forces Urged," Atlanta Journal-Constitution, Aug. 12, 2005, D3. But see, Doug Nurse, "Milton Council Seeks Therapy, But Only in the Dark," Atlanta Journal-Constitution, July 11, 2007, A1, A8 (a psychologist's meeting with council members to promote conflict resolution would not qualify as a privileged doctor-patient relationship and thus would not be exempt from open meeting requirements).

> To err in favor of openness will not result in
> the imposition of penalties on public officials;
> however, to err otherwise may well result in
> such penalties.[58]

Yet, meetings of the Commission on Gender Bias, established by the Georgia Supreme Court in 1989, were determined to be exempt from the state's open meetings laws.[59] On the other hand, the Piedmont Park Conservancy, a private group which manages a public park, agreed to hold a public vote on building a parking garage near the park, while contending that it is not required to do so.[60] In 2008, Clayton County schools lost their accreditation, in part, because of the school board's violations of the state's code of ethics and open meetings requirements.[61] The Attorney General has concluded

---

58. Justice Norman Fletcher concurring, in Steele v. Honea, 261 Ga. 644, 409 S.E.2d 652 (1991) at 647. Emphasis in original.

59. See, "Fathers Lose Bid To Open Judiciary Hearings," Atlanta Journal-Constitution, Feb. 5, 1991, D2.

60. See, Jeffry Scott, "Meetings on Park Open to Public," Atlanta Journal-Constitution, Dec. 14, 2004, page number unknown; Ty Tagami, "Group Agrees to New Garage Vote," Atlanta Journal-Constitution, Dec. 15, 2004, page number unknown; David Pendered, "Garden Assails Lawsuit on Files," Atlanta Journal-Constitution, Feb. 23, 2007, D6.

61. See, Megan Matteucci, "AJC Challenges Clayton Schools' Closed Meeting," Atlanta Journal-Constitution, April 15, 2008, page number unknown; Megan Matteucci, "Clayton Defends Closed Meeting," Atlanta Journal-Constitution, April 16, 2008, B1, B4; Megan Matteucci, "Clayton Schools: Public Shut Out Despite Protest," Atlanta Journal-Constitution, April 17, 2008, page number unknown; Megan Metteucci, "School Board Faces AJC Complaint," Atlanta Journal-Constitution, April 24, 2008, page number unknown; Megan Metteucci, "Clayton Must Explain Closed Meetings," Atlanta Journal-Constitution, April 30, 2008, page number unknown; Megan Matteucci & John Hollis, "Judge: Yank Clayton School Board Members," Atlanta Journal-Constitution, Aug. 27, 2008, page number unknown; Megan Matteucci & Laura Diamond, "Clayton's Fears Are

that the Department of Community Health's Drug Utilization Review Board is subject to open meetings requirements.[62] And the General Assembly has stated that land banks are subject to open meetings requirements.[63] Other important Georgia court decisions clarifying the Open Meetings Act have included:

- *Red & Black Publishing Co. v. Board of Regents* - in which the University of Georgia was ordered to open the proceedings and records of its student judicial courts,[64] because they stand "in the place of" and are "equivalent to the Board of Regents and the University."[65] However, this rule no longer appears to

---

Realized," Atlanta Journal-Constitution, Aug. 29, 2008, A1, A10; Robbie Brown, "A Georgia School System Loses Its Accreditation," New York Times, Aug. 29, 2008, A12; Megan Matteucci, "Clayton Board Member Blasts Colleagues," Atlanta Journal-Constitution, Sept. 4, 2008, A14. Six months later, the Clayton school board held a closed hearing, also in apparent violation of the open meetings statute. See, Megan Matteucci, "Clayton School Officials Hold Private Disciplinary Hearing," Atlanta Journal-Constitution, March 7, 2009, C6.

62. See, 2010 Opinions of the Attorney General, U2010-1, page number unknown.

63. O.C.G.A. 48-4-111. See, 2012 Georgia Laws 1055, Senate Bill 284.

64. 262 Ga. 848, 427 S.E.2d 257 (1993). This case is the first time any state supreme court has addressed the issue of the public right of access to campus judicial records and proceedings. In addition, the state Supreme Court determined that the records sought were not "education records within the meaning of the Buckley Amendment" (also known as, the federal Family Education Rights & Privacy Act of 1974).

65. Debra Gersh, "Student Newspaper Wins Access to Campus Court Records," Editor & Publisher, March 27, 1993, 24-25, at 24. This decision extended "the open meetings law beyond its literal meaning [and stood] for the proposition that whenever a governmental agency empowers another group to act in its stead, or delegates official responsibility and authority, the open meetings law will apply to the subordinate body" ("Open Meetings - UGA Student Disciplinary Court," Georgia Press Bulletin, April 15, 1993,

be valid in the aftermath of the 2012 legislative revision of Georgia's open meetings laws.[66]

- *Bryan County Board of Equalization v. Bryan County Board of Tax Assessors* – in which deliberations over disputed property values, claimed by the board to be a "quasi-judicial function," were required to be open to the public.[67]

- *Wiggins v. Tift County* – in which a county board of commissioners must receive evidence and hear arguments against a county employee in a public meeting.[68]

- *Decatur County v. Bainbridge Post-Searchlight* – where

---

3). See also, Sandra McIntosh, "Student Newspaper Wins Legal Round Against UGA," Atlanta Journal-Constitution, Feb. 21, 1992, E10; "Court Asked to Open UGA Student Court Hearings to Public," Atlanta Journal-Constitution, Sept. 23, 1992, B2; Bill Rankin, "Ruling: UGA Student Court Must Be Open," Atlanta Journal-Constitution, March 16, 1993, C5; "UGA Court Loses Its Veil of Secrecy," Atlanta Journal-Constitution, March 17, 1993, A12; Brian O'Shea, "'Red and Black' Wins Right to Access," Society of Professional Journalists' Sunshine Report, date unknown, 3. For an opposing view, see, Dennis Gregory, "Misguided Campaigns for the Release of Students' Disciplinary Records," The Chronicle of Higher Education, April 27, 1994, section 2, 1-2. The student newspaper was also upheld in a subsequent test of the ruling. See, Dennis McCafferty, "Paper Blocked in Judicial Records Fight," Atlanta Journal-Constitution, April 30, 1993, E6; Joe Earl, "UGA Court Case Opened to Paper; Student Appeals," Atlanta Journal-Constitution, May 7, 1993, G3; Bill Osinski, "Release of Records at UGA Halted 2nd Time," Atlanta Journal-Constitution, May 8, 1993, B4; Rebecca McCarthy, "Supreme Court Hears Arguments at UGA," Atlanta Journal-Constitution, Oct. 19, 1993, G3; Rebecca McCarthy, "UGA Newspaper Wins Access to Records," Atlanta Journal-Constitution, Nov. 9, 1993, E4.

66. See, Kathleen Joyner, "Open Meetings Law Could Close Off Campus Hearings," Daily Report, Oct. 2, 2012, 1, 6.

67. 253 Ga. App. 831, 560 S.E.2d 719 (2002).

68. 258 Ga. App. 666, 574 S.E.2d 874 (2002).

pending grand jury presentments about commissioners' alleged wrong-doing and commissioners' claims of attorney-client privilege were insufficient reasons for closure, because the purpose of the executive session "was to fashion a political response, not to prepare a legal defense" to pending litigation,[69] as required by the attorney-client exception to the Open Meetings Act.

- *Cardinale v. Atlanta* – where government councils, boards, and commissions must release the names of those voting for/against/abstaining, even in non-roll-call situations.[70]

---

69. 280 Ga. 706, 632 S.E.2d 113 (2006). See, O.C.G.A. 50-14-2(1). See also, "Ga. S.Ct. Nixes Closed Meeting," Georgia FOI Access (Fall 2006), 3, 8. For the exception to apply, the threat of litigation must be "realistic and tangible." Claxton Enterprise v. Evans County Board of Commissioners, 249 Ga. App. 870, 549 S.E.2d 830 (2001) at 874.

70. 290 Ga. 521, 722 S.E.2d 732 (2012); 308 Ga. App. 234, 706 S.E.2d 692 (2011). See, Bill Rankin, "Court: Atlanta Violated Open Meetings Act," Atlanta Journal-Constitution, Feb. 7, 2012, B3; Greg Land, "Non-Lawyer Wins Case He Argued Before Ga. High Court," Daily Report, Feb. 7, 2012, 1, 5.

Open Records

With the passage of the Open Records Act of 1959,[71] the Georgia General Assembly began the process of insuring that through access, Georgia citizens would be informed of state, county, and municipal government activities. Its "purpose is not only to encourage public access to information in order that the public can evaluate the expenditure of public funds and the efficient and proper functioning of its institutions, but also to foster confidence in government...."[72]

Public records are defined as "all documents, papers, letters, maps, books, tapes, photographs, computer based or generated information, data, data fields, or similar material prepared and maintained or received by an agency or by a private person or entity in the performance of a service or function for or on behalf of an agency or when such documents have been transferred to a private person or entity by an agency for storage or future governmental use," including data, such as, e-mail.[73] The definition of public agency, given in the open

---

71. The act was approved Feb. 27, 1959 (1959 Georgia Laws 88). Section 1 was initially codified as O.C.G.A. 50-18-70(b). Section 2 was initially codified as O.C.G.A. 50-18-71(a).

72. Athens Observer, Inc. v. Anderson, 245 Ga. 63, 263 S.E.2d 128 (1980) at 66. See, generally, Mark H. Cohen & Stephanie B. Manis, "Georgia's Open Records and Open Meetings Laws: A Continued March Toward Government in the Sunshine," 40 Mercer Law Review 1 (1988).

73. O.C.G.A. 50-18-70(b). Georgia courts have readily extended the statute's definitional scope whenever necessary. See, Doe v. Sears, 245 Ga. 83, 263 S.E.2d 119 (1980), certiorari denied, 446 U.S. 979 (1980) (computer print-outs); Price v. Fulton County Commission, 170 Ga. App. 736, 318 S.E.2d 153 (1984) (computer tape); and In re: Pacific & Southern Co., Inc. d/b/a/WXIA-TV, 257 Ga. 484, 361 S.E.2d 159 (1987) (video tapes). Images and data in the state online information system for deeds and plats are also public records. 2012 Opinions of the Attorney General, No. 12-5, page number unknown. E-mails not retained on state computer systems are not an "existing public record" and thus not subject to open records request. See,

meetings statute (see, Figure 9, p. 185), was incorporated into the open records statute in 1992.

The original definition of "public record" was added to the statute in 1988 - the result of a petition filed by the Athens Observer for the release of a report prepared by paid consultants evaluating the mathematics program at the University of Georgia[74] - and expanded somewhat the common law definition set forth by the Georgia Supreme Court in *Houston v. Rutledge*.[75] The law specifically applies to "all public records ... except those which by order of a court ... or by law are specifically exempted from disclosure."[76]

This definition specifically includes records kept by private

---

Griffin Industries v. Georgia Dept. of Agriculture, 313 Ga. App. 69, 720 S.E.2d 212 (2011). See also, Alyson Palmer, "Court: Agency Didn't Violate Law," Daily Report, Nov. 17, 2011, 1, 5.

74. 245 Ga. 63, 263 S.E.2d 128 (1980). The Georgia Supreme Court ruled that the documents were public records, even though they were not actually prepared by public officials.

75. 237 Ga. 764, 229 S.E.2d 624 (1976). The *Houston* definition included "documents, papers and records prepared and maintained in the course of the operation of a public office" (id. at 765).

76. O.C.G.A. 50-18-70(a). Cases in which the law has been applied include Northside Realty Associates, Inc. v. Community Relations Commission, 240 Ga. 432, 241 S.E.2d 189 (1978) (where the statute was applied to the Community Relations Commission of Atlanta); Doe v. Sears, 245 Ga. 83, 263 S.E.2d 189 (1980) (where the statute was applied to the Atlanta Housing Authority); Richmond County Hospital Authority v. Southeastern Newspapers Corp., 252 Ga. 19, 311 S.E.2d 806 (1984) (where the statute was applied to hospital authorities). O.C.G.A. 50-18-75, however, does establish confidentiality for "[c]ommunications between the Office of Legislative Counsel and ... members of the General Assembly, the Lieutenant Governor, and persons acting on behalf of such public officers." Access restrictions on the records of constitutional officers are limited to 25 years. See, O.C.G.A. 50-18-98.

companies working on behalf of a public agency,[77] including any records kept by any "association" which has a membership made up of "counties, municipal corporations or school districts ... or their officers" and receives "more than 33 1/3 percent of its general operating budget from payments from such political subdivisions."[78]

Agencies are given three business days to comply.[79] However, agencies are not required to provide access to prepare documents "not in existence at the time of the request."[80]

In addition, records should be made available using "the most economical means reasonably calculated,"[81] although the

---

77. For an interesting application, see, Hackworth v. Atlanta Board of Education, 214 Ga. App. 17, 447 S.E.2d 78 (1994) (where records of bus drivers who work for a private company which contracts with the school district to transport students to school are public). Records may also not be "parked" at such a company and withheld from public scrutiny.

78. O.C.G.A. 50-18-70(b)(1).

79. O.C.G.A. 50-18-71(b), O.C.G.A. 50-18-71(f). See, Southeastern Newspapers v. Newsome, 260 Ga. xxx, 396 S.E.2d 907 (1990) (judgment affirmed without opinion; where court clerks could not delay public inspection of divorce records); Katie Wood, "Court Affirms Open Records Decision," Daily Report, Oct. 8, 1990, 16; David E. Hudson, "Recent Favorable Georgia Supreme Court Rulings," The GPA Bulletin, Oct. 25, 1990, 5. Actions to enforce the statute should be brought in the Superior courts of Georgia. See, O.C.G.A. 50-18-73(a). See also, Chuck Bell, "Violation of Open Records Law Alleged," Atlanta Journal-Constitution, Dec. 15, 1990, C6. The statute provides for $1,000 fine for first violation, plus the possibility of recovering attorney's fees, if agency acts "without substantial justification" (O.C.G.A. 50-18-74, O.C.G.A. 50-14-5, O.C.G.A. 50-14-6). Superior court rulings may be appealed directly to the Georgia Supreme Court. See, Georgia Constitution of 1983, Article VI, §VI, ¶III(2).

80. O.C.G.A. 50-18-71(j). See, Schulten, Ward & Turner v. Fulton-DeKalb Hospital Authority, 272 Ga. 725, 535 S.E.2d 243 (2000).

81. Rick Minter, "Judge: County Overcharged Tax Group," Atlanta Journal-Constitution, Oct. 23, 1991, B3. See, O.C.G.A. 50-18-71(c)(1). See

custodial agency may choose to provide copies or make the originals available for copying by request.[82] The state-approved charge is "not to exceed 10 cent(s) per page" for photo-copies.[83] An agency may also charge reasonable search and retrieval fees, and for other direct administrative costs beyond the first fifteen minutes,[84] but not a fee for the attorney's time involved in the review of the documents requested[85] nor an administrative fee for personnel who assist with requests for "records that are routinely subject to public inspection, such as deeds, city ordinances, or zoning maps."[86] Administrative time plus the "actual cost of the media on which the records or data are produced" may be charged for computerized records.[87]

However, public disclosure is not always required. The

---

also, Trammel v. Martin, 200 Ga. App. 435, 408 S.E.2d 477 (1991) (where a $2,231.89 fee for 5,364 pages of documents was held to be excessive).

82. 1984 Opinions of the Attorney General, No. 84-39, 82.

83. O.C.G.A. 50-18-71(c)(2). The statute does not include a provision for a fee waiver for indigents. See, McBride v. Wetherington, 199 Ga. App. 7, 403 S.E.2d 873 (1991).

84. O.C.G.A. 50-18-71(c). The hourly charge "shall not exceed the salary of the lowest paid full-time employee who, in the reasonable discretion of the custodian of the records has the necessary skill and training to perform the request."

85. See, Trammell, v. Martin, 200 Ga. App. 435, 408 S.E.2d 477 (1991). See also, "Legal Update: Copy Charges," Georgia Press Association Editor's Forum (Winter 1992), 4.

86. McFrugal Car Rental of Riverdale v. Garr, 262 Ga. 369, 418 S.E.2d 60 (1992). For "non-routine" documents, the agency bears the burden of proving the reasonableness of its charges. See, Mark Curriden, "Court: No Charge for Viewing Records," Atlanta Journal-Constitution, July 17, 1992, G2; David Hudson, "Copy Fees Not To Be Excessive Under Open records Law," Georgia Press Bulletin, Aug. 15, 1992, 3.

87. O.C.G.A. 50-18-71(c). See also, 1989 Opinions of the Attorney General, No. 89-32, 72. See, generally, Sandra Davidson Scott, "Statutory Language Needed: Access to Computerized Government Records Must Be Made Easier," Editor & Publisher, Nov. 2, 1991, 8PC-13PC.

open records statute itself provides for two types of exemptions:

- Records exempt by court order; and
- Records exempt by the requirements of another state statute.[88]

When balancing the public's interest in disclosure as opposed to non-disclosure, Georgia courts "favor open, unfettered communication and disclosure except where some limitation thereon is required in the public interest."[89] In his concurring opinion in *Houston*, Justice Conley Ingram went further, contending that the First Amendment to the U.S. Constitution strongly presumes that public records "should be made available for public inspection immediately."[90] Although recently limited,[91] rarely has the "court order" exemption been used to keep records from the public.[92] Since 1990, court-derived exclusions have been limited to those in which

---

88. O.C.G.A. 50-18-71(a).

89. Houston v. Rutledge, 237 Ga. 764, 229 S.E.2d 624 (1976) at 766.

90. Id. The Georgia Supreme Court in Northside Realty Associates, Inc. v. Community Relations Commission, 240 Ga. 432, 241 S.E.2d 189 (1978), agreed with this requirement and concluded that if the requested, "identifiable" public records were "within the appellees' possession, the burden is cast on the appellees to explain why the records should not be furnished" (id. at 436).

91. See, Atchison v. Hospital Authority, 245 Ga. 494, 265 S.E.2d 801 (1980).

92. See, Brown v. Minter, 243 Ga. 397, 254 S.E.2d 326, certiorari denied, 444 U.S. 844 (1979) (where the Georgia Supreme Court prohibited disclosure of information contained in on-going criminal investigations, of the names of informants, and - in certain limited situations - the names of those filing complaints).

disclosure would cause a perilous invasion of privacy,[93] while statutory exemptions have proliferated.

Specific exemptions within the open records statute itself include:

1. Information "specifically required by federal statute or regulation to be kept confidential;"[94]
2. "Medical or veterinary records or similar files, [when] the disclosure ... would be an invasion of personal privacy."[95]

Georgia courts have generally taken a very broad approach when defining "similar files;" this exemption now includes "any information which would invade the constitutional, statutory or common law rights of ... privacy."[96] However, the courts do realize that the right to privacy "extends only to unnecessary public scrutiny" and does not prevent any

---

93. See, Georgia Hospital Association v. Ledbetter, 260 Ga. 477, 396 S.E.2d 488 (1990); Hardaway Co. v. Rives, 262 Ga. 631, 422 S.E.2d 854 (1992).

94. O.C.G.A. 50-18-72(a)(1). See, Griffin-Spalding County Hospital Authority v. Radio Station WKEU, 240 Ga. 444, 241 S.E.2d 196 (1978) (where the court ruled that private information not relevant to the public should be eliminated from released records). This restriction does not include documents that are otherwise public but claimed to be private by means of a confidentiality agreement made with a federal agency. See, 2005 Opinions of the Attorney General, No. U05-1, page number unknown.

95. O.C.G.A. 50-18-72(a)(2). See, generally, Dennis P. Quarles, "Informational Privacy Under the Open Records Act," 32 Mercer Law Review 393 (1980); Frank M. Eldridge, "Court Caught Between Individual's Right to Privacy, Public's Right To Know," Atlanta Journal-Constitution, Feb. 5, 1989, B2.

96. Napper v. Georgia Television Co., 257 Ga. 156, 356 S.E.2d 640 (1987) at 160, quoting Doe v. Sears, 245 Ga. 83, 263 S.E.2d 119 (1980) at 86.

"legitimate inquiry into the operation of a government institution and those employed by it."[97] Yet, information of "no legitimate concern, though found in a public document [is] not subject to disclosure ... because [it is] not the subject of 'legitimate public inquiry.'"[98]

3. Law enforcement, regulatory agency, or prosecutorial records relating to confidential surveillance, investigations, or sources;[99]

4. "Any pending investigation or prosecution" of criminal activity;[100]

---

97. Athens Observer, Inc. v. Anderson, 245 Ga. 63, 263 S.E.2d 128 (1980) at 65-66. For a more modern application of this rule, see Dortch v. The Atlanta Journal-Constitution, 261 Ga. 350, 405 S.E.2d 43 (1991) (where the cellular telephone records of Atlanta city officials had to be disclosed unedited). See also, Mark Sherman, "Judge Orders City To Disclose Records of Calls on Car Phones," Atlanta Journal-Constitution, Sept. 20, 1990, C3; "Atlanta Daily Wins Access to Cellular Phone Records," Editor & Publisher, July 20, 1991, 20; "City Must Make Copies of Phone Bills Public," The News Media & the Law (Fall 1991), 19-20; Mark Sherman, "Public Foots Bill for Private Calls on City Car Phones," Atlanta Journal-Constitution, Nov.. 29, 1991, A1, A18; Mark Sherman, "City Dug in Heels for 16 Months Before Releasing Cellular Records," Atlanta Journal-Constitution, Nov. 29, 1991, A18.

98. Harris v. Cox Enterprises, 256 Ga. 299, 348 S.E.2d 448 (1986) at 302.

99. O.C.G.A. 50-18-72(a)(3).

100. O.C.G.A. 50-18-72(a)(4). See, Napper v. Georgia Television Co., 257 Ga. 156, 356 S.E.2d 640 (1987); Harris v. Cox Enterprises, 256 Ga. 299, 348 S.E.2d 448 (1986); Brown v. Minter, 243 Ga. 397, 254 S.E.2d 326 (1979); Houston v. Rutledge, 237 Ga. 764, 229 S.E.2d 624 (1976). After Atlanta newspapers requested copies of Georgia Bureau of Investigation files relating to "long-dormant" bribery charges against several state legislators, the investigation was re-opened and the open records request denied. See, Rhonda Cook, "Miller Orders State To Join Bribe Probe," Atlanta Journal-Constitution, Sept. 19, 1991, F3. Later, during an on-going federal investigation into kickbacks and bribes at Hartsfield International Airport,

5. Motor vehicle accident reports, except to those named in the report or who have a "need" for access to the report, as defined by statute.[101]

In 1999, then-Governor Roy E. Barnes signed into law Senate Bill 20, which requires anyone seeking an accident record to appear at police posts in person, submit request in writing, and pay a fee for these records. Although it was designed "to discourage the sometimes ghoulish practice of ambulance chasing by lawyers and their agents,"[102] the law has had the unintentional effect of restricting journalists and other members of the public from obtaining these records.

6. Jury list data;[103]
7. Confidential evaluations of public employees and personnel records;[104]

Atlanta city attorneys first withheld and later released minutes of City Council Finance Committee meetings that had been subpoenaed by the U.S. attorney. See, Douglas Blackmon, "City Refuses To Release Panel Minutes: Though Meetings Were Public, Attorney Says Data Confidential," Atlanta Journal-Constitution, April 15, 1993, C1, C6; Douglas Blackmon, "City To Let Paper See Finance Minutes," Atlanta Journal-Constitution, April 16, 1993, D4.

101. O.C.G.A. 50-18-72(a)(5). The statute was upheld as not an unconstitutional prior restraint on commercial speech in Spottsville v. Barnes, 135 F.Supp.2d 1316 (N.D. Ga. 2001). The statute includes 11 definitions of "need." O.C.G.A. 50-18-72(a)(5)(A-J).

102. See, "Ease Restrictions on Accident Reports," Atlanta Journal-Constitution, Oct. 18, 1999, page number unknown. See also, Michael Weiss, "New Law Restricts Who Gets to See Accident Reports," Atlanta Journal-Constitution, June 26, 1999, J1.

103. O.C.G.A. 50-18-72(a)(6).

104. O.C.G.A. 50-18-72(a)(7). For cases which define the scope of the term "personnel file," see, Athens Observer, Inc. v. Anderson, 245 Ga. 63, 263 S.E.2d 128, (1980) (where a report of outside consultants did not contain the kind of information ordinarily found in a personnel file); Irvin v. Macon

8. Investigative records related to complaints against public employees until ten days after such information is presented to an agency for action;[105]
9. Information regarding real estate appraisals or property acquisition plans of state or local governments;[106]
10. Sealed bids and bid proposals detailing cost estimates until agency action is taken;[107]
11. Information about executive searches, except that state agencies must release the names and application files of their top three finalists at least fourteen days (five days for university presidents) before any final employment decision is made and may not circumvent the law's disclosure requirements by paying outside consultants to conduct employee searches for them;[108]

Telegraph Publishing Co., 253 Ga. 43, 316 S.E.2d 449 (1984) (where the placement of investigative records into an employee's personnel file did not transform them into such); Richmond County Hospital Authority v. Southeastern Newspapers Corp., 252 Ga. 19, 311 S.E.2d 806 (1984) (where names, job titles, and salaries of public hospital employees earning more than $28,000 annually may be disclosed). See also, Goddard v. Albany, 285 Ga. 882, 684 S.E.2d 635 (2009) (holding that personnel records of municipal employees are not entitled to any blanket exemption from public disclosure); Soloski v. Adams, 600 F. Supp. 2d 1276 (N.D. Ga. 2009) (noting that the personnel file of a university dean is not exempt from public disclosure).

105. O.C.G.A. 50-18-72(a)(8).

106. O.C.G.A. 50-18-72(a)(9).

107. O.C.G.A. 50-18-72(a)(10).

108. O.C.G.A. 50-18-72(a)(11). See, "Regents Fast-Track Leadership," Atlanta Journal-Constitution, June 8, 2012, A1, A12. For an example of problems caused by this requirement, see Douglas Blackmon, "City Misses Deadline for Releasing Names of Finalists for Police Chief," Atlanta Journal-Constitution, Nov. 8, 1994, B5. The public is entitled to know immediately demographic information about the applicants. The case which prompted this 1992 exemption to the statute was Board of Regents v. Atlanta Journal-Constitution, 259 Ga. 214, 378 S.E.2d 305 (1989). See, David Hudson, "Open Government in Georgia - A 12-Month Report," Georgia Press

12. Staff services records of the Georgia General Assembly;[109]
13. Records with historical research value when access restrictions (for no more than 75 years) are a condition of the gift;[110]
14. Information about the location and character of certain historic properties,[111] when disclosure will create a risk of harm to the property;
15. Records of farm water use by individual farms;[112]
16. Agricultural records considered by the state Department of Agriculture "to be a part of the critical infra-structure;"[113]
17. National animal identification system records, which identify premises of origin and track animals through the food processing procedure;[114]

Association Editor's Forum (Summer 1989), 4; "Regents Must Release Applicants' Names," News Media & the Law (Summer 1989), 34-35. See also, Sonia Murray, "Journal-Constitution Sues To Force ACVB to Reveal Finalists' Names," Atlanta Constitution, May 24, 1991, C1; Sonia Murray, "Court Upholds ACVB's Refusal to Release Finalists' Names," Atlanta Journal-Constitution, June 1, 1991, B1; ACVB Ducks Back into Its Hidey Hole Again," Atlanta Constitution, June 5, 1991, A14; Sonia Murray, "Controversy Lingers on ACVB Selection Process," Atlanta Constitution, June 21, 1991, F7; Sonia Murray, "High Court Grills Convention Bureau About Not Disclosing Records," Atlanta Constitution, Sept. 11, 1991, C3; Sonia Murray, "Top Court Says Trial Court Should Decide Dispute of ACVB Job Search," Atlanta Journal-Constitution, Oct. 8, 1991, C3.
    109. O.C.G.A. 50-18-72(a)(12).
    110. O.C.G.A. 50-18-72(a)(13).
    111. O.C.G.A. 50-18-72(a)(14).
    112. O.C.G.A. 50-18-72(a)(15).
    113. O.C.G.A. 50-18-72(a)(16). See also, 42 U.S. Code 5195c(e).
    114. O.C.G.A. 50-18-72(a)(17).

18. Information about the location and character of certain sensitive natural habitats, when disclosure will create a risk of harm to the plants or animals on the property;[115]
19. Certain records related to personal privacy, collected in connection with neighborhood watch programs, and information revealing the security codes of those with home burglar alarm systems;[116]
20. Certain records related to personal privacy - including an individual's Social Security number and e-mail address - insurance or medical information, and personal financial information – including credit and debit card information;[117]
21. Records which reveal public employees' home address, home telephone number, day and month of birth, Social Security number, financial and medical insurance information, and mother's maiden name;[118]
22. Records of the Department of Early Care & Learning that identify children, their birthday, home address, telephone numbers and emergency contact informa-

---

115. O.C.G.A. 50-18-72(a)(18).

116. O.C.G.A. 50-18-72(a)(19). See, Kathey Pruitt, "Barnes Backs Bill to Limit Release of Personal Information in State Files," Atlanta Journal-Constitution, Feb. 15, 2001, C6; Tony Heffernan, "Governor Wants to Stop Access to Personal Information in Records," Macon Telegraph, Feb. 15, 2001, 7B.

117. O.C.G.A. 50-18-72(a)(20). See, Patrick Fox, "Ga. Bill Bolsters Privacy," Atlanta Journal-Constitution, April 3, 2012, B1, B6.

118. O.C.G.A. 50-18-72(a)(21). See, Jim Galloway, "State Wants More Data Off-Limits," Atlanta Journal-Constitution, Feb. 19, 2005, E1, E7; Alan Judd, "Bill Shields Info on Elected Officials," Atlanta Journal-Constitution, March 29, 2005, A1, A8; James Salzer, "Shield Law Signed by Governor," Atlanta Journal-Constitution, May 5, 2005, C1, C2. See also, James Salzer, "Teachers Oppose Records Release," Atlanta Journal-Constitution, Nov. 2, 2000, F5; James Salzer, "Teachers Groups File Suits Over Release of Records," Atlanta Journal-Constitution, Nov. 3, 2000, C7.

tion;[119]

23. Any component of an "electronic signature;"[120]
24. Personal information contained in carpooling and ridesharing records;[121]
25. Records which, if disclosed, "would compromise" public safety and security and are thus "necessary for the protection of life, safety, or public property;"[122]
26. Personal information gleaned from "911" emergency calls which "would endanger" life or physical safety;[123]
27. Personal information from athletic or recreational program records identifying a child age 12 or under;[124]
28. Personal information contained in records of the state Road & Tollway Authority;[125]
29. Personal information from records maintained by educational institutions and associated foundations about donors or potential donors;[126]

---

119. O.C.G.A. 50-18-72(a)(22).

120. O.C.G.A. 50-18-72(a)(23); O.C.G.A. 10-12-3. See also, "Commerce and Trade: Electronic Records and Signatures: Authorize the Use of Electronic Records and Signatures Instead of Written Records and Signatures," 14 Georgia State University Law Review 25 (December 1997).

121. O.C.G.A. 50-18-72(a)(24).

122. O.C.G.A. 50-18-72(a)(25).

123. O.C.G.A. 50-18-72(a)(26); O.C.G.A. 46-5-122.

124. O.C.G.A. 50-18-72(a)(27).

125. O.C.G.A. 50-18-72(a)(28).

126. O.C.G.A. 50-18-72(a)(29). See Kelly Simmons & Nancy Badertscher, "Bill May Cloak College Donors," Atlanta Journal-Constitution, Feb. 11, 2005, E1, E5; Nancy Badertscher, "House Oks Secrecy Bill for Donors," Atlanta Journal-Constitution, March 4, 2005, D4; Jim Galloway, "Donor Bill Faces an Uphill Battle," Atlanta Journal-Constitution, March 5, 2005, D4; Alan Judd, "Bill Hides Corporate Donors," Atlanta Journal-Constitution, March 7, 2005, A1, A6; Jim Galloway, "Committee Oks Donor Secrecy," Atlanta Journal-Constitution, March 16, 2005, B1; Jim Galloway, "Secrecy Bills Advance," Atlanta Journal-Constitution, March 25, 2005, A1, A14; Jim

30. Personal or financial information, including travel history and transit card purchase records, of any user of the Metropolitan Atlanta Rapid Transit Authority;[127]
31. Building mapping information for use in emergency situations by first responders;[128]
32. Investigative materials or physical evidence involving child abuse, exploitation or pornography;[129]
33. Public retirement system proprietary financial records for a limited time;[130]
34. Business trade secrets or proprietary information in the possession of a governmental agency;[131]
35. Knowledge generated through academic research, until

Galloway, "Donor Shield Survives House," Atlanta Journal-Constitution, March 30, 2005, B1; Charmainre Henry, "Bill Will Keep All University Donors a Secret," Georgia State University Signal, April 5, 2005, 6; James Salzer, "Perdue Enacts Shield for College Donors," Atlanta Journal-Constitution, May 10, 2005, B1.

127. O.C.G.A. 50-18-72(a)(30). See, Tom Bennett, "MARTA Transcard Next on Legislature's FOI Assault List," Georgia FOI Access (Spring 2006), 3.

128. O.C.G.A. 50-18-72(a)(31). See, O.C.G.A. 38-3-152.

129. O.C.G.A. 50-18-72(a)(32). See, O.C.G.A. 16-12-100, O.C.G.A. 16-12-100.1, O.C.G.A. 16-12-100.2.

130. O.C.G.A. 50-18-72(a)(33). See, O.C.G.A. 47-1-14, O.C.G.A. 47-7-127.

131. O.C.G.A. 50-18-72(a)(34). See, Douglas Asphalt Co. v. E.R. Snell Contractor, 282 Ga. App. 546, 639 S.E.2d 372 (2006); Georgia Road & Tollway Authority v. ETC, 306 Ga. App. 487, 702 S.E.2d 486 (2010). See also John Yates, "Technology Law: Georgia Courts Protect Computer Software," Atlanta Computer Currents (February 1993), 26; John Yates & Paul Arne, "Technology Law: Defining Trade Secrets - It's Not So Simple," Technology South/Atlanta Computer Currents (May 1994), 26. The "trade secrets" exemption is not limited to documents specifically identified as confidential at the time of their submission to the state. See, Georgia Dept. of Natural Resources v. Theragenics Corp., 273 Ga. 724, 545 S.E.2d 904 (2001).

such information is "publicly released, published, copy-righted, or patented;"[132]

36. Data or records used in higher education research, until such information has been "otherwise publicly disseminated;"[133]

37. Any record that would not be subject to disclosure under the Family Education Rights & Privacy Act (FERPA) of 1974;[134]

38. Educational testing materials or answers;[135]

39. Personally identifiable information of participants in medical research conducted by state universities or agencies;[136]

40. Probate records relating to the purchase and possession of firearms;[137]

41. Attorney-client communication;[138]

---

132. O.C.G.A. 50-18-72(a)(35). See, Robert Vickers, "Smoking Study Sparks Press-School Flap," Atlanta Journal-Constitution, Feb. 20, 1993, B3; "Professor Sues Over 'Old Joe' Ad Files," Atlanta Journal-Constitution, March 13, 1993, C2; "Georgia to Protect Privacy of Unpublished University Research," The Chronicle of Higher Education, March 17, 1993, A25.

133. O.C.G.A. 50-18-72(a)(36).

134. O.C.G.A. 50-18-72(a)(37). See, 20 U.S.C. 1232g. The state Attorney General's Office has concluded that because student educational and discipline records are now exempted from disclosure, student judicial court hearings and records may now be closed. See, Kathleen Joyner, "Student Discipline Hearings Can Be Closed to Public, AG's Office Tells UGA," Daily Report, Oct. 30, 2012, 1, 4. This conclusion appears to undermine the state Supreme Court ruling in Red & Black Publishing Co. v. Board of Regents, 262 Ga. 848, 427 S.E.2d 257 (1993).

135. O.C.G.A. 50-18-72(a)(38).

136. O.C.G.A. 50-18-72(a)(39).

137. O.C.G.A. 50-18-72(a)(40). O.C.G.A. 16-11-129 requires probate courts to keep these records. See, Scott Marshall, "Pistol-Packing Fever Side Effect of Brady Act," Atlanta Journal-Constitution, June 27, 1994, J1.

42. The resulting product of an attorney's work;[139]
43. State tax matters which are confidential under state or federal law;[140]
44. Computer programs or software "used or maintained" by a state agency;[141]
45. Records used to provide or administer liability insurance coverage of any state agency;[142]
46. Economic development materials and incentives used to recruit out-of-state companies to re-locate to Georgia;[143]
47. A company's hiring and work training programs, as part of such economic development projects;[144] and

---

138. O.C.G.A. 50-18-72(a)(41). See, O.C.G.A. 50-18-75, which provides for confidentiality for communications between legislators and state officers and the Office of Legislative Counsel.

139. O.C.G.A. 50-18-72(a)(42).

140. O.C.G.A. 50-18-72(a)(43).

141. O.C.G.A. 50-18-72(a)(44).

142. O.C.G.A. 50-18-72(a)(45).

143. O.C.G.A. 50-18-72(a)(46). See, Christopher Quinn, "Bill Shuts Public Out of Companies' Plans," Atlanta Journal-Constitution, March 3, 2011, page number unknown; Robert Williams Jr., "Scary How Secrecy Scheme Refuses to Die," Atlanta Journal-Constitution, March 13, 2011, A17; Ed Bean, "Gov. Deal Says Open Records Law Hurts Business Potential," ATLaw, Jan. 12, 2012, available at: http://www.atlawblog.com/2012/01/gov-deal-says-ga-s-open-records-law-hurts-business-potential/ (last accessed Nov. 15, 2013); Bill Rankin, "Attracting Projects Trumps Openness," Atlanta Journal-Constitution, March 20, 2012, B1, B3.

144. O.C.G.A. 50-18-72(a)(47). This exemption was challenged in Coleman v. Deal, No. 2011CV209634, Superior Court of Fulton County, Dec. 12, 2012; on appeal to the Georgia Supreme Court as Kia Motors Manufacturing v. Coleman, No. S13A1085, April 8, 2013. The Georgia Supreme Court had not yet issued a ruling as of Nov. 15, 2013. See, Kathleen Joyner, "Open Records Exemption Challenged," Daily Report, May 3, 2012, 1, 4.

48. Records of public retirement systems' assets, including certain types of alternative investments.[145]

Whether or not one agrees with the appropriateness and suitability of the particular legislative act under examination, open records exemptions found in other state statutes may generally be grouped into one of three categories: 1) those which protect personal privacy, 2) those which protect commercial competitiveness, and 3) those which protect the requirements of community security. Though not an exhaustive list like the one first compiled by Linda L. Harris,[146] a sampling of these includes:

- **Personal Privacy:** conviction data of licensed sellers of checks or money orders[147] and of applicants for check-cashier's licenses received by the state Department of Banking and Finance;[148] conviction data of mortgage license applicants;[149] criminal history of financial license applicants;[150] conviction data received by the World Congress Center to make employment decisions;[151] military service records for fifty years;[152]

---

145. O.C.G.A. 50-18-72(a)(48). See, O.C.G.A. 47-20-87 for examples of such investments.

146. Georgia Open Records and Open Meetings Statutes: A Textual Analysis (master's thesis, Georgia State University, 1999). (NOTE: The author served as thesis advisor for this project.)

147. O.C.G.A. 7-1-682(c).

148. O.C.G.A. 7-1-702(c).

149. O.C.G.A. 7-1-1004(e).

150. O.C.G.A. 7-1004(g).

151. O.C.G.A. 10-9-9(e).

152. O.C.G.A. 15-6-72(c).

violent incident reports involving juveniles;[153] juvenile law enforcement records;[154] information obtained through a legal wire tap;[155] family violence reports;[156] adoption records;[157] records of the Child Support Enforcement Agency of the Department of Human Resources;[158] annual performance evaluations of school superintendents;[159] public school attendance and disciplinary records;[160] records of students attending private schools;[161] records of hunting/fishing license applicants who fail to sign a voter registration form;[162] raw research data;[163] medical records;[164] information regarding those with Acquired Immune Deficiency Syndrome (AIDS);[165] certain library records;[166] certain veterinarian records;[167] vital records of births out of

153. O.C.G.A. 15-11-40(c). See, Rhonda Cook, "Agency Pushes Juvenile Lockup Secrecy," Atlanta Journal-Constitution, March 22, 2013, B3.

154. O.C.G.A. 15-11-58 and O.C.G.A. 15-11-66. See, Linda Jacobson, "Educators Link Record Access to Safety: Juvenile Offenders - School Officials Want To Avoid Violence; Others Fear Effects of Too Much Disclosure," Atlanta Journal-Constitution, March 19, 1993, D3.

155. O.C.G.A. 16-11-62.

156. These records may be made public if arrests are made. See, O.C.G.A. 17-4-20.1.

157. O.C.G.A. 19-8-8.

158. O.C.G.A. 19-11-30.

159. O.C.G.A. 20-2-210.

160. O.C.G.A. 20-2-697 and O.C.G.A. 20-2-757.

161. O.C.G.A. 20-14-29.

162. O.C.G.A. 21-2-221.1(h).

163. O.C.G.A. 24-12-2.

164. O.C.G.A. 24-12-11, O.C.G.A. 24-12-12, O.C.G.A. 24-12-13, O.C.G.A. 24-12-14. See also, O.C.G.A. 33-59-11.

165. O.C.G.A. 24-12-20, O.C.G.A. 24-12-21.

166. O.C.G.A. 24-12-30.

167. O.C.G.A. 24-1-31.

wedlock;[168] Department of Labor employment records;[169] state Board of Workers' Compensation records;[170] criminal history, except that limited access to records of in-state felony convictions maintained by the Georgia Crime Information Center is now available;[171] mental health records;[172] clinical records relating to alcohol or drug abuse;[173] motor vehicle registration records;[174] information of driver's licenses

---

168. O.C.G.A. 31-10-25(d). These records are also exempt from disclosure when "temporarily kept or maintained in any file or with any other documents in the office of the judge or clerk of any court prior to filing with the Department of Public Health." See, O.C.G.A. 50-18-76.

169. O.C.G.A. 34-8-121(a) and O.C.G.A. 34-8-121(b)(3). Exceptions to these rules are provided for in O.C.G.A. 34-8-124 through O.C.G.A. 34-8-128. The commissioner of labor is authorized to control all access to departmental records. See, O.C.G.A. 34-8-123. Records may be released if all identifying information is first deleted. See, O.C.G.A. 34-8-129.

170. O.C.G.A. 34-9-12. The records of the board are not "open to the public but only to the parties satisfying the board of their interest in such records and their right to inspect them" (id.).

171. O.C.G.A. 35-3-30 through O.C.G.A. 35-3-40. Criminal history information may also be disclosed if it is contained in a law enforcement agency's investigatory file, unless the disclosure would violate a person's right of privacy. See, Napper v. Georgia Television Co., 257 Ga. 156, 356 S.E.2d 640 (1987) at 167.

172. O.C.G.A. 37-2-11.2(b), O.C.G.A. 37-3-167(d), and O.C.G.A. 37-4-125(a-c). See, Southeastern Legal Foundation, Inc. v. Ledbetter, 260 Ga. 803, 400 S.E.2d 630 (1991) (where clinical records of a former state mental patient charged in a shooting spree at an Atlanta area mall shortly after his release need not be disclosed). See also, "Court: File on Mental Patient Is Protected," Atlanta Journal-Constitution, Feb 24, 1991, C4.

173. O.C.G.A. 37-7-166(a-c).

174. O.C.G.A. 40-3-23, O.C.G.A. 40-2-130, O.C.G.A. 40-5-2(j). Included are drivers' histories, compiled by the State Department of Public Safety. See, Katie Long, "A Public Service: Open Driving Records." Atlanta Journal-Constitution, Jan. 19, 1992, C5. These records may be disclosed if they are found in a law enforcement officer's investigatory file. See, Napper

and in the possession of the Department of Public Safety;[175] information regarding prison inmates with communicable diseases;[176] information identifying companies providing drugs used in executions and prison staff who carry out executions;[177] probation records;[178] pardon and parole records;[179] professional

---

v. Georgia Television Co., 257 Ga. 156, 356 S.E.2d 640 (1987) at 166.

175. O.C.G.A. 40-5-1, O.C.G.A. 40-5-2, O.C.G.A. 40-5-105. The department may disseminate information to other government agencies to facilitate the prevention of fraud. O.C.G.A. 40-5-2(f) See, "Motor Vehicles and Traffic - Drivers' Licenses: Comply with the Provisions of the Federal Driver's Privacy Protection Act; Provide Strict Guidelines for the Release of Personal Information from Drivers' Licenses and Other Records of the Department of Public Safety," 14 Georgia State University Law Review 196 (December 1997).

176. O.C.G.A. 42-1-7(c).

177. O.C.G.A. 42-5-36(d). 2013 Georgia Laws 333, unofficially known as the "Lethal Injection Secrecy Act of 2013." Such information is "classified as a confidential state secret." See, Bill Rankin & Melissa Abbey, "Lethal Injection Info Would Be Secret Under Bill," Atlanta Journal-Constitution, March 22, 2013, B1, B10; Arlinda Broady, "Bill Would Keep Execution Info Secret," Atlanta Journal-Constitution, March 31, 2013, B4; Rhonda Cook, "Lethal Drug Secrecy Tested," Atlanta Journal-Constitution, July 20, 2013, A1, A8; "State Appeals Execution Ruling," Atlanta Journal-Constitution, July 27, 2013, B3. See also, Manny Fernandez, "Executions Stall as States Seek Different Drugs," New York Times, Nov. 9, 2013, A1, A3.

178. O.C.G.A. 42-8-40. "However, the commissioner may by written order declassify any such records" (id.).

179. O.C.G.A. 42-9-53. Such records are "classified as confidential state secrets." When a convicted felon is paroled, the pardons and parole board files a document with the court stating the conditions of parole, including the address of the parolee. This document is a public record. See, Rhonda Cook, "Parole Board Votes Are Kept a 'State Secret'," Atlanta Journal-Constitution, Jan. 30, 1992, D1; Carlos Campos, "Group Pushes To Open Parole 'Secrets,'" Atlanta Journal-Constitution, Nov. 18, 2005, E1, E8. But see, "Web Site Finds Ga. Parolees," Atlanta Journal-Constitution, March 14, 2003, C4; Carlos Campos, "Web Site Keeps Track of Felons," Atlanta Journal-Constitution, Nov. 27, 2003, E1, E8. See also, Georgia State Board

license applications and related information;[180] records of the rehabilitation of impaired health care professionals;[181] records of investigations of physicians;[182] psychologist-patient communication;[183] material subpoenaed by the coroner or medical examiner, including autopsy and crime scene photographs;[184] state employee payroll records;[185]

---

of Pardons and Paroles (undated), available at: http://thelmalou.pap.state.ga.us/pls/web/georgia_profile_pkg.entry_form (last accessed Nov. 15, 2013).

180. O.C.G.A. 43-1-2(k).

181. O.C.G.A. 43-34-5.1.

182. O.C.G.A. 43-34-37(d). See, Carrie Teegardin, "Secrecy Laws Shield State's Physicians," Atlanta Journal-Constitution, May 2, 1999, A1, A14. See, generally, David Pace, "Secret File Lists Disciplined M.D.s," Atlanta Journal-Constitution, June 30, 2000, A17. For a listing of publicly disciplined medical doctors, see, Georgia Composite Medical Board, List of Monthly Public Board Orders (undated), available at: http://medicalboard.georgia.gov/list-monthly-public-board-orders (last accessed Nov. 15, 2013).

183. O.C.G.A. 43-39-16. However, a witness' communications during hypnosis conducted for prosecution purposes may be disclosed. See, Emmett v. Ricketts, 397 F.Supp. 1025 (N.D. Ga. 1975).

184. O.C.G.A. 45-16-27(c) and O.C.G.A. 45-16-34(b). In R.W. Page Corp. v. Kilgore, 257 Ga. 179, 356 S.E.2d 870 (1987), the Georgia Supreme Court ruled that the transcript of an inquest which was open to the public was a public record. Autopsy photographs are not subject to disclosure since 2002. See, O.C.G.A. 45-16-27(d). Crime scene photographs are not subject to disclosure as a result of the Meredith Emerson Memorial Privacy Act of 2010. See, O.C.G.A. 45-16-27(e)(1). See also, Bill Rankin & Aaron Sheinin, "Hustler Magazine Photo Request Sparks Uproar," Atlanta Journal-Constitution, March 8, 2010, available at: http://www.ajc.com/news/local-govt-politics/hustler-magazine-photo-request-sparks-uproar/nQc9w/ (last accessed Nov. 15, 2013); Bill Rankin & Aaron Sheinin, "DeKalb Judge Bars Release of Photos of Slain Biker to Hustler," Atlanta Journal-Constitution, March 10, 2010, available at: http://www.ajc.com/news/dekalb-judge-bars-release-of-photos-of-slain-hiker/nQdC5/ (last accessed Nov. 15, 2013); Bill

results of drug tests of state employees;[186] confidential taxpayer information;[187] income tax information;[188] records of the Department of Human Resources on juvenile delinquents;[189] and records of child abuse and neglect, including child drug abuse.[190]

Rankin, "Public Access to Private Agony," Atlanta Journal-Constitution, March 14, 2010, B1, B4; Walter Jones, "House Passes Bill To Block Graphic Crime Scene Photos," Athens Banner-Herald, March 16, 2010, available at: http://onlineathens.com/stories/031610/ bre 591538793.shtml (last accessed Nov. 15, 2013); Ernie Suggs, "Senate Passes Sex Offender Bill," AJC.com's Gold Dome Live, April 21, 2010, available at: http://blogs.ajc.com/gold-dome-live/2010/04/21/senate-passes-sex-offender-bill/ (last accessed Nov. 15, 2013); Nancy Badertscher, "So-Called 'Hustler' Bill Wins Final Approval," AJC.com's Gold Dome Live, April 29, 2010, available at: http://blogs.ajc.com/gold-dome-live/2010/04/29/so-called-hustler-bill-wins-final-approval/ (last accessed Nov. 15, 2013).

185. O.C.G.A. 45-18-36. However, records of monies paid state employees during each calendar year are available. See, Georgia Dept. of Audits and Accounts, "Open Georgia: Transparency in Government" (2008), available at: http://www.open.ga.gov/ (last accessed Nov. 15, 2013).

186. O.C.G.A. 45-20-92.

187. O.C.G.A. 48-2-15.1.

188. O.C.G.A. 48-7-60 and O.C.G.A. 48-7-61.

189. O.C.G.A. 49-5-10.

190. O.C.G.A. 19-7-5, O.C.G.A. 49-5-40, O.C.G.A. 49-5-41, and O.C.G.A. 49-5-186. Exceptions to this rule are provided for in O.C.G.A. 49-5-41. Penalties for improper access are outlined in O.C.G.A. 49-5-44. Napper v. Georgia Television Co., 257 Ga. 156, 356 S.E.2d 640 (1987) at 166, illustrates the circumstances under which such records may be disclosed. However, O.C.G.A. 19-1-6, which opened records of child abuse investigations in cases where the children have died was weakened by a federal-state agreement to delete the children's identities from those files. See, Charles Walston, "Agencies Make Deal on Opening Records: Grant Will Help State in Child Abuse Probes," Atlanta Journal-Constitution, Oct. 3, 1991, D7; Diane Loupe, "Ga. Agency Still Keeps Child Abuse Files Closed: Says Federal Law Prevents Release," Atlanta Journal-Constitution, Oct. 15, 1992, D2; Alan Judd, "Child Safety: Law Conceals Information on Child Deaths," Atlanta Journal-Constitution, April 23, 2013, A1, A20. See also,

- **Commercial Competitiveness:** information which is a "trade secret" and used in the registration of a pesticide;[191] trade secrets of commercial feed;[192] information furnished the Milk Commission;[193] animal disease data;[194] records of the Department of Banking and Finance;[195] bank examination records;[196] examination reports of out-of-state banks;[197] mortgage lender and broker investigation records;[198] trade secrets of antifreeze;[199] waste disposal secrets;[200] information about hazardous waste generators and transporters;[201] information about secret processes, devices or methods of manufacture obtained by the Department of Natural Resources;[202] records relating to the Georgia Underground Storage Tank Act;[203] records evaluating health care providers;[204] insurance rate investigation or financial condition evidence;[205] proprietary insurance

---

Celia W. Dugger, "Fatal Child Abuse Is Hidden by Laws on Confidentiality," New York Times, May 18, 1992, A1, A12.

191. O.C.G.A. 2-7-68(a)(1).

192. O.C.G.A. 2-13-5.

193. O.C.G.A. 2-20-1(15)(b).

194. O.C.G.A. 4-10-7.3(a). The agriculture commissioner may release reports about animal diseases in Georgia for research and other purposes he deems appropriate.

195. O.C.G.A. 7-1-70(a).

196. O.C.G.A. 7-1-625(c).

197. O.C.G.A. 7-1-628.5(b)(1).

198. O.C.G.A. 7-1-1004(l).

199. O.C.G.A. 10-1-207.

200. O.C.G.A. 12-8-29.2(a).

201. O.C.G.A. 12-8-64.

202. O.C.G.A. 12-9-19.

203. O.C.G.A. 12-13-1; O.C.G.A. 12-13-21.

204. O.C.G.A. 31-7-133.

205. O.C.G.A. 33-1-16(e); O.C.G.A. 33-2-14(g).

company information;[206] documents relating to the Worker's Compensation Guaranty Trust Fund;[207] "information secured ... incident to the administration of any tax;"[208] "information provided to a local government by a business ... for the purpose of determining the amount of occupation tax for the business;[209] and information relating to the operation of the state lottery.[210]

- **Community Security & Stability:** grand jury deliberations;[211] courthouse security plans;[212] and bomb technicians' and law enforcement training manuals.[213]

The Georgia Supreme Court has also identified as "confidential state secrets" information of wrongdoing provided by inmates to the Department of Corrections, confidential information provided to the state Board of Pardons & Parole, and information on subversive activities provide to special assistant attorneys general.[214]

---

206. O.C.G.A. 33-9-20(b).

207. O.C.G.A. 34-9-388(c).

208. O.C.G.A. 48-2-15.

209. O.C.G.A. 48-13-15(a).

210. O.C.G.A. 50-27-2; O.C.G.A. 50-27-24. See, Charles Walston, "Secrecy on Bids Raises Questions About Lottery and Open Records Law," Atlanta Journal-Constitution, April 15, 1993, C5.

211. O.C.G.A. 15-12-67(a).

212. O.C.G.A. 15-16-10(a)(10).

213. O.C.G.A. 35-8-25(e). See also, "Law Enforcement and Other Agencies - Employment and Training of Peace Officers: Restrict Public Access to Bomb Technicians' Training Materials," 14 Georgia State University Law Review 179 (December 1997).

214. These are codified in O.C.G.A. 42-5-36 (information on wrong-doing by inmates and identities of those who make and supply lethal injection drugs used in executions), O.C.G.A. 42-9-53 (confidential information provided the parole board), and O.C.G.A. 16-11-9 (information on

A few types of records are specifically required to be open to public inspection. These include:

- Records of the official proceedings of local school boards;[215]
- Campus police records at both public and private institutions;[216]
- Records relating to primary and general elections;[217]
- Voter registration name lists, but not other personally identifying information;[218]

---

subversive activities). See, Hardaway Co. v. Rives, 262 Ga. 631, 422 S.E.2d 854 (1992). See also, David Hudson, "Georgia Open Records: 'State Secret' Rejected," Georgia Press Bulletin, Feb. 1, 1993, 3.

215. O.C.G.A. 20-2-57(a).

216. O.C.G.A. 20-8-7. This statute negates the effects of the ruling in Mercer University v. Barrett & Farahany, 271 Ga. App. 501, 610 S.E.2d 138 (2005) (where police records at private universities were determined not to be public records). See, Jonathan Ringel, "Open Records Law Doesn't Apply to Private University Cops," Daily Report, Feb. 8, 2005, 1, 3; Andrea Jones, "Opening Up the Books," Atlanta Journal-Constitution, March 18, 2005, D1, D8; Richmond Eustis, "Hopes Rise for Change in Campus Cop Secrecy," Daily Report, June 1, 2005, 1, 3; Laurie Lattimore-Volkmann, "Campus Crime Docs Issue for '06 Assembly," Georgia FOI Access (Fall 2005), 1, 7; Allison Retka, "Georgia Legislature Passes Bill Increasing Access to Campus Police Records," Student Press Law Center News Flash (April 5, 2006), available at: http://www.splc.org/newsflash.asp?id=1233&year=2006 (last accessed Nov. 15, 2013); Tom Bennett, "Anti-Gang Bill Requires Private School Crime Disclosure," Georgia FOI Access (Fall 2006), 2.

217. O.C.G.A. 21-2-72. Not included in these records are the contents of voting machines.

218. O.C.G.A. 21-2-225(b). However, addresses of voters who are also victims of domestic abuse may now be kept confidential. See, Shelia Poole, "Abuse Victims Will Get Privacy," Atlanta Journal-Constitution, Jan. 8, 2010, B1, B5. To participate, an individual must be a resident of Georgia, a registered voter in the state, and must qualify under O.C.G.A. 19-13-4, O.C.G.A. 16-5-94, or O.C.G.A. 19-13-20. See, Georgia VoteSafe Program,

- Vital records located in county government offices;[219]
- Carnival ride variances;[220]
- Criminal history records, specifically, felony convictions;[221]
- Local government audits;[222]
- Names of convicted sex offenders registered in Georgia;[223]

---

available at: http://www.sos.ga.gov/votesafe/ (last accessed Nov. 15, 2013). See also, O.C.G.A. 21-2-225.1.

219. O.C.G.A. 31-10-25(f). Access to these records at the state level is more restrictive. See, generally, O.C.G.A. 31-10-25 and O.C.G.A.50-18-76. "When 100 years have elapsed after the date of birth or 75 years have elapsed after the date of death or application for marriage, or divorce, dissolution of marriage, or annulment," the Department of Archives & History controls these records and makes them available to the public in a manner which assures their continued safe keeping. See, O.C.G.A. 31-10-25(e).

220. O.C.G.A. 25-15-93.

221. O.C.G.A. 35-3-35(d.1). See, Georgia Crime Information Center, Criminal History Records (undated), available at: http://gbi.georgia.gov/obtaining-criminal-history-record-information (last accessed Nov. 15, 2013); Georgia Technology Authority, Georgia Felon Search (undated), available at: http://gta.georgia.gov/georgia-felon-search (last visited Nov. 15, 2013). See also, Sarah Huntley, "Criminal Records Coming to Web," Atlanta Journal-Constitution, Dec. 11, 2000, A1, A11.

222. O.C.G.A. 36-81-7(e-f).

223. O.C.G.A. 42-1-12. To access the registry, see, Georgia Bureau of Investigation, Georgia Sex Offender Registry (undated), available at: http://gbi.georgia.gov/georgia-sex-offender-registry (last accessed Nov. 15, 2013); see also, Georgia Bureau of Investigation, Sexual Offender Search Form (2013), available at: http://services.georgia.gov/gbi/gbisor/ControllerServlet (last accessed Nov. 15, 2013). See also, Andria Simmons, "Sex Offender Info Gets Upgrade," Atlanta Journal-Constitution, Dec. 13, 2012, B1, B6. County sheriffs also maintain lists on their own web sites. See, for example, Gwinnett County Sheriff's Office, Offender Watch (undated), available at: http://www.sheriffalerts.com/cap_main.php?office=54503 (last accessed Nov. 15, 2013). See also, Jessica Turner, "Gwinnett County Sex Offender

- Lists of inmates kept by county sheriffs;[224]
- Public officials and employees' yearly disclosure statements concerning business transactions with the

---

Registry," Gwinnett Citizen, September 2005, 1, 9-11. Other counties have similar sites. See, for example, Office of the Sheriff, Fulton County, Atlanta, Georgia (undated), available at: http://www.fultonsheriff.org/ (last accessed Nov. 15, 2013) and click on the "GBI Sex Offenders" or "FCSO Sex Offender Registration Database" link on the left side of the page. See, generally, Georgia Sex Offender Maps & Alerts (2004), available at: http://www.georgia-sex-offenders.com/index.php (last accessed Nov. 15, 2013). See also, Thomas J. Schramkowski, "A Mandate without a Duty: The Apparent Scope of Georgia's Megan's Law," 15 Georgia State University Law Review 1131 (Summer 1999). Deficiencies in the registration process have been revealed in recent years. See, Alan Judd, "More Than 200 Sex Offenders Can't Be Found," Atlanta Journal-Constitution, Dec. 20, 2009, B1, B5; Cameron McWhirter, "Sex Crime Registry Flawed," Atlanta Journal-Constitution, Aug. 29, 2010, A1, A13. However, the Georgia Supreme Court upheld the state statute in Ranier v. Georgia, 286 Ga. 675, 690 S.E.2d 827 (2010). See, Bill Rankin, "Ga. Supreme Court Rebuffs Sex Offender Registry Challenge," Atlanta Journal-Constitution, March 15, 2010, available at: http://www.ajc.com/news/news/loca/ga-supreme-court-rebuffs-sex-offender-registry-cha/nQdLQ/ (last accessed Nov. 15, 2013). O.C.G.A. 42-1-18 prohibits registered offenders from photographing children without the consent of their parents.

224. O.C.G.A. 42-4-7(a). See, for example, Office of the Sheriff, Fulton County, Atlanta, Georgia (undated), available at: http://www.fultonsheriff.org/ (last accessed Nov. 15, 2013) and click on the "Inmate Information" link on the left side of the page. Other counties have similar sites. See, for example, Gwinnett County Sheriff, Detention Center Docket Book (undated), available at: http://www.gwinnettcountysheriff.com/Docket%20Book.htm (last accessed Nov. 15, 2013). One Web site offers a live law enforcement radio scanner feed, coupled with local police information. See, ScanGwinnett, Live Gwinnett County Police and Fire Radio (2004), available at: http://www.scangwinnett.com/ (last accessed Nov. 15, 2013). See also, Lindsay Jones, "Get Scoop on Arrested Neighbors via E-Mail," Atlanta Journal-Constitution, Feb. 24, 2003, J1, J6.

state;[225]

- Initial accident or arrest reports - "incident" reports[226] - although portions of the report "that might endanger people's lives or disclose confidential investigations" may be withheld;[227]
- Athletic records;[228]
- Records of the Harbor Pilot Commission;[229]
- Names of attorneys against whom formal disciplinary action has been taken by the State Bar of Georgia;[230]

---

225. O.C.G.A. 45-10-26.

226. O.C.G.A. 50-18-72(a)(4). See also, "Sheriff Ordered to Give Newspaper Incident Reports," News Media & the Law (Summer 2000), 29-30. However, a state statute requiring that the identifying information contained in such records not be used for commercial purposes was found to be unconstitutional in Statewide Detective Agency v. Miller, 115 F.3d 904 (11th Cir. 1997) (involving motor vehicle accident reports).

227. Peter Mantius, "Police Can Withhold Crime Report Details," Atlanta Journal-Constitution, May 23, 1995, B4. See, Brunswick v. Atlanta Journal-Constitution and Florida Publishing Co., 265 Ga. 413, 457 S.E.2d 176 (1995). See also, Jingle Davis, "Papers Sue Brunswick to Get Reports: Information Sought About Series of Attacks," Atlanta Journal-Constitution, Oct. 7, 1993, D4; Jingle Davis, "Both Sides Unhappy with Ruling on Access to Police Reports," Atlanta Journal-Constitution, June 17, 1994, B11; "Incident Report Access Clarified with Ruling," Georgia Press Bulletin, July 1994, 3; "Police Secrecy vs. Public Safety," Atlanta Journal-Constitution, May 28, 1995, B4.

228. O.C.G.A. 50-18-72(a). See, Macon Telegraph Publishing Co. v. Board of Regents, 256 Ga. 443, 350 S.E.2d 23 (1986) (where records relating to the financial operation of the University of Georgia Athletic Association were held to be public, without regard to who prepared them or how they were prepared).

229. O.C.G.A. 52-6-10.

230. Rule 4-219, Judgments and Protective Orders, Georgia Rules of Professional Conduct, State Bar of Georgia (2013), available at: http://www.gabar.org/barrules/handbookdetail.cfm?what=rule&id=150 (last accessed Nov. 15, 2013). See also, State Bar of Georgia, Recent Discipline

- Names of doctors against whom formal disciplinary action has been taken by the State Board of Medical Examiners;[231] and
- State-owned "trade secrets".[232]

Academic course evaluations prepared for faculty by students, "including performance evaluations of individual faculty members," are open for public review, according to an opinion of the attorney general,[233] as are decisions of the Office of State Administrative Hearings.[234] And although not exactly an "open records" issue, persons who have been convicted for driving under the influence of alcohol two times are required to have their name and photograph published in their local newspaper.[235]

(2013), available at: http://www.gabar.org/forthepublic/recent-discipline.cfm (last accessed Nov. 15, 2013).

231. For a listing of publicly disciplined medical doctors, see, Georgia Composite Medical Board, List of Monthly Public Board Orders (undated), available at: http://medicalboard.georgia.gov/list-monthly-public-board-orders (last accessed Nov. 15, 2013).

232. "[T]he trade secrets of any state department, agency, board, bureau, commission, or authority are not exempt from public disclosure under the open records act. [However,] information in the possession of such entity which is a trade secret of others must be protected from disclosure." 1994 Opinions of the Attorney General, No. 94-15, page number unknown. Regarding state protection of the trade secrets of others, see, Georgia Trade Secrets Act of 1990, codified in O.C.G.A. 10-1-760 through O.C.G.A. 10-1-767.

233. See, 1988 Opinions of the Attorney General, No. 88-3, 10. See also, Chris Parmelee, "New Book Grades GSU Professors," Georgia State University Signal, Aug. 9, 1994, 1, 2.

234. See, 1999 Opinions of the Attorney General, No. 99-13, page number unknown.

235. O.C.G.A. 40-6-391(j). See also, "Access Varies to Metro DUI Records," Atlanta Journal-Constitution, Dec. 19, 1993, A8.

The Open Records Act was rarely tested until the 1970s, when the notoriety of the 1973 Watergate scandal brought about a general distrust of government and governmental agencies. More and more media organizations and citizens groups have relied on open records laws to keep themselves informed about governmental activity.[236] Important Georgia court decisions clarifying the Open Records Act have included:

- *United States v. Napper* - in which the Atlanta police department was ordered to return to the Federal Bureau of Investigation files on Atlanta's missing and murdered children, almost ten years after Wayne Williams was convicted of two of the murders, the result of a lawsuit filed by the Atlanta Journal-Constitution, WSB-TV, and ABC News to have the files released to the public.[237]
- *Harris v. Cox Enterprises* - in which the Georgia Bureau of Investigation was required to release the report on its probe of the Georgia State Patrol.[238] The Georgia Supreme Court ruled that "information reflecting upon an individual's performance of official duties would not be exempt from open records" requirements.[239]

---

236. See, Marc Rice, "Getting Tough: Georgia Newspapers Aggressive in Fight for Open Government," Georgia Press Association Editor's Forum (Summer 1989), 1, 24.

237. 887 F.2d 1528 (11th Cir. 1989). The Georgia Supreme Court had previously affirmed a ruling that Atlanta police had to make the files public under Georgia's open records law. See, Napper v. Georgia Television Co., 257 Ga. 156, 356 S.E.2d 640 (1987). See also, "State Ordered To Return FBI Documents," News Media & the Law (Winter 1990), 6-7.

238. 256 Ga. 299, 348 S.E.2d 448 (1986).

239. Id. at 302.

- *Macon Telegraph Publishing Co. v. Board of Regents*,[240] *Dooley v. Davidson*,[241] and *Cremins v. Atlanta Journal-Constitution*[242] - in which the university system was required to release records showing the assets, liabilities, income, and expenses of the University of Georgia Athletic Association, as well as its coaches' salaries and outside income.[243]

- *Bowers v. Shelton* - in which confidential tax information contained in a closed criminal investigation file was not subject to disclosure;[244]

- *Hoffman v. Oxendine* – where records regarding the investigation of an insurer was not a "pending investigation" and should not have been withheld by the

---

240. 256 Ga. 443, 350 S.E.2d 23 (1986).

241. 260 Ga. 577, 397 S.E.2d 922 (1990).

242. 261 Ga. 496, 405 S.E.2d 675 (1991).

243. See, Tony Barnhart, "Court Opens Records on Income of Coaches," Atlanta Journal-Constitution, Nov. 30, 1990, E2; David Davidson, "UGA To Do All TV Deals for Coaches," Atlanta Journal-Constitution, Feb. 26, 1991, E1; David Davidson, "Tech Coaches' Income Public Record, Court Says," Atlanta Journal-Constitution, April 25, 1991, F4; David Davidson, "Cremins Had $400,000 Income Besides Salary," Atlanta Journal-Constitution, Sept. 8, 1991, E1; David Davidson, "Despite Ruling, Coaches Uncooperative: Request Concerning Ross Bounced From Agent to Attorney to Accountant," Atlanta Journal-Constitution, Sept. 8, 1991, F3; David Davidson, "Bobby Ross' Income: Players' Pleas Led to Switch to Nike Shoes," Atlanta Journal-Constitution, Sept. 8, 1991, F3; David Davidson, "Homer Rice's Income: TV, Radio Shows Provide the Bulk of Extra Money," Atlanta Journal-Constitution, Sept. 8, 1991 F3; David Davidson, "Bobby Cremin's Income: Nike Provides $130,000 a Year, Other Benefits," Atlanta Journal-Constitution, Sept.8, 1991, F3; See also, Mark Schlabach, "SEC, ACC Salaries a Surprise in Survey," Atlanta Journal-Constitution, June 20, 2003, D1, D2; "ACC, SEC Football Coaching Salaries," Atlanta Journal-Constitution, March 13, 2009, page number unknown.

244. 265 Ga. 247, 453 S.E.2d 741 (1995). See, O.C.G.A. 50-18-70(a)(43).

state Insurance Commissioner;[245]

- *Central Atlanta Progress v. Baker* – where proposals for Atlanta to host the NASCAR Hall of Fame and the 2009 Super Bowl, made by private entities, were found to be public records, "in light of the significant involvement of public officials, public employees, public resources, and public funds" involved in preparing the proposals.[246] This meant that the private entities were "working on behalf of public offices or agencies;"[247]

- *Fulton-DeKalb Hospital Authority v. Miller & Billips* – in which documents generated during an internal investigation of sexual misconduct, as a routine inquiry into external complaints and not in anticipation of

---

245. 268 Ga. App. 316, 601 S.E.2d 813 (2004).

246. 278 Ga. App. 733, 629 S.E.2d 840 (2006) at 734. This ruling also appears finally to settle the question of whether the records of the private entity which managed the 1996 Olympics in Atlanta are public records. See, Walter Woods, "Atlanta NASCAR Web Site Remains Coy About Plans," Atlanta Journal-Constitution, July 9, 2005, F1; Walter Woods, "NASCAR Hall of Fame: Georgia Sues on Secrecy," Atlanta Journal-Constitution, Aug. 19, 2005, F1, F3; Walter Woods, "Ruling Says Bids Can't Be Secret," Atlanta Journal-Constitution, Nov. 8, 2005, D1, D7; Walter Woods, "Groups Evaded Open Records Act, Judge Rules," Atlanta Journal-Constitution, Nov. 18, 2005, page number unknown; Walter Woods, "NASCAR Bid Open to Public, Court Says," Atlanta Journal-Constitution, April 13, 2006, A1, A12; Nancy Badertscher, "Attorney General: Keep Files Public," Atlanta Journal-Constitution, April 19, 2006, B2; Tom Bennett, "Attorney General Wins Case for NASCAR Hall of Fame Records," Georgia FOI Access (Summer 2006, 1, 3. For arguments on both sides of the issue, see, Sam Williams & A.J. Robinson, "NASCAR Museum Bid: Sealed Lips Needed for Now To Gain Edge," Atlanta Journal-Constitution, July 11, 2005, A9; "No Wiggle Room on Open Records," Atlanta Journal-Constitution, Aug. 7, 2005, B6; Angela Tuck, "It's Not OK to Keep a Secret with the Public's Money," Atlanta Journal-Constitution, Aug. 20, 2005, A11.

247. Id. at 737.

litigation, were determined to be public records and not exempt from disclosure as an attorney's privileged work product.[248]

In recent years, Georgia courts have also been called upon to decide whether "restructured" hospitals, those which are publicly owned but privately managed, are governed by the state's sunshine laws.[249] Promina Health Systems first claimed it was not subject to the laws, then agreed to comply with them while claiming that its policy "in no way implies the [hospital alliance] is legally obliged to conduct its business in public."[250] After the state attorney general's office sided with the *Marietta Daily Journal* in a lawsuit to force the "mega-network" of ten Atlanta area hospitals to comply with the law and a Cobb County Superior Court judge agreed, Promina appealed.[251] The judge stated that despite the private, nonprofit status of the defendants, the defendants were ordered to disclose the requested documents. The court held that the defendants were subject to the Open Records Act as they had "contractually agreed to operate public hospital authority assets for the public good."[252]

---

248. 293 Ga. App. 601, 667 S.E.2d 455 (2008).

249. See, Laura Williamson, "Health Alliance Defends Move to Keep Records, Meetings Private," Atlanta Journal-Constitution, Nov. 2, 1994, G2.

250. Laura Williamson, "Health Systems Will Let Sunshine In," Atlanta Journal-Constitution, Nov. 10, 1994, page number unknown.

251. See, Laura Williamson, "State Official Joins Publisher in Opposing Secrecy in Hospital Records," Atlanta Journal-Constitution, Jan. 6, 1995, B4; "Sunshine Laws Apply to Hospital Alliance," Atlanta Journal-Constitution, Feb. 14, 1995, C5; Laura Williamson, "Appeals Court May Open Secret Plans of Hospital Group," Atlanta Journal-Constitution, May 11, 1995, C4.

252. Northwest Georgia Health System, Inc. et al v. Times-Journal, Inc., 218 Ga. App. 336, 461 S.E.2d 297 (1995). See also, O.C.G.A. 50-14-1 and O.C.G.A. 50-18-70.

The open records statute is an imperfect one, subject to continuous revision and amendment, for "just as old as the principle of open government is the desire of public officials to tailor the principle to suit their own ends - permitting access to only such information as will portray their decisions in the best possible light, and denying access to information that will subject them to public criticism."[253] The open records law provides that recalcitrant public officials may be fined $1,000 for the first violation of the law.[254] In addition, the attorney general may bring a civil or criminal action to force compliance with the law.[255] Whether even further revision is needed in the aftermath of the 2012 modifications is an open question, though Georgia could choose to follow Virginia's lead in restricting access to public records to in-state residents and citizens, with which the U.S. Supreme Court recently agreed in *McBurney v. Young*.[256]

---

253. Attorney Peter Canfield, quoted in Sam Hopkins, "Pending Sunshine Case Reflects Openness Trend," Atlanta Journal-Constitution, April 23, 1989, B1, B8. See, Harris v. Cox Enterprises, 256 Ga. 299, 348 S.E.2d 448 (1986).

254. O.C.G.A. 50-18-74(a). However, the statute does not permit recovery of compensatory or punitive damages. See, Chisolm v. Tippens, 289 Ga. App. 757, 658 S.E.2d 147 (2008) at 762.

255. O.C.G.A. 50-18-73. Members of the public can bring a civil action to enforce the law.

256. ___ U.S. ___, 133 S.Ct. 1709 (2013), available at: http://www.supremecourt.gov/opinions/12pdf/12-17_d1o2.pdf (last accessed Nov. 15, 2013). See, Adam Liptak, "Supreme Court Backs State Restrictions on Who Can Ask for Information," New York Times, April 30, 2013, A11. For pre-2012 critiques of Georgia's sunshine laws, see, Lucy Soto, "Enforcement Hassles Make Records Law a Toothless Tiger," Atlanta Journal-Constitution, July 16, 2001, B1, B5; Rebecca Carr, "Access Denied: There's 'No Cop on the Beat' To Enforce Information Law," Atlanta Journal-Constitution, March 12, 2006, C1, C4.

Overall, the fundamental problem with Georgia's commitment to open meetings and open records has been that its
commitment has not been shared equally by all levels and areas
of government - especially law enforcement agencies, school
boards, and city councils.[257] Many times agencies and boards
have misinterpreted the law to restrict public access, with
unauthorized fees, delays, and excuses.[258] The development of
the Internet may make access to public information easier,[259]

---

257. See, Tom Bennett, "'Open' Records Often Stay Closed," Atlanta
Journal-Constitution, Dec. 12, 1999, H5. See also, Heather Vogell, "AJC
Files Complaint with State," Atlanta Journal-Constitution, Nov. 20, 2010,
B1, B7; "Probe Hits City, Again," Atlanta Journal-Constitution, April 19,
2011, B7; John Thompson, "Ruling Finds Violation of Ga. 'Sunshine Law',"
Atlanta Journal-Constitution, July 16, 2011, B6; Kristina Torres & Jaime
Sarrio, "School Board Hit with State Sanctions," Atlanta Journal-
Constitution, July 26, 2011, A1, A8; Kathleen Joyner, "APS Avoids
Penalties for Violations of Open Government Laws," ATLaw, July 27, 2011,
available at: http://www.atlawblog.com/2011/07/aps-avoids-penalties-for-
violations-of-open-government-laws/ (last accessed Nov. 15, 2013); Patrick
Fox, "Details of Closed Meetings Leaked," Atlanta Journal-Constitution,
Feb. 22, 2012, B1, B7; Dan Whisenhunt, "Dunwoody Leak Highlights
Closed Meetings," Reporter Newspapers, May 31, 2012, available at:
http://www.reporternewspapers.net/2012/05/31/dunwoody-leak-highlights-
closed-meetings/ (last accessed May 31, 2012).
258. See, Lucy Soto, "Agencies Make Their Own Rules on Open
Records," Atlanta Journal-Constitution, Aug. 14, 2000, B1-B2; Lucy Soto,
"Open Records Quests Good, Bad and Ugly," Atlanta Journal-Constitution,
Sept. 18, 2000, B1, B6.
259. See, "Internet May Prove Best Access for Public Records," Atlanta
Journal-Constitution, Sept. 8, 1997, D5; Patrick Fox, "Local and Streaming
Local Government," Atlanta Journal-Constitution, Jan. 19, 2011, page
number unknown. See also, Office of the Attorney General of Georgia
(undated), available at: http://law.ga.gov/ (last accessed Nov. 15, 2013) and
click on the "Open Government" link. See also, Data.Gov (undated),
available at: http://www.data.gov/ (last accessed Nov. 15, 2013). As
examples of privately developed Internet applications which collate public
data, see, the Atlanta Journal-Constitution's web site which allows users to

but a commitment to open government requires a long-term devotion to education,[260] media publicity,[261] and constant diligence to ensure the law is properly and fully enforced.[262]

"Search Metro Atlanta Home Appraisals," available at: http://myproperty.ajc.com/ (last accessed Nov. 15, 2013); FelonSpy.com – which notes that "safety starts with good information, even if it ends with a loaded .44 caliber pistol" – available at: http://www.felonspy.com/ (last accessed Nov. 15, 2013); and Criminal Searches – with Criminal History Check, Neighborhood Watch, and Sex Offender Finder links – available at: http://www.criminalsearches.com/ (last accessed Nov. 15, 2013). See, Brad Stone, "If You Run a Red Light, Will Everyone Know?" New York Times, Sunday Business section, Aug. 8, 2008, 4; David Goodman, "Outcry over a Newspaper's Map of Handgun Permit Holders, New York Times, Dec. 27, 2012, A17; David Carr, "Guns, Maps & Data That Disturbs," New York Times, Jan 14, 2013, B1, B6. Privacy advocates, however, contend that "at the very least, the Internet has made it far easier for anyone to obtain not only someone else's birth date or Social Security number but also, liens, lawsuits, divorces and other personal and potentially embarrassing – but technically public – information." Brian Bergstein, "Data-Mining Tools Fuel Concerns about Privacy," Atlanta Journal-Constitution, Jan. 4, 2004, C2. O.C.G.A. 10-1-393.5 sets out procedures for seeking the removal of publicly available arrest photos or "mug shots" from non-government websites. See, 2013 Georgia Laws 613, House Bill 150. See also, Aaron Sheinin, "Commercial Use of Mug Shots Targeted by Bill," Atlanta Journal-Constitution, March 8, 2013, A8; Aaron Sheinin, "Mug Shot Legislation Heading to Deal's Desk," Atlanta Journal-Constitution, March 29, 2013, A10; Emma Lacey-Bordeaux & Gavin Godfrey, "Published Mug Shots: A Constant Reminder of One Man's Past," CNN.com, May 29, 2012, available at: http://www.cnn.com/2012/05/29/us/mug-shot-websites.html (last accessed May 31, 2012); David Segal, "Mugged by a Mug Shot," New York Times, Oct. 6, 2013, Sunday Business section, 1, 4.

260. This is the goal of the Georgia First Amendment Foundation which may be reached online at: http://www.gfaf.org/ (last accessed Nov. 15, 2013). As an example of its educational outreach, see, Hollie Manheimer, "Exercising Your Right To Know: Getting Access to Government Information," a paper presented at "Media Law in the Digital Age" (a conference sponsored by Harvard Law School's Berkman Center for Internet & Society and Kennesaw State University's Center for Sustainable Journalism), Sept. 25, 2010, Kennesaw, Ga., available at:

http://vimeo.com/17123259 (last accessed Nov. 15, 2013) The foundation's first book, the "red" book, Georgia's 'Sunshine Laws' - A Citizen's Guide to Open Government (4th ed., 2008) is available at: http://www.gfaf.org/resources/sunshine laws.pdf (last accessed Nov. 15, 2013). Its second book, the "blue" book, Georgia Law Enforcement and the Open Records Act: A Law Enforcement Officer's Guide to Open Records in Georgia (2d ed., 2005) is available at: http://www.gfaf.org/resources/resourcesBlueBook.pdf (last accessed Nov. 15, 2013). Its third book, the "green" book, Georgia Public Schools and the Open Records Act: A Citizen's Guide to Accessing School Records (2007) is available at: http://www.gfaf.org/resources/greenBook.pdf (last accessed Nov. 15, 2013). The foundation's "2008 Georgia Student Sunshine Audit: Testing Statewide Compliance [with] the Georgia Open Records Act" (2009) – previously available at: http://gfaf.org/newsletter/doc/StudentAuditGeneralSummary.pdf (copy on file with author) – revealed what appeared to be a substantial misunderstanding and ignorance of (or simply noncompliance with) the law's requirements by public officials statewide, in that only 65 percent of public records requested were made available. In the "2010 Georgia Student Sunshine Audit: Testing Statewide Compliance with the Open Records Act" – available at: http://gfaf.org/resources/2010 GeorgiaStudentSunshineAudit.pdf (last accessed Nov. 15, 2013) – compliance increased to 80 percent.

261. See, for example, Teresa Borden, "Open Records Empower Citizens," Atlanta Journal-Constitution, Feb. 13, 2005, A1, A19; "Freedom of Information: The State of Open Records Around the World," Atlanta Journal-Constitution, Feb. 13, 2005, A18; "Sunshine Sunday: Open Records," Atlanta Journal-Constitution, March 13, 2005, F1-F5; "Open Government," Atlanta Journal-Constitution, March 12, 2006, C1-C4; "Sunshine Sunday: Open Government," Atlanta Journal-Constitution, March 11, 2007, E1-E4; Angela Tuck, "Open Government Clearly a Freedom Georgians Count On," Atlanta Journal-Constitution, March 17, 2007, A17; "Sunshine Sunday: Open Government – Finding the Key to the Kingdom," Atlanta Journal-Constitution, March 16, 2008, C1; "Here's How We Used the State Open Records Act in the Past Year To Keep You Informed," Atlanta Journal-Constitution, March 16, 2008, D10-D11; Shawn McIntosh, "Sunshine Laws Light Way for Journalism," Atlanta Journal-Constitution, March 13, 2010, A2; "Sunshine Week: The Public Matters," Atlanta Journal-Constitution, March 20, 2011, A18, A19; "Sunshine Week: Warmed by Progress of Ethics Movement," Atlanta Journal-Constitution, March 20,

2011, A21; "Sunshine Week: Linchpin of Democracy," Atlanta Journal-Constitution, March 11, 2012, A16, A17, A18; Kevin Riley, "Open Governance: Sunshine Laws Light Our Way," Atlanta Journal-Constitution, March 11, 2012, A23.

262. Procedures for requesting public records are available at the following web sites: Georgia Press Association, "Georgia Sunshine Laws" (undated), available at: http://www.gapress.org/sunshine.html (last accessed Nov. 15, 2013); Reporter's Committee for Freedom of the Press, Open Government Guide – Georgia (2011), available at: http://www.rcfp.org/georgia-open-government-guide (last accessed Nov. 15, 2013). A model open records letter is available at: http://www.gfaf.org/wp-content/uploads/2012/05/model-open-records-request-april-2012.pdf (last accessed Nov. 15, 2013). See, Georgia First Amendment Foundation, Resources & Links (2013), available at: http://www.gfaf.org/resources/ (last accessed Nov. 15, 2013). See also, Meri K. Christensen, "Opening the Doors to Access: A Proposal for Enforcement of Georgia's Open Meetings and Open Records Laws," 15 Georgia State University Law Review 1075 (Summer 1999).

QUESTIONS

1. How much funding must organizations receive before they are subject to Georgia's open records/open meetings laws?

2. What general conclusion regarding open meetings did the Georgia Supreme Court reach in *Coggin v. Davey* (1975)?

3. How many business days do Georgia public agencies have to respond to open records requests?

4. What two types of health records, "which would invade personal privacy," are statutorily exempt from disclosure under Georgia's open records law?

5. What happens to official actions taken by public agencies in meetings improperly closed to the public?

6. What rule of law was established as a result of the decision in *U.S. v. Napper* (1989)?

7. What two-part test may be used to determine when a particular government meeting should be an "open" meeting?

8. What rule of law was established as a result of the decision in *Central Atlanta Progress v. Baker* (2006)?

Thought Question:
What types of records are presumptively not open in Georgia? Why? What competing interests is the state attempting to balance with such a rule? Are there other, better ways to balance these interests?

Index

COURT RULINGS

TERMS, CONCEPTS & NAMES

Made in the USA
Lexington, KY
20 August 2014